THE BALLAD OF "BLIND" WILLIE JOHNSON

TEXAS MUSIC SERIES
Sponsored by the Center for Texas Music History
Texas State University
Jason Mellard, General Editor

THE BALLAD OF "BLIND" WILLIE JOHNSON

*Race, Redemption, and
the Soul of an American Artist*

SHANE FORD

TEXAS A&M UNIVERSITY PRESS
College Station

Library of Congress Cataloging-in-Publication Data

Names: Ford, Shane, author.

Title: The ballad of "Blind" Willie Johnson / Shane Ford.

Other titles: Texas music series.

Description: First edition. | College Station: Texas A&M University Press,
    [2025] | Series: Texas music series | Includes bibliographical
    references and index.

Identifiers: LCCN 2024045209 (print) | LCCN 2024045210 (ebook) | ISBN
    9781648432774 (cloth) | ISBN 9781648432781 (ebook)

Subjects: LCSH: Johnson, Blind Willie. | Gospel singers—Texas—Biography.
    | Blues musicians—Texas—Biography. | Guitarists—Texas—Biography. |
    African American gospel singers—Texas—Biography. | African American
    guitarists—Texas—Biography. | Gospel music—History and criticism. |
    Blues (Music)—History and criticism. | LCGFT: Biographies.

Classification: LCC ML420.J72695 F67 2025 (print) | LCC ML420.J72695
    (ebook) | DDC 782.25/4092 [B]—dc23/eng/20241001

LC record available at https://lccn.loc.gov/2024045209

LC ebook record available at https://lccn.loc.gov/2024045210

For the unnamed rebels, both past and present

"Thou shalt not oppress a stranger: for ye know the heart
of a stranger, seeing ye were strangers."
—EXODUS 23:9

In the Sahara Desert of northern Africa there exists a people who have walked for over a thousand years, traversing the harsh desert sand dunes, camels by their side, navigating the scorched earth by the light of the stars. They are nicknamed the "blue people" for the indigo dye their clothing leaves on their skin, and they are our new practitioners of the blues: the rebel music first brought to life by Blacks in the American South. They are the mystics who tramp beneath the heavens in solitude, embarking on their own journey in the spiritual wilderness before eventually returning to us with the gifts of their odyssey: the tribulations of the soul articulated through song. With the assistance of the most basic, portable instruments, their sound punctures through the veil of self, inviting us to share in this common humanity, this necessary connection: of rhythm, love, and resistance. This is the music, disseminated through time, that pulses in the veins of the politically and socially marginalized poets as they feel their way through the darkness. It is a sound that, for many reasons, died out in America many years ago.

CONTENTS

ACKNOWLEDGMENTS

There are many people to whom I owe a debt of gratitude for making sure we were able to get a book on "Blind" Willie Johnson finally completed. They include Anna Obek, who was there when this whole thing began and made every word possible. There's Thom Lemmons—without his blind faith, even through a plague, you wouldn't be reading this now. For having the passion and admiration for this great artist long before I was born, I owe Sam Charters the reverence he so rightly deserves. The same goes for Dan Williams, who through our correspondence, I have come to recognize as one of our truest artists of life. I also want to give a special thanks to Julien Bresson, who endured my craziness on this subject and made this book infinitely better than it would have been. Particular appreciation is also extended to Ann Charters, who personally approved the use of Angelina's photograph for inclusion in the work, and who I revered long before I had any particular interest in the blues. For Kristin Eshelman at the UConn Library Archives & Special Collections, Terese Austin at the University of Michigan William L. Clements Library, and Aimee Brooks of the Columbus Museum, all of whom treated my questions and requests with an abundance of humanity and not simply as a chore. That especially goes for Todd Harvey of the American Folklife Center, who always entertained my requests with passion and curiosity. There are several people who took my random calls in the course of this writing—they were unselfish with their time and a joy to speak with. Most of them probably don't remember me, but I will never forget them. They are Glenda Goodson, the founder of the Center for African American Church History and Research, Jeannie McWilliams of the Sabine Tabernacle, Clarice Weeks of Paul Quinn College, and Brian Simmons of the Texas Collection at Baylor University. For providing his expertise, time, and patience, I want to thank Matt Cornelia. And for their willingness to lend images or pieces of their archives to support this project, I wish to acknowledge the Morgan Library & Museum, New York; the James Avery Lomax Family Papers, Dolph Briscoe Center for American History, University of Texas at Austin; William L. Clements Library, University of Michigan; the Columbus Museum, Georgia; the Robert "Mack" McCormick Collection at the National Museum of American History, Smithsonian Institution; and the Samuel and Ann Charters Archives of Blues and Vernacular African

American Musical Culture, and Thomas J. Dodd Research Center, both at the University of Connecticut Library. To all the people and institutions above, as well as to the artists who have impacted my life in ways that I will never be able to repay, I dedicate this work.

INTRODUCTION

Dark clouds rolled, and the wind did moan. A train conductor punched out following his last stop for the evening for the old Santa Fe, or "Santa Fee" as they said, before mingling into a small crowd lingering around the cramped depot station. It's mid-September 1945 in Texas, the second World War is finally coming to a close, and in a burned-out house on the side of a dead-end dirt road in Beaumont, a growing city eighty miles east of Houston, a man lay on a bed in a blanket made of newspapers suffering from a horrible fever, dying. His name is Rev. Willie Johnson.

He is one of history's greatest travelers—a beggar, a maker of songs. He is a musician and a preacher. It is in this home that, before the fire, he would play his guitar and minister. Setting up on street corners and in rural churches, he sang, from experience, of motherless children having a hard time, of Samson tearing the building down, and of the Great Ship that went down. He sang of the soul of man and of the Crucifixion. He had been through the storms, the floods, and all the red-light district towns. But at four in the morning on September 18, the final trumpet sounded and, just like that, he was gone. Virtually unknown at this point outside of his small community of shotgun shacks and patchwork of African American churches in Southeast Texas, he was buried by the Southern Pacific tracks, four miles south of where he last lay from the illness. And with him also went his history—his days growing up in Temple, Texas, the real story of his blinding, and his memories of various East Texas towns on Saturday afternoons as he played for the passers-by strolling down crowded sidewalk streets. His last recordings had been fifteen years earlier, and although he still sang some of these old songs, there were also new ones that almost no one would hear.

Early that same morning, as the sun rose, the conductor reported for work in the same unwashed uniform from the night before. Soon the passengers boarded, the signal turned from red to green, and the train pulled out of the station. No one had heard the news of Johnson's death. There was no obituary, no tributes, no time to mourn.

Some things catch on right away and others take a long time. The list of artists who the public did not immediately accept, but who were rediscovered long after death are too numerous to recount here. Timing certainly plays a part in what the culture is willing to accept at any given moment, and usually the great artists are always ahead of theirs. There are also all sorts of critics, journalists, and historians who, although it may not be purposeful, are already too indebted to the old ideas, or to their tailor-made education to have their eyes wide open. They've already made up their minds to what is important, and any new work is simply too radical or inconvenient. And sometimes, as is the case with much of the blues and early Black religious music, because it was Black music made in Black neighborhoods for Black people, the mainstream is just unaware, late, stuck having to play catch up. But things are always in flux, and beautiful truths can't be buried forever. There are cracks, and eventually a flood of light is able to break through. As D. H. Lawrence put it, "We move, and the rock of ages moves."[1]

In Johnson's case, the first opening came when the inventor and filmmaker Harry Smith included one of Johnson's songs on the *Anthology of American Folk Music*, released in 1952 on Folkways Records. The *Anthology* was a groundbreaking compendium that would lead to critical rediscoveries of not only early American folk songs but also some of the forgotten performers, some of whom would be brought out of the coal mines, back alleys, cotton fields, or rural churches and onto concert stages. The next break in introducing Johnson's music across the racial barrier would come a few years later when, in 1955, a young student who would play blues records after his jazz rehearsals at college in California drove to Texas to seek out a couple of the men who made some of those records: Robert Johnson and "Blind" Willie Johnson. His name was Samuel Charters, and he would later write about his findings in his seminal 1959 book, *The Country Blues*. Then, in 1977, as NASA prepared to launch its twin Voyager spacecraft, it also decided to include music as a way of conveying our human feeling should any life form intercept the craft as it traversed the solar system. The folklorist Alan Lomax, who had his roots in Texas but who had also recorded folk music ranging from the work songs of the Black convicts in the Mississippi State Penitentiary to the rhythm in the fields of Haiti, was enlisted as an advisor on the project. One of Lomax's selections was Johnson's 1927 recording of "Dark was the Night—Cold was the Ground."

By the time I found Johnson's music thirty years later, I assumed such a significant artist would already have his name permanently carved in the place where they memorialize all the best prophets of the heart. But, as I was about to discover, it was clear he still remained virtually obscure outside a select population of musicians and blues record collectors. And while at first there seemed to be some agreed upon story of Johnson's life, I quickly found there was hardly any consensus, and almost everything that was written wasn't true at all.

Interstate 10 is the highway that will lead you straight to Beaumont from San Antonio. And if you keep going it runs further east right on into Louisiana. I ended up on this highway in 2007 after first hearing Johnson's "The Soul of a Man." This sort of original, deep blues was a new language for me. I was always attracted to artists who stood outside the mainstream, who had something to say, told you something new, or made you feel different than what everybody else was trying to convince you was true when you knew it to be otherwise. Johnson's sound did that. Discovering that song and others later was like finding ancient scrolls with the meaning of life on them. But instead of any explanation or concrete answers, they contained just the sort of raw truth and revelations only a feeling can provide. To me, his songs could have been recorded a thousand years ago or in the present day.

The asphalt burned under the car tires as I turned toward the path where people had written Johnson had been buried. There were cemeteries but none labeled as Blanchette, the place listed on his death certificate. And at the corner of Forrest Street and the highway (I-10), where Johnson last lived, the house was gone too. Nothing but a field of grass and a knoll remained where the house likely stood, a hill now adorned with three wooden crosses, like those on Calvary. It may have been the first time someone had returned to this address looking for Johnson in over sixty years, and I had no idea at that moment that I would spend time on and off over the next three years running in circles, hitting dead ends, and almost going crazy putting together some of the critical pieces necessary to honor his legacy.

The main issue with the research into Johnson's story is that no one was able to interview Johnson while he was alive. Instead, it was the recollections of two women who lived with him who provided the most insight. The first was Angelina, Johnson's wife at the time of his death, who Charters interviewed in 1955. The second was Willie B. Harris, who Dan Williams—a young artist and researcher—spoke with twenty years later. So, by the 1980s, we were able to have some minimal details—mostly written in some liner notes and some contradictory—of Johnson's biography. But there were still many more questions than anything definitive.

We also had the issue of Johnson's music being very much under the radar of serious researchers. This was the case with Johnson and other most early blues or religious musicians who did not originate from what has come to be defined as the Deep South. Most music researchers focused on Mississippi and the surrounding states. And while we are lucky today to have an abundance of conversations and writings on some of the Texas artists, so much was left unfinished.

I suppose that many in the blues scholar community looking for research on Texas were relying on the work of intrepid investigator Mack McCormick who, in the late 1950s and '60s, walked the streets of many of East Texas' African American neighborhoods knocking on doors and seeking out the stories of the disenfranchised communities who were creating all these sounds. And he made incredible discoveries. In fact, one could argue that if it wasn't for McCormick, Texas may have been completely left out of the major blues conversation (at least the pre-war blues conversation). And although his friendships with the researcher Paul Oliver and future Arhoolie Records founder Chris Strachwitz spawned additional recordings and research, McCormick himself mostly withdrew from publishing any additional material after the 1960s. But even McCormick did not conduct any serious research into Johnson's life. In fact, from the time of Johnson's death in 1945 to 2009, no significant, meaningful research had been conducted on Johnson other than the already mentioned critical field work of Charters and Williams.[2]

Another major reason for the lack of Johnson scholarship is Johnson's overall lack of recognition as a great artist outside of scattered mentions here and there by musicians, or through the avenues already described. In fact, as of this writing in 2020, Johnson's music has never been brought to greater prominence in the mainstream press. He has never been posthumously honored with awards or hall of fame inductions. The only people who really paid attention to his work in a way that amounted to any sort of original writing or research were individuals (including myself) who were moved by the music he made.

This lack of real scholarship has led to the Johnson narrative being framed through the eyes of the researchers themselves. Sam Charters began this method in his chapter on Johnson in *The Country Blues*. Precisely because so little was known, I took this same route in 2011 when I needed to release my research. Even as I am writing this, it has been the gaps in information that have defined Johnson's biographical story. If one was to read about Johnson, the author would always preface the piece by stating that "little is known about Johnson's life."

Because there has not been one cohesive and agreed-upon narrative of Johnson's life, guesses have replaced truth, while myths and falsehoods have been used as placeholders for facts. This began with the release of *His Story Told, Annotated and Documented*, an album consisting of a series of interviews Charters conducted in 1954 and 1955 and released on Folkways in 1957. The centerpiece of the research was a lengthy interview with a woman Charters identified as Angeline, Johnson's widow. In the liner notes for the release, Charters writes that Johnson was born outside of Temple in 1900, that his father was George Johnson, that Angeline and Johnson married in 1927, that she was the one who sang on the last records in 1930, that they recorded in Beaumont, and that Johnson died in 1949. Two years later, in a chapter on Johnson for his book, *The Country Blues*, Charters changed some of the narrative, writing that Johnson was born on a farm outside Marlin, and that, in addition to the 1930 records, Angeline had also sung on the 1928 recordings. This confusing framing of Johnson's story *became* Johnson's life. The problem is not only that Charters's accounts were inconsistent or inaccurate. We were also led to believe that he derived the facts from Johnson's widow, when, in truth, they were assembled by Charters.[3] Thus, a story was constructed from a patchwork of material, and what was released to the public was a highly edited version of Charters's interview with none of the omissions disclosed. To this day, new articles are introduced, but lacking in any original research, they merely echo Charters's assumptions. One such error that was finally corrected was the identity of the singer on both the 1928 and 1930 recording sessions, something we learned when Dan Williams interviewed Willie B. Harris in the 1970s.[4]

This is the world I walked into in 2010 when I was taking a serious look at the Johnson biography. That year, even after I discovered the forgotten cemetery where Johnson was buried and finally proved who Johnson's parents were and that his birthplace was Pendleton, Texas, near Temple, and not Marlin or Brenham, as most had written, the information was virtually ignored, proving that verifiable facts are no match for myth.[5] But this never should have been the case, because, besides the location of the cemetery, we should have had more accurate information years before. The reason is both women we know to have been with Johnson said that Johnson was from Temple, the main city just south of Pendleton and where Johnson would move very early in life. Willie B. Harris told Dan Williams that Johnson was from Temple in her 1977 interview with him, and Angelina told Samuel Charters that he was from Temple. Furthermore, even though Charters received conflicting statements, Angelina said that Johnson's father's name was Dock (not George) in unreleased audio included in their 1955 interview.[6]

Additional misstatements that are endlessly repeated include why Johnson employed his false bass while singing, and that Johnson and Harris lived together at 817 Hunter Street in Marlin.[7] The latter was a trap I also fell into, but when I looked further into it, it was obvious that it was not true. Not only is there no evidence of it, but the house at Hunter Street was not even constructed until 1951, six years after Johnson's death, according to deed records, something that I am correcting with this work. And finally, to this day, oftentimes in articles and videos, "Blind" Willie McTell's photo stands in place of Johnson's—something that would never happen with say, Robert Johnson, who has become well-known even outside of blues history circles.

But ultimately what is missing is the bigger picture: the actual life of the man and the music he gave us. The above errors are still only fragments, a skeleton outline of points like stars in the sky before we know there are constellations to unite them. My goal in conducting my initial work was simply to pay tribute to Johnson—that's why I established where Blanchette Cemetery was, to honor his unmarked grave.[8] That is why I fought to have a historical marker placed along that dirt road in Beaumont where Johnson died in 1945, and that is why I pursued his story.

But none of us did enough. The things I brought were a way to memorialize Johnson, to pay tribute to him as a person and to say to future generations that he was not forgotten. But we had not told the story; the story that needed to be told—*his story*. Man-made objects cannot last forever and they cannot speak to us in the way hearing him can. Johnson was a traveler; he preferred to play on the streets, and everything he sang was about feeling. We didn't go deep enough. It's the feeling we need to get back to if we are to truly meet Johnson on his level.

It took a little cooling off period on my part following my research and a little more listening to all kinds of what I now call *The Real Blues* to understand that. I didn't even have to go too far back either. I found the field recordings to be the most captivating—those raw sounds captured outside the studio environment, stuff like what George Mitchell recorded along with the emotion of Cecil Barfield's "Bottleneck Blues," recorded by Art Rosenbaum. And the deeper I got, even though the songs didn't need to be about anything specifically religious, it was clear these voices expressed a profound spiritual connection, a force that gets at the root of it all, a response to devastating crimes perpetrated upon the culture.

We have to remember that the initial recordings that took place on record in the American South were of people who never thought their music would be heard outside of farms, coal country porches, church houses, or Saturday night celebrations. This was functional music. These songs were about life. Polly did drive steel like a man, Railroad Bill was a mighty mean man, and the cane along the Brazos had been all ground to molasses. All of these seeds were planted in slavery, and the roots and branches grew from a specific time period and a confluence of specific political, economic, and societal factors. All the factors that gave birth to this music will never arise in the same way ever again.

So, when we write or talk about this music, we cannot do so just from our current period looking back. We must meet the people and the artists on their soil. We must always go deeper, because the music and the people who performed this music were just that. That is why, when Carl Sagan and his team were assembling the Voyager Golden Record for NASA, they were not asking writers to describe the wind, laughter, or the human heartbeat—they wanted a recording of these things. And when they were looking for music, they were searching for the sounds that were as deep as the feeling of the wind across one's skin, or of the beautiful involuntary laughter that, like the rhythms of the heart, have more to tell us about the way we feel than possibly we even understand. Beethoven, Bach, Louis Armstrong, and Johnson were as deep as thunder. That's why they were included. These sounds are the lived experience; they are cosmic truths that can never be pinned down, not to any singular articulate understanding, or compressed to fit any one particular religion. Without naming things, these are the sounds, and this is the music that reveal that God is everywhere. And after understanding that—not intellectually—but only after having all this incredible, sublime music dancing in my brain for some time, I felt like there was only one thing I could do, and that was to go back and give Johnson another look—this time from the eyes of an artist and not just someone who was looking to honor the artist.

Any serious study of Johnson's life and music must be rooted in the African American traditions of his time. It seems obvious, while at the same time never seriously attempted. Through my research it became clear that those who grew up entrenched in the sounds of the Black church, even knowing nothing of Johnson, would be able to answer more articulately what he was doing than the journalists who could recite lyrics or the musicians who attempted to imitate note for note what he was doing on guitar, but who were culturally alienated. Thus, guesses replaced research and popularity determined importance. So-and-so rock band covered this, and that is why it is important. And while this may not always be why one felt moved by the music, it's too often how writers wrote about Johnson when signifying cultural importance. So, the main areas I will explore all have their roots in the African American traditions in the South. They include themes of protest and resistance, the necessary act of physical movement, and the struggle for freedom both within and outside established institutions with a focus on the importance of finding one's own voice within the tumult. This is the place where Johnson and his music were born.

My goal with this book is to assemble the facts that I know to be true of Johnson's life and reframe the narrative, putting it back in the world Johnson inhabited. To tell the story—from the sun-drenched fields of slavery to the cold living room floor where Charters listened intently to the story of Johnson's widow. We did what we could before, thinking that the answers resided in places that could be mined with the intellect, but that is because we were never asking the right questions. I'm not interested in trivia, but with engaging deeper with the mystery of the spirit. For too many Black musicians of the earliest blues era who were not lucky enough to survive into the folk revival era, their biographical lives will always remain merely a sketch. This work will fill in many missing facts as it pertains to Johnson's life, but overall I am reaching for something much deeper. While Johnson's life story may have been marginalized or omitted from the greater American story while he lived, he did leave us something that carries with it a more profound truth that resides in that more abstract realm, something of what it means to be human.

So now it is time to set the story straight.

The book is constructed in two distinct sections that, I believe, complement each other. The first, "The Ballad," represents the bulk of the work and tells the narrative of Johnson and his contemporaries in, as much as I could, linear time; the second, "A Love Supreme," encompasses the final chapter and looks at Johnson's influence following his death. For the title, I have chosen the ballad theme for several reasons. The first is that one of the most frequently asked questions as it relates to Johnson's songs pertains to authorship. But this has always been a question that completely misses the mark on what Johnson's (or most blues or religious) music was about. It was not the words that were most important to Johnson, but the emotion and most importantly, it was the unique mark he could impart on the song; it was his *individual voice* he gave to that music that mattered. The Texas folklorist Dorothy Scarborough wrote that a Black singer of folk songs is not interested in the author of the song but "the story, in the incident and character the song relates. A collector may ask in vain as to authorship, for he finds nothing."[9] These are songs that moved with the singers, across borders of various counties and states as they picked up and moved, traveled in the various circus or medicine show circuits, worked on the levees or railroads, and performed in the network of churches. Characters and locations in the songs may change to fit the individual singer's perspective or mood; it's a loose-fitting pattern that allows the singer to improvise with lyrics while commenting on current events.

This is a tradition stretching back centuries to the medieval British and Scottish ballads printed as broadsides and sung by traveling minstrels. The themes were often rooted in the concerns of the "common man," and ranged in subject matter from the personal to the social and topical events of the day. And as more immigrants made their arrival in the United States, these ballads and hymns traveled with them and over time were recomposed in the folk tradition. Recent events replaced ones from an old country, and names from the past were exchanged with the more familiar. But the idea was the same—that of communal composition. So while a song leader may begin a song, it is expected that it will evolve over time.[10]

But it is the newly freed Black slave who would help to give form to some of America's greatest and enduring ballads. Some, like "St. James Infirmary" and

"The Gallis Pole," evolved from British origin. Others, like the ballad of John Henry—the account of the steel-driving railroad worker racing against technology and time to outpace the steam drill—appear as uniquely American creations.[11] Some ballads were religious in nature, employing similar themes of perseverance, strength, and wit, but the heroes are biblical, in the cases of Jonah, Noah, and Samson. These ballads were favorites of the religious street singers, many of whom would add their own lines, and have a local printer produce them into ballad sheets they could turn around and sell for five or ten cents a copy. And although there is no evidence Johnson sold these broadsides himself, there is ample evidence that several of his songs were variants of the ballads that circulated in his time.

The second reason for choosing the title is that Johnson's life story could fit the definition of the ballad itself. Searching for information on Johnson became like trying to track down all the details of the real John Henry. For, like Henry, whose real identity and story may never be known, Johnson's narrative became something of a myth, built mostly around the point of view of the researchers, and only grew more cemented with each retelling of it. Unfortunately, not only was much of the information inaccurate, but hardly any attention was paid to the actual work he created. So, while I dedicated an enormous amount of effort to correct the biographical record, my true focus remained on what the artist had to say. The ballad makers, after all, were not journalists but artists. They did not seek only what was factually true but used facts to get at something deeper and more profound: what was essentially true. And it is the artist "Blind" Willie Johnson who I am seeking to reveal.

As is true of most great artists, Johnson, the artist, was molded by the time and the world he lived. It is precisely because of the musical heritage and the social circumstances from which he was born that we have the exact expression that Johnson gave to us. Without the institution of slavery, without Jim Crow, without formal education or access to the healthcare system we now have today, Johnson's music, as we know it, would not exist. Without his close relationship to spirituality and the denominations of the Black church, Johnson's music, as we know it, would not exist. Unlike some of the secular musicians of his day, Johnson likely never saw his role as strictly an entertainer or his highest aim coming in the form of a record deal. The recordings themselves resulted from the major companies' business decision to sell to new audiences as well as serendipitous timing that coincided with when this form of music was being widely performed. But it was not an avenue that many Black musicians at the time, particularly religious singers, thought could be a stable career that would provide all their income.[12] The music was Johnson's response to living in particular historical circumstances within a broader musical tradition, and the way in which that response was unique is what makes Johnson the artist he was. Russian filmmaker Andrei Tarkovsky's remarks on the artist Andrei Rublev could just as easily apply to all the truly timeless artists, including Johnson.

> If they [ideal conditions] existed, his work wouldn't exist, for the artist doesn't live in a vacuum. Some sort of pressure must exist: the artist exists because the world is not perfect. Art would be useless if the world were perfect, as man wouldn't look for harmony but simply live in it. Art is born out of an ill-designed world.[13]

The critical element necessary for creation in most artists is found through the journey of self-discovery. This discovery can best be compared to the Spanish mystic St. John of the Cross's "Dark Night of the Soul"—the concept that love and union with God can be achieved without light from anywhere but that which burns in the soul.[14] But in order to achieve this state, one must venture into the painful purification of the *dark night*. It is then, through this journey, that the soul is transformed and brought closer to God and love:

> This blessed night, though it darkens the mind, does so only to give it light in everything; and though it humbles and makes it miserable, does so only to raise it up and set it free.[15]

Thus, in Johnson's case, it is because he chose or was chosen to take this spiritual journey that he was able to create such a rendition of a song such as "Dark was the Night," pairing his own trials in union with Jesus in the garden of Gethsemane. This rejuvenation and new insight by the soul is reminiscent of the great bard and poet William Blake's savior in *Jerusalem* when he sings:

> *Awake! awake O sleeper of the land of shadows, wake! expand!*
> *I am in you and you in me, mutual in love divine.*[16]

This is a journey that always must be undertaken alone. For while singing—especially in the case of spirituals or work songs—was communal, it was also an individual act centered around finding one's own voice outside the group setting. If nothing else, this is Johnson's most important contribution to music—this mastery in blending the collective voice of the spirituals with the individual expression of the blues. This ultimate freedom of expression is where the *dark night* can eventually lead, but along the road, as one is looked upon as separate from the ever-amassing herds, one is sure to be met with misunderstanding or worse. But the reward, if one survives, is to experience the ultimate redemption: a unique, fully developed "self" and a fearlessness to stand in protest when called as there is nothing anymore on this material plane that can harm you.

That's why a crucial component of early African American spirituals and life was rooted in this protest. It is also why many of the civil rights leaders were preachers within the Black church. These songs told the story that led to redemption, internal freedom, and hopefully one day on Earth, political freedom. Is it any wonder then that the face of the Black civil rights movement in the United States was a minister and an activist or that many of the songs that fueled the movement were the same songs sung a hundred years before by their ancestors. Even listening back now to the sermons of Black preachers recorded during the 1920s, there can be no mistaking—from the rhythms of the voices and response from the assembled congregations—what is happening. The words may seem innocent enough, but there is no misunderstanding what is meant as the voice of the preacher rises and falls and growls. This is the lineage from which "Blind" Willie Johnson emerges.

Thus, it only seems natural that it was the Black American music tradition that gave birth to what we know today as rock 'n' roll or that it ascended in the same political period as the American civil rights movement. For in it we can feel the attitude, the rebelliousness, and the inner freedom that seeks nothing other than to free others. This is the spirit Johnson possessed at least as early as his first recordings. Not only were the songs he chose to sing deeply rooted in the spirituals of resistance, but he also adopted the fiery vocal expressions of the preachers and song leaders that led the Black Baptist and Church of God in Christ congregations he frequented. And while there are other recordings of street singers and congregants of these churches, these singers did not choose to sing in the same way as Johnson.

Like the prodigal son, venturing out on one's own was the only option for many newly freed slaves and many of the sons and daughters of slaves. No place was home in the United States, and if there was to be one, it would have "to be one that he created for himself."[17] It is this forced pilgrimage into the unknown to build new societies, both as a community and as individuals, that led to whole new religions, modes of expression, and a musical language that spoke to the souls of the alienated as they went tramping in the wilderness. That is why it is the stranger "who just blew into town" who gets dogged around and why "you've got to cross that river of Jordan" and "walk that lonesome valley" for yourself. It's why Bessie Smith sang of the "Long Old Road," and why we all oughta treat a stranger right. What the road meant for many African Americans seeking their own voices was an affirmation of humanity, a freedom that is not granted by the oppressor but won through faith itself. "Freedom is an inalienable possession of the Christian," Leo Tolstoy wrote in his treatise on modern Christianity. "A Christian cannot fail to be free, because the attainment of the aim he sets before himself cannot be prevented or even hindered by anyone or anything."[18]

This is the vein Johnson flows from. While many blues songs dealt with personal matters, Johnson and other gospel-tinged performers combined elements of the Black church and blues guitar languages to deal with something else altogether. In these songs there is rarely any naming of the performer's origin geographically, but rather those regions mapped internally, spiritually. They were on a different mission than their blues counterparts. These songs were ultimately about freedom and would be sung for political freedom, but if that was not to be achieved, they still would be sung for inner freedom.

> *Before I'd be a slave*
> *I'll be buried in my grave*
> *And go home to my Lord and be free.*

Johnson's music and voice convey many things, but at its core reside the themes of movement and resistance. He lived his life as an itinerant evangelist—a blend of John who wrote the book of Revelation and the traveling preacher, John the Baptist—and his voice was that of the rebel, one who refuses to allow the absurdity of existence to overcome the truest experience of living. This is the rebel's story, the journey through the *dark night* of the blind bard who, not unlike the Greek poet Homer or his character, Demoducus, was robbed of his sight but given the gift of song—a song that gets at the real mysteries of existence, not the superficial ones that we may locate in the archivist's accounting. For too long we have chosen to remain deaf as we fumbled around for answers in the wrong locations, leaving us poorer as a result.[19] Let us no longer choose to ignore what the artist has revealed to us already through his voice, his life, and his music.

The Ballad of "Blind" Willie Johnson

PROLOGUE
Dark Was the Night

O He gives to us His joy,
That our grief He may destroy:
Till our grief is fled and gone
He doth sit by us and moan.
—WILLIAM BLAKE[1]

It has been written that on the night before the Crucifixion, while Jesus was in Gethsemane and he prayed, that his agony was so deep "his sweat was as if it were great drops of blood falling down to the ground." It was also in this sacred garden where Christ was arrested and the following day executed in the way Romans dispersed of their rebels—by hanging him from a piece of wood in the public square for all to see as they mocked and tortured him.

The purpose of this section is to give a very brief overview of song structures, both secular and spiritual, in the times of Black slavery in the United States in order to provide critical context to the origins of Johnson's music. But it is merely a prologue, an overview of the musical traditions that were born as a result of slavery. The meanings, though, extended long after and were continually affirmed in the face of oppression. It is imperative that, in order to come close to where Johnson's music originated, one must be able to hear the history of a nation and of a people, a people who sang in beautiful antiphonal patterns and lined-out hymns.

Slavery and Song

These early spirituals could be heard on the plantations in work songs Black laborers, working in groups, would call out in timed responses to the lead man with either sung lines or with grunts as their axes fell. And in their worship services, one of the few places in Black life where one could feel the freedom to emotionally express themselves, the congregation would respond to the stirring sermons with soft affirmative moans, hand claps, and shouts of "Hallelujah!" or "Well."

The Moan

Johnson's ballad begins with a moan. It is the same moan that was forced to America on the slave ships; the same moan of the men, women, and children who stood upon the auction block; and the same moan used to convey the deepest of human emotion as voices cried out through work songs and field hollers. It is the same moan that emanated from a people as they labored on the levees, in sawmills, or on the railroad. And these are the voices that communicated the deepest of hums in the houses of worship. It is that long, glorious moan—full of love and trauma and a belief in something better despite the wounds that time may never heal—that still endures under the weight and in the gaps. It is the moan that built America.

The moan is a language, but it transcends speech; it's both a protest and prayer. It is "[t]he only sound that would carry Africans over the bitter waters."[2] The folklorist Howard Courlander, in his study of African American folk songs, grouped the moans with the vocal expression of humming and found this style of singing was not limited to religious songs but could also be found in work songs, the "old-style blues," and the field cries. On the meaning of the moan in African American singing, he wrote that it "does not imply grief or anguish; on the contrary, it is a blissful or ecstatic rendition of a song." The moan, he wrote, occasionally is rendered with mouth open, sometimes with closed lips (humming), and other times in falsetto.[3]

The great Leadbelly (Huddie Ledbetter), who grew up at the turn of the twentieth century on a Louisiana plantation remarked, "Before the people could sing it they'd moan."[4] And "Blind" Willie McTell, the blues songster, echoed these sentiments in his recorded interview with folklorist John Lomax in 1940 when he moaned a deep moan in an Atlanta hotel room before singing a medley of hymns he'd heard around the house and learned from his mother and father.[5]

The moan began with the first deep human expression where words were insufficient. An utterance both of pain and jubilation, the moan found a home on the slave plantations, in the blues and gospel, and later in Louis Armstrong's trumpet and John Coltrane's saxophone.

The moan was a response. The moan was joy. And the moan was a tool to disguise the words when an oppressor got too close. What carries the moan is the inflection, the attitude, and the feeling or mood of the singer or singers. But the moan could also be a deep cry, a vocal response either to accompany the physical labor or to replace a more violent, instinctive reply. In all forms, the moan emanated from, the scholar and collector of African American folk songs John Wesley Work wrote, "the very tissue of their souls."[6]

Call and Response—the Work Song

Antiphonal exchanges in music date back at least to the singing of psalms in English churches, but it was the West Africans and the slaves in America who would come to define what it meant when we speak about call-and-response: the pattern of singing built around a song leader calling out and a chorus answering in response. From the plantation to the blues, it was this democratization of voices that became the dominant mode of singing whether in play, worship, or work. Amiri Baraka, in his seminal book on early Black music, described the basics of the performance of antiphonal singing in African American life.

> A leader sings a theme and a chorus answers him. These answers are usually comments on the leader's theme or comments on the answers themselves in improvised verses. The amount of improvisation depends on how long the chorus wishes to continue.[7]

The call-and-response songs in the antebellum South were about rhythm and—particularly with the work songs—about the practical and physical act of work paired in rhythm with song. The pulse of the rhythm is in sync with the activity of the participants; the music is paired with the physical body, like dance, in movement. The songs, while providing an emotional outlet in addition to being functional, were not an escape from life but a plunge further into it.

The majority of work songs during slavery were religious in nature, but they were not innocuous in the way that many slave owners or early white song collectors, embedded in a racist narrative, interpreted them. Although many were moved by the feeling of hearing the songs, both the plantation owners and the song collectors mistakenly confused the spirituals as evidence of a "primitive" culture and of an acceptance of enslavement. It was because of this—as well as the idea that the songs facilitated more production of work—that singing was most often encouraged.[8] It would take cultural shifts as well as Black intellectuals, writers like W. E. B. Du Bois, and song collectors like James Weldon Johnson to shift this distorted narrative. Arguments that the spirituals were not limited in meaning to freedom in a life elsewhere but justice in this one opened the door to further scholarship during the civil rights movement. This contributed to what we now understand about not only the singing, but the topics of the songs themselves. That is, of course, that—even amid the unthinkable—the spirituals were both a confirmation of slaves' own humanity and a defiance of the horrors of their captivity.[9] As Frederick Douglas wrote, "Every tone was a testament against slavery, and a prayer to God for deliverance from chains."[10]

The Song Leader and the Importance of the Voice

Key to the functionality and performance of the call-and-response pattern is a superior song leader. This role was a critical one because they not only had to sometimes have the necessary superior physical skills to set the work pace, but they also had to possess a deep knowledge of songs. The experienced voice was preferred over the most eloquent, and the way in which this maturity was revealed was through the singer's melodic diversity, a style that survived through the slave trade from Africa. The main two ways to convey this diversity is through the actual arrangement of notes as well as the singer's vocal interpretation. Emphasizing what an experienced voice may sound like, Baraka wrote:

> The tense, slightly hoarse-sounding vocal techniques of the work songs . . . stem directly from Western African musical tradition. . . . In African languages the meaning of a word can be changed simply by altering the *pitch* of the word, or changing its stress—basically, the way one can change the word *yeh* from simple response to stern challenge simply by moving the tongue slightly.[11]

Echoing Baraka's assessment of the value of melodic diversity in African music, Courlander described the value of a "throaty" voice and also referenced West African influences in the determination of what makes a good singer:

> In most traditional singing there is no apparent striving for the "smooth" and "sweet" qualities that are so highly regarded in Western tradition. Some outstanding . . . singers have voices that can be described as foggy, hoarse, rough, or sandy. Not only is this kind of voice not derogated, it often seems to be valued. Sermons preached in this type of voice appear to create a special emotional tension.[12]

An English priest wrote of the interplay of the various voices of both the song leader and "basers" after his visit to a Georgia plantation shortly after the close of the Civil War:

> It is the way they *sing* the words, and the natural seconds they take. . . . The leading singer starts the words of each verse or line, often improvising, and the others who base him . . . strike in with a refrain. The basers seem often to follow their own whims, beginning when they please and leaving off when they please, striking an octave above or below . . . or hitting some other note that chords, so as to produce the effect of a marvelous complication and variety, yet with the most perfect time and rarely with any discord.[13]

Following emancipation, the work song endured in the freedman communities as Black workers began migrating across the country in search of employment. This uprooting in a physical way also had the effect of liberating the songs even further. As men and women moved, so did various lines of songs. With the inherent emphasis on personal expression in folk songs, hundreds of songs were deconstructed and quilted back together with new names and locales in place of the old lines, one song being built into another, forcing new meanings to emerge. In addition, the songs more often became secular in nature and were freed up to include more direct commentary of work and working conditions. On the docks, in the railroad work gangs, and in logging camps, singers sang to relieve tension inherent in the backbreaking physical labor in the burning sun, and oftentimes the new Satan was the work boss.

The Field Holler

The field holler was just a call. It went by many names, but it was about the same thing regardless of circumstances—a solo cry sent with desire across the vast, open sky and through boiling fields, awaiting a reply. The field holler was the secular moan, an a cappella "Amazing Grace" from the gut, sung with or without words in the fields while picking cotton.

> *Ohhhhh [a long moan]*
> *I won't be here long.*
> *Ohhhhh*
> *Oh, dark gonna catch me here,*
> *Dark gonna catch me here.*
> *Ohhhhh*[14]

The sustained moan, sung here in long meter, where the "[v]ocal tones are drawn out and embellished as desired" were typical of the field holler granting a sense of freedom for the singer as they worked, the song continuing "as long as the singing impulse lasts."[15] Frederick Law Olmsted, while traveling on a train one night through the antebellum South for his writings on slavery, came to the end of a railroad line where he fell asleep and was awakened by the laughter of a slave work gang loading cotton bales onto a rail car:

> Suddenly, one raised such a sound as I never heard before; a long, loud musical shout, rising, and falling, and breaking into falsetto, his voice ringing through the woods in the clear, frosty air, like a bugle call.[16]

Like the work song—and due to the substandard living conditions of African Americans who still relied on the agricultural economy for subsistence before mechanization fully supplanted a total reliance on physical labor—the field holler survived in the margins of the American South long after the pronounced end of the institution of slavery. The folklorist Harold Courlander described some of the details in the singing he heard that had survived long after slavery.

> The simplicity of conception, the humming and moaning, the occasional use of falsetto, the rhythmic "ah hmm" heard elsewhere in Negro preaching, and the impression that the singer is singing to himself seem to relate it to the field songs that must have been commonplace in plantation days.[17]

One of the finest examples recorded of a such a field holler was sung by Vera Hall Ward and her song "Black Woman." Ward was an Alabama singer who first met the folklorist John Lomax in the 1930s and later sang "Black Woman" for Alan Lomax in his New York apartment in 1948. Her voice moaned the first lines, and as each line closed, the tone lifted into falsetto "effortlessly as a bird in the wind."[18]

> *Ah-hmmm, I say run here Black woman,*
> *I want you to sit on Black daddy's knee, Lord!*
> *M-hmmm, I know your house feel lonesome,*
> *Ah don't you hear me whoopin,' Oh Lordy!*
> *Don't your house feel lonesome,*
> *When your biscuit roller gone,*
> *Lord help my cryin' time don't your house feel lonesome.*
> *I'm goin' to Texas mamma,*
> *Just to hear the wild ox moan.*[19]

The Instruments

Many plantation owners feared that allowing slaves to possess certain musical instruments may, like the subversive ways religion was used in slave rebellions, lead to insurrection. That is why it did not take long in South Carolina, following the Stono Rebellion in 1739, to enact a series of measures reinforcing the already existent slave codes (codes that, in many cases, affected Native Americans as well) including the ban against learning to write; limiting the amount of slaves gathering in a group to seven (unless accompanied by a white person) especially on Saturday nights and Sundays; and making it punishable by death if any slave shall "wound, maim, or bruise any white person." The white planters, also realizing that many of the African instruments, especially the talking drum, could be made to "speak," forbid slaves from keeping them.[20] Such a rule was even codified into law, prohibiting the "using or keeping of drums, horns, or other loud instruments, which may call together or give sign or notice to one another of their wicked designs and purposes."[21] These laws eventually would be a model for the entire South. But there were instruments that were allowed and often encouraged.

In place of the drum, other instruments gained prominence on the plantations. Among them were bones, quills or panpipes, and the tambourine. But the most frequently mentioned instruments in both the Works Progress Administration's *Slave Narratives* and writings in the eighteenth and nineteenth century by those who either lived on or visited the plantations were the fiddle and the banjo.[22] Often played when slaves were allowed some leisure time, most often on Sundays and Christmas, both instruments were staples of the breakdowns, or dances, a tradition that would survive into the 1900s as a regular Saturday night event. The ability to play the instruments often afforded musicians both an esteemed reputation on the plantation as well as added protections.[23] Speaking on some of the privileges his talent on the fiddle provided him, Solomon Northup, author of *Twelve Years a Slave*, wrote:

> It introduced me to great houses—relieved me of many days' labor in the field—supplied me with conveniences for my cabin—with pipes and tobacco, and extra pairs of shoes, and oftentimes led me away from the presence of a hard master, to witness scenes of jolly and mirth. It was my companion—the friend of my bosom—triumphing loudly when I was joyful, and uttering its soft, melodious consolations when I was sad. Often, at midnight, when sleep had fled affrighted from the cabin, and my soul was disturbed and troubled with the contemplation of my fate, it would sing me a song of peace.[24]

The banjo, originating from the African banjar and constructed from a half a gourd and animal skin, was another staple of the minstrel on the plantation.[25] The status of the banjo player, like the fiddle player, was of more social prominence than his peers. In describing a plantation scene in his 1832 novel, *Swallow Barn*, John P. Kennedy details his encounter with Carey, a banjo player on the plantation who would play for dances and was known as a "seer" who would improvise songs "weaving into song the past or present annals of the family."[26] Following emancipation (but also occasionally during slavery), both the banjo and fiddle—while still finding a home with the wandering roustabouts and Black songsters from the medicine shows to the country breakdowns—would also accompany the singing of spiritual songs. But for many, the instrument's painful association with slavery and its appropriation by blackface minstrel performers as a "tool of cultural exploitation, serving as an emblem of racist slander and stereotyping" eventually led many of the Black banjo players to retire the instrument.[27] In its place, a younger generation of Black performers traded the banjo for another affordable instrument that could just as easily be carried from one town to the next—the guitar.

Also during the slave era, some musicians played the saw as an instrument, using a case knife to change the pitch, a possible precursor to the use of a knife on the guitar during the blues era. George Strickland, a former slave, was ninety-one years old when someone from the Federal Writers' Project interviewed him in Alabama in the mid-1930s. He detailed the abuses he witnessed but also his favorite time—the harvesting or "shuckin'" of corn ritual, which took place in November and was a rare time of celebration on the plantations. It was an event, usually initiated by the owner of the plantation, that included the choosing of teams and team captains who would lead the husking activity and function as the song leaders for the group. After a traditional ceremony, the two leaders, or captains, would sit upon a pile of corn and motivate their teams by leading them in call-and-response chants. Following the event, "chairing" took place—the act of lifting the planter, his son, or overseer around the yard or the house, accompanied by singing.[28] Strickland recalled one such event:

> Old Master took a jug of liquor roun' and got 'em tight and when they got full they would hoist him up and down, tote him round and holler. Then the fun started and they would play the old gourd and horse hair dance, the hand saw and case knife. They could run their hand up and down the saw to change the tune and the leader was on top of the pile of corn singing while all the others would follow.[29]

The Preacher

On the plantations in the antebellum South there was no greater leader than the Black preacher. Due to restrictions and laws on literacy, those who were enslaved relied on, ironically, the same teachings their oppressors claimed to follow— the books of the Bible. And for the oppressed there could not be a more fitting text, as in it the slaves saw *themselves* as the chosen people. The biblical heroes showed them a way out of this most existential terror. In the stories of Jonah, Noah, and Samson they felt a power rise, and what was needed was a leader who could embody the true meaning of these stories—to demonstrate both with voice and expertise the *feeling* of their conviction. Through the door steps the Black preacher, a figure who possesses a superior memory of sermons, a penchant for improvisation, and what W. E. B. Du Bois called "the most unique personality developed by the Negro on American soil. A leader, politician, an orator, a 'boss,' an intriguer, an idealist."[30]

Rebellion

Three of the largest slave revolts were led by Black preachers or religious leaders within the slave communities, and none had a bigger impact on the laws or the course of the country as it veered toward Civil War than that of the revolt of the Virginia slave Nat Turner in 1831.[31]

For Turner, who considered himself more a prophet than a preacher, it was a matter of divine intervention. Deciding early on that he could never be a slave, he devoted his time both to religion and the goings-on of his own imagination.[32] It was during one of these times, at his plough, that he had his first vision from a spirit saying to him, "Seek ye the kingdom of Heaven and all things shall be added unto you."[33] Turner prayed on this revelation for two years before receiving it once more, only affirming in him his greater purpose and union with God. His third calling arrived in 1825 when he witnessed, as part of a vision, white and Black spirits engaged in battle, the sun darkened, and the streams running with blood. Turner retreated to serve this spirit and "obtain true holiness before the great day of judgment should appear." That is when he knew the Holy Ghost spoke to him, and looking toward the heavens, he witnessed the "lights of the Savior's hands, stretched forth from east to west . . . as they were extended on the cross of Calvary for the redemption of sinners."[34] Turner awaited the next eclipse, which he took to be the final sign to begin his work, and thus prepare to "slay my enemies with their own weapons."[35]

By August of 1831, Turner had assembled a small group of men who would carry out the revolt. Commencing with Turner's slave master's family, the rebels killed more than fifty people over four days, sparing not even the young. When the white militias organized, the reaction was swift. All of Turner's men abandoned him, splitting up in different directions. Many were killed or captured. Nat hid under a pile of fence rails in a field for six weeks, only leaving in the darkness of night to get water. Meanwhile, the militias and white citizens took full revenge. As rumors of other insurrections spread, militias fanned out, indiscriminately slaughtering Blacks not just in Virginia but other Southern states. Many of those suspected of participating in Turner's rebellion were beheaded and their heads displayed on poles as warnings to others.[36]

Turner was eventually located on October 30 in a hole he had dug into the earth. He surrendered his sword at gunpoint and was brought into prison for the charge of conspiring to rebel and making insurrection. He pleaded "not guilty" but confessed the entire incident to his lawyer, Thomas Gray. Four days later,

Turner's trial was held and concluded on the same day. When asked at the conclusion of the trial if he had any reason that he should not be executed, Turner answered that his confession was given and there was nothing else to be said. Turner was hanged six days later. He was thirty-one years old. In his confession to his lawyer, Turner was asked, now that he had been captured, if he had been mistaken in his visions. Turner answered by responding, "Was Christ not crucified."

Nothing would ever be the same. A new paranoia was planted in the minds of many slave owners. Two of the ways Southern legislatures sought to deal with preventing future insurrections was by passing anti-literacy laws and restricting or banning slaves from holding religious meetings. In addition, slave patrols were stepped up, and the plantation owners would hire their own preachers to hold service for slaves, preachers who would subvert the meaning of the Bible to suit the owner's needs and quell their fears. A woman named Charity Bowery, quoted by Thomas Wentworth Higginson in his 1861 Atlantic article on the rebellion, noted:

> At the time of the old Prophet Nat the colored folks was afraid to pray loud; for the whites threatened to punish 'em dreadfully, if the least noise was heard. The patrols was low drunken whites, and . . . if they heard any of the colored folks praying or singing a hymn, they would fall upon 'em and abuse 'em, and sometimes kill 'em, afore master or missis could get to 'em. The brightest and best was killed.[37]

> *O some tell me that a nigger won't steal*
> *But I've seen a nigger in my cornfield*
> *O run, nigger, run, for the patrol will catch you,*
> *O run, nigger, run, for 'tis almost day.*[38]

Camp Meetings

Occasionally, the enslaved would hold religious meetings in a cabin, but more often they would take place at what they called "brush arbors," worship spaces in the woods crudely constructed from reeds and brush cane. In the evenings, and with great risk of getting caught and whipped or killed, they would "steal away" to worship. Most often occurring on Sundays, the services were active affairs that required participation from the congregants both physically and vocally with expressions modeled from the field call-and-response chants and shouts.[39] The preacher would lead the service as he would "begin slowly and softly, then build to an unbelievable frenzy," all the while his sermon infused throughout with the cries of the members' shouts of "Oh Lord," "Yeah," and groans. Peter Randolph, a former slave who was freed in 1847 after his owner's death, and who would end up becoming a leading figure in the Black Baptist Church, wrote about a typical service on a plantation.

> Not being allowed to hold meetings on the plantation, the slaves assemble in the swamps, out of reach of the patrols. They have an understanding among themselves as to the time and place of getting together. This is often done by the first one arriving breaking boughs from the trees, and bending them in the direction of the selected spot. Arrangements are then made for conducting the exercises. They first ask each other how they feel, the state of their minds, etc. The male members then select a certain space, in separate groups, for their division of the meeting. Preaching in order, by the brethren; then praying and singing all round, until they generally feel quite happy. The speaker usually commences by calling himself unworthy, and talks very slowly, until, feeling the spirit, he grows excited, and in a short time, there fall to the ground twenty or thirty men and women under its influence.[40]

In 1936 former slave Silvia King, who was born in Morocco but was kidnapped and enslaved in Texas after being bought off the auction block in New Orleans, recalled the worship services on a Fayette County, Texas, plantation where she was held:

> The black folks get off down in the bottom and shouts and sings and prays. They get in the ring dance. It's just a kind of shuffle, then it gets faster and faster and they get warmed up and moans and shouts and clap and dance. Some get exhausted and drop out and the ring gets closer. Sometime they sing and shout all night, but come break of day, . . . [we] got to get to the cabin.[41]

The services relied on oral rather than written communication, often making the words secondary to the *feeling* of the event. "There is a joy on the inside and it wells up so strong that we can't keep still. It is the fire in the bones," recalled an old slave preacher.[42] This emotional devotion was expressed with the raspy, hoarse voice of the preacher, and improvisation of lyrics and utterances by the congregants. The singing itself, also influenced by African culture and its independence of written notation, allowed for a greater freedom of emotional expression through pitch. This bending of pitch and sliding between the notes, as opposed to Western music's faithfulness to a fixed pitch structure, was a concept that seemed foreign to some early observers:

Like birds, they seem not infrequently to strike sounds that cannot be precisely represented by the gamut [scale], and abound in slides from one note to
the other, and turns and cadences not in articulated notes. It is difficult . . . to
express the entire character of these negro ballads by mere musical notes and
signs. The odd turns made in the throat, and the curious rhythmic effect produced by single voices chiming in at different irregular intervals.[43]

Like in the call-and-response patterned work songs in the field, oftentimes
the songs themselves were led not by the preacher but by a designated song leader
who would direct the group in song before the sermon. By calling out a line, the
song leader invited other singers to join in, or to "base" him. Other times, there
would be "no singing in parts," as was on plantations shortly after the Civil War,
when the leader would begin a line and then stop partially finished "leaving the
rest of the words to be guessed at."[44]

The Line Hymn

The lining-out of a hymn is when a preacher or song leader sings or calls out the
hymn one line at a time, followed by the congregation answering in unison a cappella by restating the entire line back, drawing out each word almost to a slow
moan. It endures as one of the most profound religious styles of singing molded
into the Black tradition. The practice, originating in seventeenth century British
churches to assist illiterate white parishioners, was brought to the United States
and was an encouraged form of worship for slaves on antebellum plantations.[45]
Sometimes referred to as the "old one hundreds," the lining-out of hymns in
slave churches—and later free Black churches—became more widely referred to
as "Dr. Watts hymns" after the prolific English hymn writer Isaac Watts, whose
hymn books were widely circulated in the American colonies (though there are
multiple hymns in this style not written by Watts).[46] It was the slaves, many of
whom could also not read due to the strict enforcement of literacy laws, who
would adopt the form and make it their own, distinct from the white tradition.
By blending the African call-and-response style with the long meter field holler,
the responses in this new tradition transformed beyond a mere pleasing sound of
voices reciting the words during a service and became yet another opportunity
for the expression of deep emotion, each song almost always concluding with the
members moaning the melody as they awaited the preacher. The solo hum from
the voice behind the plow in the fields now united with the wider community in
solidarity and prayer.

Remarks on the Burial of a Child on a Plantation in Virginia in the Late 1800s

Near the river, a planter's son and a friend stood still as a funeral procession made up of former slaves and their children passed. Walking two by two and in solemn fashion, the mourners and three preachers followed a horse-driven wagon carrying a child's casket draped in a black cloth as it approached the burial site. Years later, the son would recall what transpired next, beginning with a description of a line hymn while also making an early distinction between the preacher and the song leader.

> While we were gazing intently upon the . . . striking scene, the leading preacher, who had been reading from the Scriptures, closed the book, and the brother on his left raised a hymn. The others joined in, singing with the long, weird whining rhythm. . . . The notes became louder and louder and still more thrilling, ranging from the high-pitched screams of the women to the deep, resonant tones of the men. Wail after wail ascended, one voice beginning the refrain anew when another drawled out its end, and all uniting in the climax. . . . It possessed a pathos and power which went to the heart before the mind could render a cold judgement.[47]

The writer also described the group entering the woods and preparing for the burial, and he remarked on the preacher's "genuine oratory," which he defined as "the power which moves the heart in spite of all resistance." The preacher read from the book of Revelation before closing the Bible and moving into the eulogy.

> At first his voice is calm, and the utterance slow and distinct . . . but continuing his voice grows louder, his sentences are poured out more rapidly while the eyes of all are fastened upon him with attentive reverence. The dew of the mental work drips from his forehead, his arms are moved passionately to assist in the expression of his emotion, his head is thrown spasmodically backwards, his eyes are firmly closed, and after finishing the sentence he sucks in the air with that . . . gasp and groan so effective with his people. Women and children are in tears, the men moan out their responses.[48]

As the ceremony came to a close, the preacher, a vocal and physical embodiment of the transitory stresses and momentary releases of life, restored a sense of calm to the proceedings. His body was still once more and his vocal tones that were just at a growl were smoothed again to a speaking level as the mourners stared, hushed:

A feeling of relief follows when the preacher, with a voice hoarse from the tension at which it has been kept, ends his discourse and steps back from the open grave. Once more a hymn is sung, earth is shoveled upon the coffin, the mound is shaped off, a prayer is made, the group disperses.[49]

The Art of the African American Slave Spiritual

The type of service described above was common in the antebellum South as well as in the early Black churches and communities in post-Civil War America. And although the Black practitioners took from the same sources as the white Christians, their meanings, symbols, and way they practiced the religion was utterly foreign to the white observers. The enslaved Blacks, seeing the similarities between themselves and the oppressed in the Christian Bible, took the themes of the persecuted and merged them with the emotional religious rituals of their rich African heritage and produced what W. E. B. Du Bois called "the most beautiful expression of human experience born this side of the seas."[50]

Freedom from oppression was at the heart of nearly every spiritual. For many during slavery that freedom would come only with death, which was a constant threat. That is why we see death almost as an individual figure in the spirituals. Lines like "When death comes creepin' in my room," and "Before this time another year I may be gone," and "Death's black train is coming" were not just symbols but a literal reality in both slave and post-slavery life. But freedom was not limited to death. The churches and early worship services on the plantations were sometimes "the only place where they could be free from white man's domination."[51] Here the congregation, many of whom were "motherless children" deprived of natural familial bonds when sold away from their parents, found a common union and cohesion within community.

Here they could also sing of freedom not just as a spiritual conquest but as a practical one in the form of escape from the plantation both mentally and physically. Their spirituals were songs of resistance and also life affirming. "The spirituals are songs about black souls . . . affirming that divine reality which lets you know you're a human being," the theologian and author James Cone wrote.[52] They sang lyrics like, "Keep your lamp trimmin' and a-burnin'" as a watch sign for the Underground Railroad, but the lamp was also a symbol for the soul to stay alive and ready when the time would arrive to either fight or leave the plantation. "Joshua Fit de Battle of Jericho," is a reference to the biblical Joshua leading the Israelites in the conquest of the city of Jericho in Canaan and a clear allusion both lyrically and emotionally, through the rhythm, to physical freedom from bondage.[53] It is no coincidence that many of the chosen heroes of the slave songs are those who overcame their trials through faith and with God's help—the God

SPIRITUAL SONG.

Good morning brother Pilgrim, what marching to Zion,
What doubts and what dangers have you met to-day,
Have you found a blessing, are your joys increasing ?
Press forward my brother and make no delay ;
Is your heart a-glowing, are your comforts a-flowing,
And feel you an evidence, now bright and clear ;
Feel you a desire that burns like a fire,
And longs for the hour that Christ shall appear.

I came out this morning, and now am returning,
Perhaps little better than when I first came,
Such groaning and shouting, it sets me to doubting,
I fear such religion is only a dream ;
The preachers were stamping, the people were jumping,
And screaming so loud that I neither could hear,
Either praying or preaching, such horrible screaching,
'Twas truly offensive to all that were there ?

Perhaps my dear brother, while they pray'd together,
You sat and consider'd and prayed not at all,
Would you find a blessing, then pray without ceasing,
Obey the command that was given by Paul,
For if you should reason at any such season,
No wonder if Satan should tell in your ears,
The preachers and people they are but a rabble,
And this is no place for reflection and pray'rs.

No place for reflection, I'm fill'd with distraction,
I wonder that people could bear for to stay,
The men they were bawling, the women were squaling,
I know not for my part how any could pray ;
Such horrid confusion, if this be religion,
Sure 'tis something new that never was seen,
For the sacred pages that speak of all ages,
Does no where declare that such ever has been.

Don't be so soon shaken, if I'm not mistaken,
Such things have been acted by christians of old,
When the ark was a-coming, King David came running,
And dancing before it by scripture we're told,
When the Jewish nation had laid the foundation,
And rebuilt the temple at Ezra's command,   rais'd,
Some wept and some prais'd, and such a noise there was
It was heard afar off, perhaps all through the land.

And as for the preacher, Ezekiel the teacher,
Was taught for to stamp and to smite with his hand,
To shew the transgression of that wicked nation,
That they might repent and obey the command.

For scripture quotation in the dispensation,
The blessed Redeemer had handed them out,
If these cease from praying, we hear him declaring,
The stones to reprove him would quickly cry out.

The scripture is wrested, for Paul hath protested,
That order should be kept in the houses of God,
Amidst such a clatter who knows what they're after,
Or who can attend to what is declared ;
To see them behaving like drunkards a raving,
And lying and rolling prostrate on the ground,
I really felt awful and sometimes was fearful,
That I'd be the next that would come tumbling down.

You say you felt awful, you ought to be careful,
Least you grieve the Spirit and make it depart,
For from your expressions you felt some impressions,
The sweet melting showers has tender'd your heart ;
You fear persecution, and that's the delusion,
Brought in by the devil to turn you away ;
Be careful my brother, for bless'd is no other,
Than creatures who are not offended in me.

When Peter was preaching, and boldly was teaching,
The way of salvation in Jesus' name,
The spirit descended and some were offended,
And said of the men they were fill'd with new wine.
I never yet doubted but some of them shouted,
While others lay prostrate by power struck down,
Some weeping, some praying, while others were saying,
They are as drunk as fools, or in falsehood abound.

Our time is a flying, our moments a dying,
We are led to improve them and quickly appear,
For the bless'd hour when Jesus in power,
In glory shall come is now drawing near,
Methinks there will be shouting, and I'm not doubting,
But crying and screaming for mercy in vain :
Therefore my dear Brother, let's now pray together,
That your precious soul may be fill'd with the flame.

Sure praying is needful, I really feel awful,
I fear that my day of repentance is past ;
But I will look to the Saviour, his mercies for ever,
These storms of temptation will not always last,
I look for the blessing and pray without ceasing,
His mercy is sure unto all that believe,
My heart is a glowing, I feel his love flowing,
Peace, comfort, and pardon, I now have received.

Printed for and Sold by the Rev. RICHARD ALLEN, No. 150 Spruce Street, Philadelphia.

Figure 1. *Bishop Richard Allen's broadside "Spiritual Song," published prior to 1801. Courtesy William L. Clements Library, University of Michigan.*

of love but also vengeance. The God of the Old Testament and the God of the book of Revelation was the God of the persecuted. It was the Old Testament God who saved Daniel from the lion's den and sacrificed his persecutors instead. It was Pharaoh's army who got drowned by the Red Sea after the Hebrew slaves were led safely across by Moses. These are the lines that make up the spirituals, and while many lines may have also been used as code for specific places in the pursuit of freedom, on their face they were not veiled or coded messages. In fact, many slaves at the outbreak of the Civil War were jailed or threatened with violence when singing many of these lyrics.[54] These were very clear messages. The enslaved believed that it would not be in another life that freedom would come but, like their biblical companions, they would be "delivered in this world."[55]

With the spirituals functioning both as an emotional release and a shout for political emancipation, it is natural that the Black preacher became both leader and healer. On the plantations, the preachers served to instill a spiritual and sometimes physical rebellion, as was the case with Nat Turner. Outside the plantations, including prior to emancipation, some former slaves were able to purchase their freedom, form their own churches, and preach on subjects such as abolition and colonization. Some, like Denmark Vesey, were accused and hung on suspicion that they were plotting slave revolts. Bishop Richard Allen, who was able to purchase his freedom and co-founded the African Methodist Episcopal Church, actively worked for Black education and freedom; his church even functioned as a station on the Underground Railroad. Allen also published the first compilation of hymns specifically for African American congregations. His "preaching style was almost never expository or written to be read, but the subject delivered in an evangelical and extemporized manner that demanded action, rather than meditation."[56] Allen advocated for this active, joyful approach to preaching in a broadside ballad he published, a call-and-response dialogue between a confused parishioner (Brother Pilgrim) and a figure who is most likely Allen himself.

With music being an inextricable and vital component of the service, it was incumbent on the preacher to be both guide, griot, and sometimes musician.[57] Baraka wrote that the Black preacher:

> contributed the most musical and most emotional parts of the church service. The long, long, fantastically rhythmical sermons of the early Negro Baptist and Methodist preachers are well known. These men were singers, and they sang the word of this new God with such a passion and belief."[58]

These songs were imbued with emotion and had to be sung with feeling. "In a word, the capacity to *feel* these songs while singing them is more important than any amount of artistic technique," the great writer and civil rights activist James Weldon Johnson wrote.[59] They were also about justice.

> Through all the sorrow of the Sorrow Songs there breathes a hope—a faith in the ultimate justice of things. The minor cadences of despair change often to triumph and calm confidence. Sometimes it is faith in life, sometimes a faith in death, sometimes assurance of boundless justice in some fair world beyond.[60]

Faith in God then becomes the answer to the ultimate evil and terror. But this faith also had to be acted upon. It was not an idealist faith but a pragmatic one. It "comes only in and through the struggle for righteousness—not in passivity," wrote theologian James Cone.[61] That's why the experienced singer was valued over the inexperienced, the hoarse voice of the preacher cherished over the smooth. And the spirituals were the expression of this faith, this bold declaration that freedom was not up to the so-called "masters" or profiteers but came from the divine. So, in the face of cruelty, they made up their minds to "set up an altar dedicated to the God of love."[62]

Am I Born to Die

> *When you feel like moanin'*
> *It ain't nothing but love,*
> *When you feel like groanin'*
> *It ain't nothin' but love.*[63]

It was through the redemptive nature of Jesus' death on the cross and faith in his Resurrection that they assuaged the fear of death. By placing themselves at the scene of the Crucifixion, as they did in the spiritual "Were You There," those who were enslaved were affirming the death not of a distant God but of a physical, human man who lived on Earth and suffered and died at the hands of his persecutors. "The death of Jesus meant that he died on the cross for Black slaves. His death was a symbol for their suffering, trials, and tribulations in an unfriendly world," Cone wrote.[64] And it was Christ's Resurrection that meant death was not the end, and that one day Jesus would return and judge the sinners of the world, liberating the enslaved from bearing that heavy weight themselves.

Jesus walked with them, bestowing upon his companions unconditional love and by doing so granting mercy to the otherwise abandoned. In turn, those who were kept in bondage responded to brutality with resistance—not always through insurrection but also through love. Through faith, Jesus would stay with them and even heal them like he did Blind Bartimaeus, the blind beggar who would have his eyesight restored by Jesus near Jericho. With their capacity for love over hate manifested through the forging of an identity that affirmed their humanity, the enslaved repudiated any definition of them constructed by their captors. Not dissimilar from the innocent victims of systematic oppression in prisons and internment camps who are aware that death is always a constant threat—they had to choose how to respond. Viktor Frankl, a doctor who survived the Nazi death camps, wrote on the healing power of finding meaning and love in spite of the worst of human atrocities:

> I grasped the meaning of the greatest secret that human poetry and human thought and belief have to impart: The salvation of man is through love and in love. I understood how a man with nothing left in this world still may know bliss, be it only for a brief moment.[65]

This choice was critical and was the foundation to achieving a freedom the slave masters never could. Because although they possessed no political power and may have been institutionally enslaved, they were not slaves at all. The real slaves—the ones with the whips, the ones who owned other human beings for profit—hid in their mansions only steps from the slave cabins, and yet they had a difficult time comprehending the unmistakable sublime nature of the sounds and spirit of those who were actually free. This was art in its truest sense; it was the ultimate faith. It did not dwell in the house of logic but in beauty. As Andrei Tarkovsky wrote, "Art acts above all on the soul, shaping the spiritual structure."[66] This "spiritual structure," this freedom, originated within both the individual "I" and the communal "I."[67] And while the individual "I" would be further developed in the era of blues music, the deep moans in the fields and worship houses were about forming that identity, about people locating their own voices as strangers in America in conjunction with a greater truth than their immediate existence. They understood that they were never alone, because they saw the nature of God like the philosopher Saint Augustine did, "as a circle whose center was everywhere, and it's circumference nowhere."[68]

⁛

It is for all these reasons, and the fact that Jesus' Resurrection, for the slaves, meant "the divine guarantee that Black people's lives" were in God's hands that, in song and spirit, they placed themselves beside Jesus when he died—at the site of the Crucifixion.[69] "In Jesus' death Black slaves saw themselves," wrote James Cone.[70] They also had been "pierced in the side," "whupped up the hill," and "nailed to a tree." So, it seemed natural to sing of his death as if they were there. So, they sang:

> *Were you there when they crucified my Lord (Were you there?)*
> *Were you there when they crucified my Lord?*[71]

The other song most often sung about Jesus' death by the slaves was composed by Thomas Haweis, an English clergyman in the eighteenth century. It concerns Jesus' prayer as he knelt in the garden just prior to his betrayal and eventual death. It is likely they never knew the author of this hymn as they stood, hunched in the fields as the evening sun set. Even the precise words as they were written were of less importance than what sprang from that inner voice. Something always remains from the experience, and it is this residue that can be accessed at any point that provides the emotional knowledge that one cannot be defeated by the external forces. It is an internal feeling, and what emanates outwardly is the cry of the soul.

They knew a new day was coming. They were God's chosen people, and one day soon, like the Israelites, the Lord would make a way and they too would cross that Red Sea.[72] So, in their distress, they continued to stare, with faith, to the east as they shouted, hollered, rejoiced, all the while listening for the Lord's footsteps, for the God of love, and they moaned:

> *Dark was the night and col' de groun'*
> *On which de Lord was laid,*
> *His sweat like drops of blood ran down,*
> *In agony he prayed.*
> *Am I born to die,*
> *Am I born to die,*
> *Am I born to die,*
> *To lay dis body down.*[73]

TELL 'EM I'M GONE

Jubilee: The period described in the book of Leviticus (Chapter 25) when, at the end of every fifty years, slaves and prisoners would be freed, debts would be forgiven, and the trumpets would sound.

I'm a-rolling, I'm a-rolling through an unfriendly world,
I'm a-rolling, I'm a-rolling through an unfriendly world,
O Brothers, O Sisters, O Preachers, won't you help me?
—from "I'm A-Rolling," collected in American Negro Spirituals,
J. W. Johnson and J. R. Johnson, 1925

Mark Twain, in a letter prior to the Fisk Jubilee Singers arriving in London in 1873, wrote of the group, "I do not know when anything has so moved me as did the plaintive melodies of the Jubilee Singers."[1] But it was not only the author, who would end up seeing the group in concert multiple times, who was moved by the Singers. As they traveled through the northern United States, this mix of both male and female students from the fledgling Fisk University—even while often hungry and denied lodging—stood and sang before rapt audiences, on a mission to not only save their university but also to reclaim their history through their voices. Through them it would be the first time the world, outside the plantation system, would hear the cry of both the private and collective spirit of those who were enslaved. It was not only the students' voices that could be heard on the platforms but a million souls were lifted through deep anthems like "Steal Away," "Keep Your Lamp Trimmed and Burning," and the Union marching song "John Brown's Body." These spirituals, which had been lampooned by the blackface minstrels already for too long, were now being unmasked and redeemed. What once was kept hidden and private was now visible; their voices rising together, a cappella, like a thousand ships, constructed from the blood of the fields, now sailing out of the troubled water bringing the good news, proclaiming that the trumpet has sounded.[2]

William Doctor ("Dock") Johnson was born in the summer of 1869 to former slaves Dock Johnson and Ellen Whitaker in the now defunct East Texas town of Eutaw. Named by the first settlers in the region, who had ventured from Eutaw, Alabama, the town was situated in the southernmost point of Limestone County about twenty miles east of Marlin. The most populous town in the area for a time, depopulation began to occur about the time of the younger Dock Johnson's birth when the Houston and Texas Central Railway (H&TC) bypassed it for Kosse, a city named for the railroad's chief engineer. It would be the end of the line for the H&TC railroad at the time. A year later Eutaw's post office relocated to Kosse as well, and not long after many of its citizens would do the same. For the freedmen though, there was a more pressing reason to flee Limestone County altogether.

∷

The day of Jubilee was finally announced in Texas on June 19, 1865. The declaration, while officially emancipating the enslaved, still encouraged the newly liberated to stay on their current plantations to work for wages.[3] Nine days later an order was issued restricting the movement of the freedmen by prohibiting them from traveling without passes or permits from their newly defined employers. Idleness was a vice, it warned, that would be met "using every means" necessary. This, of course, was only the beginning.

In his report in early January 1866, the inspector general of the Freedmen's Bureau in charge of Texas, William Strong, reported that east of the Brazos River—where the majority of the plantation economy of the state flourished—many of the freedmen were still being held in slavery.[4] Outlining his grave concerns not only for the economic freedom of the former slaves but also for their safety, Strong wrote:

> The freedmen are in a worse condition than they ever were as slaves. When they were held in bondage . . . cases of extreme cruelty were very rare; it was for the interest of the master to take care of them, and not to ill treat them. Now it is quite different; they have no interest in them, and seem to take every opportunity to vent their rage and hatred upon the blacks. They are frequently beaten unmercifully, and shot down like wild beasts, without any provocation, followed with hounds, and maltreated in every possible way. It is the same old story of cruelty, only there is more of it in Texas than any southern State that I have visited.[5]

That same year, after failing to ratify the Thirteenth Amendment, the Texas legislature convened to pass laws governing Black labor and life in what came to be known as the Texas Black Codes. These statutes prohibited Blacks from attending public schools, voting, holding office, or marrying whites. The bulk of the laws, though, related to labor contracts and defined punishment for disobedience for those under such agreements that mirrored the discipline they may have endured while enslaved.[6] The laws also codified the vagrancy decree issued during emancipation making such "idleness" cause for arrest, and the penalty a fine, or if one was unable to pay (as most so-called vagrants would certainly be unable to do), imprisonment. It also became legal to lease convicts at the moment of arrest—not conviction—to public utility works such as roads and bridge construction, work which previously had been the domain of slave labor. The statute defined a vagrant as "an idle person, living without any means of support, and making no exertions to obtain a livelihood, by honest employment." Examples of vagrants cited in the statute included fortune tellers, prostitutes, gamblers, those who beg for money who are not disabled physically, and "persons who stroll idly about the streets of towns or cities, having no local habitation."[7]

In the ensuing years, particularly in East Texas, the terror perpetrated on the freedmen only increased, and at the state's 1868 Constitutional Convention reports were submitted warning that the "murder of negroes is so common as to render it impossible to keep an accurate account of them."[8] Most of the violence was attributed to the rise of an armed group calling itself the Ku Klux Klan, which targeted not only freedmen, but Mexicans and federal troops as well. Meanwhile, the lawmen, many of whom were members of the Klan themselves, were impotent in its wake.[9] "Texas, as a whole, is in a state of outlawry . . . where murder and persecution of loyal men and disregard for the law is the order of the day," the report read.[10]

For the Black citizens of Limestone County, the violence perpetrated on them at this point was beyond levels of control. For example, in the county seat of Springfield, located about twenty miles north of Eutaw, the freedmen were terrorized and murdered at rates that were too numerous to count.[11] Klan members and gangs indiscriminately murdered all freedmen or Union soldiers they encountered. One man in particular, Simpson Dixon, nicknamed "Dixie," was one of the most feared. Acting as a one-man Klan, Dixon's reign of terror was so murderous he forced many of the freedmen to sleep in the woods at night to evade detection before he himself was finally murdered in 1870.[12]

It was this same year, in June 1870, that the elder Dock, a thirty-year-old tenant farmer, and his wife, Ellen, twenty-five, took their children Sarah, Charity, Elvira, and young William "Dock" and made their way sixty miles west to the town of Valley Mills in southern Bosque County.[13] But even though they had made their way west of the Brazos River, they couldn't have known what the

Daily State Journal out of Austin was reporting at the time: that the county they were fleeing to was averaging two killings a week.[14]

::

John Lomax was born in Mississippi and was only two years old when his parents, James and Susan Lomax, set out for the foreign country of Texas in the winter of 1869. Their destination was the edge of the Bosque River just north of Meridian, the county seat, in Bosque County, located about twenty-five miles north from where Dock and Ellen would reside six months later in Valley Mills. It was here, near a branch of the Chisholm Trail, where the couple would raise their children and work the land, and where John would experience the "hellfire and damnation brand" of religion and first hear the songs that would stay with him a lifetime.[15] As he labored through the heat and dust on the long days on the farm, his constant companions were the cowboy songs and yodels sung by the cattle ranchers along the trails and the field hollers and work songs sung by the hired Black field hands, including Nat Blythe.[16]

Nat was around seventeen and a bond servant to James Thomas Blythe, a Kentucky planter turned banker, when he was brought to Bosque County in 1875.[17] In a scenario that wasn't atypical at the time, Nat had been bonded to Blythe until the age of twenty-one following the death of his mother when he was still an infant. John was nine when he first met Nat in 1876. John's father had hired him to assist around the farm, and even though Nat was twice his age, according to John, he was almost like a brother to him. John Lomax later claimed to have spent hours teaching Nat basic reading and writing skills while "[f]rom Nat I learned my sense of rhythm."[18] With Nat's fondness for jig tunes, field hollers, and the patting Juba dance, Lomax would later recall that "[Nat] danced rather than walked."[19]

But by 1879, when he turned twenty-one, Nat was freed from his servitude to the Blythe family and upon his departure, handed a sum of $1,000. Taking the money, he and John went into town, even taking a couple pictures as a way of remembering each other. It would be the last time John would see him. Regarding Nat's disappearance, John Lomax later wrote, "His negro friends think he was murdered for his money, and his body, bound with baling wire and weighted down with scrap iron, thrown into the Bosque River."[20] If true, it was a fate that would not have been unique in Bosque County or in Texas. It was only a couple of years following Nat's disappearance that an eighteen-year-old Black laborer in Meridian was accused of rape and was dragged from the county jail by a dozen or so vigilantes and hung from a pecan tree nearby.[21] Then, a few years later, at the trial of Sidney Davis in 1866—in what one newspaper reported as "The Texas

Method"— a mob of five hundred overtook the sheriff in a Meridian courtroom and dragged Davis to the Bosque River bridge to be lynched.[22] Just before his murder, Davis made one last plea for a preacher to come and pray for him. The request was swiftly denied, and Davis was promptly strung up with rope and hanged.

> *Were you there when they nailed him to the tree? (Were you there?)*
> *Were you there when they nailed him to the tree?*
> *O sometimes it causes me to tremble! tremble! tremble!*

The elder Dock Johnson also disappeared or died sometime before the mid-1870s. Ellen, now alone with the kids, remarried in January 1876 to a sharecropper named Albert Stewart, and together they and the children drifted a few miles south along the Bosque River to McLennan County. It was here where, at the age of ten, the younger Dock continued to labor as a farm hand for his stepfather. He wasn't attending school and couldn't read or write. John Lomax, meanwhile, sometime before his twentieth birthday, took some money and escaped in the opposite direction, heading fifty miles north along the Brazos to further his education. The world was split in two with Dock going one way and John the other.

INTERLUDE 1
Keep Your Lamp Trimmed and Burning

The first time the hymn "Keep your Lamp Trimmed and Burning" appears to have been written down was in the 1850s after it was heard on James Island, near Charleston, South Carolina. Recorded as "Breddren, Don' Git Weary," it was a group song "sung by the boatman as they rowed," but its most prominent usage was likely as a symbol for readiness in the Underground Railroad, ensuring those enslaved that "the work is almost done":

> Breddren, Don' Git Weary,
> Breddren, Don' Git Weary,
> Breddren, Don' Git Weary,
> Fo' de is work 'mos done.
> Keep yo' lamp trim an' a burnin,'
> Keep yo' lamp trim an' a burnin,'
> Keep yo' lamp trim an' a burnin,'
> Fo' de is work 'mos done.[1]

Ten years later, during the Civil War, it was a marching song titled "This World Almost Done" for the first recognized Black slave regiment in the United States. Assisted by Harriet Tubman and overseen by the white minister and abolitionist Col. Thomas Wentworth Higginson, the men advanced two by two, the soldiers shouting:

> Brudder, keep your lamp trimmin' and a-burnin,'
> Keep your lamp trimmin' and a-burnin,'
> Keep your lamp trimmin' and a-burnin,'
> For dis world most done.[2]

A decade later, the song would be one of the ones chosen by the Fisk Jubilee Singers as part of their fundraising concerts in 1873 and '74.[3]

KEEP YOUR LAMP TRIMMED AND BURNING

Willie Johnson

(CHORUS)
Keep your lamp (trimmed and burning)
Keep your lamp (trimmed and burning)
Keep your lamp (trimmed and burning)
See what my Lord has done

Sister, don't get worried
Sister, don't get worried
Sister, don't get worried

Brother, don't get worried
Brother, don't get worried
Brother, don't get worried
For the work is almost done

Heaven's journey on before
Heaven's journey he's gone before
Heaven's journey
See what my Lord has done

Elders don't get worried
Elders don't get worried
Elders don't get worried
For the work is almost done

Almost over
It's almost over
Almost over
See what my Lord has done

Brother, don't get worried
Brother, don't get worried
Brother, don't get worried
For the work is almost done

BLIND MAN SAT IN THE WAY AND CRIED

The Preacher and the Song Leader

He had heard of this sort of thing happening to others, but never did he believe it could happen to him. In fact, he was always a little suspicious of the stories they would tell. How fantastical they seemed, these visions. And of course, he had heard of St. Paul, who was blinded on the road to Damascus, and Jonah in the belly of the whale, of John of Patmos, of Nat Turner, and of the poor daughter of tenant farmers from France, "The Maid of Orleans," but certainly this sort of thing was quite rare. And although he attended the services where they would sometimes shout out with such fervor, he had never been so moved himself to act out in such ways. But then one day, while plowing in the fields as he had done a hundred times, he heard a voice calling him from the east. He stood for a minute and looked around, but the closest person to him must have been several hundred yards away. Suddenly, his knees became weak, and he felt his body begin to sink down almost to a kneeling position as he descended into the dirt. The entire atmosphere seemed to go silent, and he listened more intently. And that is when he heard the voice again, just as it had come the first time only this time much louder, calling his name. "Now there could be no doubt, his time had come," he thought to himself. Then, suddenly, an intense light encompassed him, blinding him in an instant. When he managed to open his eyes once more, he could see that he now adorned a pair of wings, and within moments he was lifted out of his present condition and began to glide over the field where he just had stood, over the big house, and into a sea of radiant light. But just as soon as it all began it came to a halt, and when he came down he landed in the same spot from where he had departed. He immediately felt an overwhelming sense of peace, and his burdens lifted. He knew that he had been converted. And that's when he heard the voice again calling out to him, saying, "Go forth and preach the Gospel."

Madkin Butler was called when, according to him, God put his eyes out at the age of twenty-two while he was working as an orderly at the Houston Infirmary. The date was August 26, 1895, and, "he felt that the Lord took his sight because he had heard the 'call' to the ministry and had not heeded it, and so the Lord took his sight and called him again," his last wife would later recall.[1] One of the finest hospitals in Texas in the late 1800s, the infirmary was located within a few blocks of the Houston and Texas Central tracks and its Grand Central Station, so close that one could hear the steam engines blowing down the track as they pulled in and out of the station. He had bent over to cleanse his face in a bowl of what he thought was water and got the sting of poison instead.

The conversion experience was often a necessary component of the religious experience for the Black Baptist or Methodist, creating a sharp distinction from the white traditions. While the white tradition may seek out God, "it was not so much the Negro who sought out God as God who sought out the Negro."[2] To be converted meant that your life would be put on a different course, pointed away from the material and toward the heavenly road, but more precisely it was a call to express oneself with all one's beauty and with the gifts that had been bestowed upon you to do so. "God had literally to struggle with him, not to persuade him to give up his sins but to force him to be willing to express himself, to fulfill his mission, in other words to attain individuation."[3] It may have taken his blinding, but this time Butler answered the call, and within a year of this tragedy at the infirmary he was on his way, pursuing that narrow way of the traveler, the evangelist, an original voice joining the order of bards of this burgeoning society— one that was structured on both class and on an artistic scale, and one where within the church hierarchy, the preacher stood at the top.

::

The Missionary Baptist Church, by the time Butler decided to fully dedicate his life to it, had grown to over 110,000 members in Texas since its formation separate from the white tradition of Texas Baptists.[4] In the state, the church was established in fledgling form in early 1866, shortly after emancipation. The seeds had been sown for years, but it was when former slaves were joined by Baptist missionaries that things really began to flourish. In Houston, Baptist minister Israel (I. S.) Campbell and Reverend I. Rhinehart paved the way for what would later become Antioch Baptist Church. It was a church that—in the coming years under the leadership of a young ordained freedmen named Rev. John "Jack" Yates—would reside at the heart of Houston's distinguished Freedmen's Town and transform the lives of many former slaves who flocked to the city from the surrounding plantation communities.

Reverend Campbell, meanwhile, made his way from Houston to the island of Galveston to assist in organizing the First Regular Missionary Baptist Church (later known as Avenue L Missionary Baptist Church). And it would be these two churches that would form the foundation of the Lincoln Missionary Baptist Association, the first independent Black Baptist association in the state. Soon, Baptist churches all over Texas, from Galveston to across the Brazos in McLennan County, were member churches of the association.

Out of the brush arbor and into the church structure, these developing networks and expanding congregations were at the center of this new Black existence. The church was where property and political decisions would be made, and it was one of the few places that the newly liberated could truly be free of surveillance to express themselves. The services took on the emotional exuberance of the slave days, but now, unencumbered by fears of the slave patrol, they could worship with a new sense of freedom. And like in the days of bondage, the congregation required the impassioned presence of a preacher who was able to fill the multiple roles demanded of him. They had to be able to speak with hushed yet affecting tones, but also be skillful enough to rouse the fire from their soul as the spirit sees fit, reminiscent of the ring shouts they grew up with. Music and song were inextricable from the worship experience going all the way back to Africa, and here it was no different. In these first few steps, out from under the direct boot of slavery (but into other oppressive systems), it was the preacher who stood ready to help guide the way through the treacherous path both externally, through institutional commitments, and internally through the language of the soul. So out of the wilderness and into the hands of this stirring orator, the congregation erupts in ecstatic outbursts of joy in the hands of their fervent preacher.

> The stamping, shrieking, and shouting, the rushing to and fro and wild waving of arms, the weeping and laughing, the vision and the trance. All this is nothing in the new world, but old as religion. . . . And so firm a hold did it have on the Negro, that many generations firmly believed that without this visible manifestation of the God there could be no true communion with the Invisible.[5]

Most of the preachers would maintain a base close to home, and they limited travel except to attend the annual association meetings. But others would garner such a wide reputation for their commanding sermons and voice that they demanded to be heard outside their home territory, although mostly at churches within the Baptist associations. Then there were others who, although they may have their own church, preferred the more itinerant path and remained fiercely independent. They saw their mission as more far-reaching and took every opportunity to roam to spread their message or song. Their chosen venue was not the local church but the wide-open spaces that provided the possibility of reaching a mass audience. It was here, at the camp meetings and revivals, where sometimes for weeks at a time and mostly in the summer, thousands would gather to hear electrifying sermons by some of the greatest orators and to be baptized.

Rev. John (J. L.) Griffin was one of the most popular, yet controversial, of these firebrand Baptist preachers in the late 1800s and early 1900s. Born in Shreveport, Louisiana, around 1865, he said he got his nickname from a local reporter around Shreveport who began referring to him as a "sin-slaughterer"—later changed to "Sin-Killer"—after attending one of Griffin's first revivals and river baptisms.[6] By the 1880s he had already established himself as a minister in the Baptist Church in North Texas, but after some trouble and with a vision to become more than a preacher heading a single congregation, he decided to take to the road and become what he termed an "Independent Baptist." Extremely popular, he traveled widely in Texas, and he also spent time in Los Angeles, Oklahoma, and Kansas City, Missouri, leading fervent tent revivals that attracted thousands, both white and Black.

He traveled with his own group of singers and often employed a popular song leader, all of whom would lead the crowds in song and prayer prior to the appearance of Griffin himself. In his ministerial dress and long black coat that extended past his knees, Griffin would make his entrance onto the platform to face the thousands who had traveled to see him. With his searing voice, often at the pitch of a deep growl, he would begin the ceremonies by leading the congregants in an old spiritual. At the close of the song he would launch into the evening's sermon, his preaching centered on saving souls, his voice fluctuating from hushed tones to a rapid fire eruption of speech while the enthralled congregants wailed and answered Griffin's enthusiasm with shouts of "That's right" or "Amen!"[7] One of his favorite recurring themes was that of the Resurrection, and he would end every evening with a stirring rebuke against wickedness, moving the members to rise from their benches in excitement.

> He set out in a well modulated tone, but had not proceeded far until his voice had reached a high pitch, his words poured forth in senseless volubility and his whole demeanor was that of one who had either lost control of his own faculties or was bent on depriving his hearers of theirs. The gyrations he executed, the terror inspiring utterances he vented. . . the excessive physical exertion he underwent, combined to form a mesmeric and hypnotic influence which no doubt has achieved for Sin Killer Griffin the reputation he bears.[8]

By the close of the sermon, Griffin's voice would be so hoarse from exertion that he could barely whisper, but the many who were there to witness him would be so moved they would clap hands, shout, and dance in the aisles. He would frequently close the events by leading the congregants down to the river for baptisms or through a laying on of hands ceremony where many would claim to be healed. Griffin's popularity at the time was immense. Newspapers reported on his revivals often, and his services were also in demand in political circles, including in 1892 when he led the prayer at the Republican State Convention in support of an anti-prohibition candidate. It was a sentiment that, years later, would end in prison time for him, a twist of fate that would change the way we interpret American music.[9]

Griffin was just the newest in the long line of historical bards tracing back to Europe or to the griot in Africa; the gifts of stories and song were critical to their role as keepers of tradition and oral history. These were the protectors of the past but also the poets of the present and the future. And so, in the precarious context of post-slavery, when few had any possessions and many were displaced from familial bonds or illiterate, the new Black bard leapt into the unknown with a fresh song and poetry that was never still long enough to become routine or pinned down. Like the singers themselves, their words remained alive and open to the influence of the fast-moving engine of time and the nature of the artistic spirit, which could be tossed and driven in any direction at any moment.

⁚⁚

A new bardic tradition was emerging in this fertile landscape, but there was a hierarchy beginning with the preacher and song leaders, who often assisted the preacher during church services or revivals, at the top, and the modern-day minstrel or street singer at the bottom. The latter was more of a traveler, and while admired, frequently suffered from an impairment and often had to contend with the derogatory title of beggar. While sometimes the definitions could overlap, James Weldon Johnson, the

Figure 2. *Rev. J. L. "Sin-Killer" Griffin. Austin Daily Statesman, May 20, 1907.*

writer and civil rights activist, classified them into an order of bards in which he distinguished between the "makers of songs" on the one hand and the "leaders of singing" on the other.

> [There] were makers of songs and leaders of singing. They had to possess cer-
> tain qualifications: a gift of melody, a talent for poetry, a strong voice, and a
> good memory. Here we have a demand for a great many gifts in one individ-
> ual; yet, they were all necessary. The recognized bard required the ability to
> make up the appealing tune, to fashion the graphic phrase, to pitch the tune
> true and lead it clearly, and to remember all the lines.[10]

At least one leader of singing, Johnson wrote, could be found in every congregation, but it was the maker of songs who was the most in demand. It was
these singers, traveling from congregation to congregation, who would impart
upon the churchgoers the latest iteration of song. Brought forth from the fire that
resides in the heart and forged with the fortitude that only the life of the traveler
could produce, these were messengers of emotional truths.[11] In James Weldon
Johnson's youth, it was a local laundress, "Ma" White, who led the singing and
"Singing" Johnson who was a maker of songs.

> I can still recall her shrill, plaintive voice quavering above the others. . . . Even
> as a child my joy in hearing her sing these songs was deep and full. She was
> the recognized leader of spiritual singing in the congregation to which she
> belonged and she took her duties seriously. . . . She knew scores of Spirituals,
> but I do not think she ever "composed" any songs.
>
> On the other hand, singing was "Singing" Johnson's only business. He
> was not a fixture in any one congregation or community, but went from one
> church to another, singing his way. I can recall that his periodical visits caused
> a flutter of excitement akin to that caused by the visit of a famed preacher.
> These visits always meant the hearing and learning of something new. I recol-
> lect how the congregation would hang on his voice for a new song.[12]

"Singing" Johnson was both a maker of songs and a leader of singing, "a man
who could improvise lines on the moment" and who "sang with his . . . eye . . .
closed, and indicated the tempo by swinging his head and body." James Weldon
Johnson believed that these were the singers who "made the original inventions
of story and song, which in turn were influenced or modified by the group in
action."[13]

In the late 1920s, folklorist Mary Virginia Bales, while looking for African

American folk songs, happened into a compact Baptist Church in Hearne, Texas, where she witnessed the raw energy produced by the local congregation as they sang "When the Saints Go Marching In." She would later recall the experience of hearing the song, as sung by the members, as having "such a sweep of rhythm to it that one can hardly keep from swaying to the music and joining in with the lusty voiced singers."[14] During this visit, Bales learned of a great aging song leader who lived in the area reminiscent of James Weldon Johnson's depiction of bards: of "Singing" Johnson and the song leader. Bales wrote:

> The songs that show more complicated verse structure and more variation of theme are built upon the "call and response" plan. The "leader" calls out the leading verse, and the group answers with a refrain. The "leader," who goes from one community to another, has to be a man of some talent for singing and verse making, as well as a man who can rise to the demands of a hundred different occasions. . . . There are still a few of these men in Texas. . . . M. B. Butler, of Hearne, is one . . . I am thinking of. He is known as "Blind Butler" by a third of the Negroes of the state. He is a preacher but is more famous as a song leader.[15]

> *When de saints go marchin' in,*
> *When de saints go marchin' in,*
> *When de saints go marchin' in,*
> *Good Lord, I wanna be in dat numbah!*[16]

Marian Madkin Butler was, like Dock Johnson, the child of former slaves. He was born near the convergence of the International-Great Northern Railroad and the Houston and Texas Central Railway lines, forty-five miles northwest of Navasota in Hearne on April 15, 1873. It was in the middle of cotton country in a railroad town, and Madkin was the fourth child born to James and Rachel Butler, who had taken to tenant farming following emancipation. Hearne would be a constant home base for Butler throughout his life as his prominence as a singer flourished into the early twentieth century. Following his blinding in 1896, the Black newspapers at the time detailed an extensive travel schedule as Butler offered his talents to the various revivals within the Baptist Church and the Lincoln Association, including numerous association meetings and conventions from Oklahoma to Iowa. Butler was known by several names including his initials, M. B, and was more frequently referred to as "Blind Butler." Like most of the leaders of the church, he seemed to always be dressed in a suit and was an imposing figure according to his 1918 draft card, which listed him as tall and "stout." His voice was always unaccompanied, preferring the solo route, which the newspapers at the time described as "jubilee style" singing.[17]

Butler's role as song leader with the church entailed working hand in hand with all the prominent church leaders of the district. These included preachers Rev. I. R. Richardson and Rev. Isaac (I. S.) Golden, both of whom served as pastors in Butler's home city of Hearne, as well as Rev. J. D. Leonard, who for a time served as pastor at Butler's home church of New Elam Baptist.[20] He also would have worked with some of the most influential preachers and social reformers of his time including Rev. H. M. Williams, who in 1904 took over the esteemed Avenue L Baptist Church in Galveston following the 1900 hurricane and was recognized as one of the "best scholars of the race and one of the recognized leaders of the denomination."[18] Williams also served as moderator of the Lincoln Association for many years when Butler would have been the most active and played a prominent role in advocating for social reform and was a vocal critic of the social conditions he saw his race experiencing in the South. Writing in the *Houston Daily Post* in 1917, Williams addressed many of the issues he saw around him.

> A surface view of the negro people which shows him generally jolly and good-natured, with some schooling, a little property accumulated by men and women among us, a partial right of suffrage makes him appear to be "doing well," when really, he is sick at heart from ill treatment and poverty. He needs two things and needs them badly—that is, encouragement and protection. He does not need social equality with white folks, and he does not want it. . . . No, that is not what he needs or wants. He wants something better than social equality. He wants legal equality—equality before the courts of justice. He wants equality of opportunity to work and make an honest living without being shut out from so many places of industry and employment simply because he is black.[19]

These are the types of men Butler was routinely surrounded by and would assist in his role as a song leader within the church, in preparing the congregation, emotionally, for worship. His duty was to take charge of the devotional section, the commencement of most Missionary Baptist services of the day. The devotional entailed several parts, most of which Butler would lead, beginning with the line hymn, the antiphonal call and response song that was, following slavery, a staple at formal undertakings like funerals and would set the emotional tone for the Missionary Baptist service.[21] With its abbreviated utterances and moaning responses, the line hymn was an integral component of the devotional section, acting as an emotional bridge for the congregation as members made

their entrance into the church, carrying them across the threshold from whatever was on the outside into the spiritual domain. Following this opening section of the devotion, usually a prayer would follow as well as a welcoming to the
church members. Tithes or offerings would be collected, and finally the song
leader would once again lead the congregation in song, this time a number more
energetic in tone than the lined-out hymn which began the service. All of this,
of course, would precede the grand entrance of the preacher who would stir the
members to an all-out fury of the senses for the next sixty to ninety minutes as he
exerted every last ounce of energy in service of the spirit—sometimes high, sometimes low, but always moving. The intensity poured out of his physical body and
hoarse voice before he brought it to a more sustainable level and finally came to a
halt or sometimes closed with another line hymn.[22]

This was the rhythm of the Baptist service: to begin with the deep moan and
build to ecstatic joy, and to leave your spirit filled with love. Like Mozart modu-
lating melodies through different keys and keeping the listener awake with sud-
den harmonic shifts, these two bookends of the song leader and preacher's tones
were perpetually in motion, hitting every note of the human emotional scale. The
entire church would be constantly engaged and alert, and if both the preacher and
song leader were of extreme talent, a rarity, it could be something to experience.

::

It was because of his talents that Butler's services were in such high demand.
Accounts place Butler visiting many locations inside his home state and out, collecting money from part of the collection to help assist with travel and living
expenses, much in the same way "Singing" Johnson did.[23] "Wherever Blind Butler goes the people gather," one announcement read.[24] "Brother Butler, the blind
man, led in a fervent prayer," reported another paper from an association meeting
in 1910.[25] By this time, Butler had dedicated himself to his role as a "singer," as
he listed himself in the census of that year, and was only at the beginning of the
success he would enjoy over the next decade. The Black newspapers of the time
printed detailed reports on many church functions, members, and travels of the
most in-demand preachers, but Butler is one of the only song leaders who was
consistently mentioned as a regular visitor at various Baptist churches within the
Lincoln Association. In 1904 he married Hannah Steward in Fayette County,
south of Hearne, but the marriage lasted only seven years, ending in February
1911 with her early death. She was buried in the all-Black Greater Riverside
Cemetery in Robertson County, and the inscription on her marker read: "Hannah Wife of M.P. Butler Died Feb. 5 1911 Age 43 Years."

::

In June of 1911, a grand two-day celebration was convened at Emancipation Park in Houston's Third Ward to celebrate the annual holiday of Juneteenth, a commemoration of the official end of slavery in Texas announced from Galveston in 1865.[26] The festivities brought in leaders of the Lincoln and Southwestern Baptist associations as well as thousands of attendees. A magnificent parade strolled through the Black communities of the city, prayers were read, new members were chosen for church leadership, music was played, and a fireworks display concluded the celebration on June 20.[27] It was here that Butler most likely met his second wife, Ophelia, with whom he would spend the rest of his natural life. They were married by the Reverend Hilliard (H. R.) Johnson, who at the time was a leading preacher of his day as well as the pastor of St. John's Baptist Church in Houston, located not far from Emancipation Park.[28]

A few months after the Juneteenth celebration, Butler worked as the song leader for "Sin-Killer" Griffin in Victoria, Texas, at a camp meeting that was so successful it lasted over a week.[29] He was welcomed all over the state and was frequently referred to as "the noted evangelist singer" or the "great blind evangelist."[30] In addition to invitations to perform across Texas, there are reports from Langston, Oklahoma; Eldora, Iowa; and Kansas City, Missouri. "The greatest Negro Evangelist Singer in the world," is how the Reverend Arthur (A. A.) Moore, a preacher from Austin who accompanied him, announced his participation in a monthlong trip in a Kansas City newspaper in June 1917. In the advertisement, Moore described Butler's oratory as "capturing because of the poetry and music in his singing (fig. 5)."[31] At events like this, in addition to being a featured singer, Butler would be in charge of running and hosting the revival for the local preacher.[32]

Butler made good money from his services, enough for him and Ophelia to invest in property as advised by the teachings of Rev. Jack Yates at Antioch Baptist Church.[33] His earnings were accumulated, in part, from the church collections taken up on his behalf at the various services and revivals, and also from the sale of his broadside ballad sheets, which he printed and carried with him while on the road to the various association meetings. It was here, at the meetings, that Butler would "generally take up a position on the lawn of the church, outside the building, and . . . would sing as the people were gathering" and afterwards would sell his "ballet" sheets.[34]

Butler, as a maker of songs, was the religious version of the secular minstrel singers. He picked up variants of melodies or lyrics of songs from hymn books or along the long railway lines on his way to sing for a new congregation in some faraway town, and then he altered them to fit his mood or the current state of life that he found himself in. For ballad makers, the songs were not written in stone, but instead were something always breathing, begging to be released from formal ownership and renewed through consistent communal and individual improvisation. This is the folk tradition, and although anyone who could spare a nickel may be able to purchase a ballad sheet from a rambling street singer or from Butler at an association meeting, the popularity of each song was dependent on the talents and singing of the individual singer. To both the composers and the audience, authorship was secondary to performer's ability to improvise and convey the *meaning* of what had been written. The ballad, according to the Texas folklorist Dorothy Scarborough, was "started by some unknown soldier of song, and kept alive by thousands of others. A song passed from lip to lip, till it is almost unrecognizable, and yet it is the same."[35]

Butler's unique versions of these otherwise familiar hymns were printed on paper about two inches wide and eleven inches long as broadside ballad sheets (fig. 3, 4). He also carried a calling card emblazoned with his image. The card reveals a sober looking man with a restrained look on his face. He is dressed in his suit of black and white with his blinded eyes hidden behind a pair of glasses appearing to almost stare out from the paper. The card also included a brief biography and highlighted his expertise as an evangelist—"He has been the means of thousands turning from the dark," and "his prayers pierces the hardest hearts and melts the eyes to tears."[36] While the popular ballads sung by Texas songsters included tales of gambling, like "Jack O' Diamonds," or murder, like "Ella Speed," Butler's ballads were all of a religious nature. Most likely carried with him in a briefcase, they consisted of "Old Time Religion," the old slave patrol song "Run, Sinner, Run," and "Amazing Grace," which he most likely would have sung as a line hymn to start many services.[37] There were versions of the Titanic ballad circulated almost immediately following the disaster in 1912, but Butler is thought to have distributed the Texas version under the title "God Moves on the Water."[38] In addition to other ballad sheets like "I Am Working in the Lord," "Lead Me On," and "Christ Went on Man's Bond," he was also known for singing a version of the spiritual "Little Boy How Old Are You" that included lyrics inspired by the story of Jesus in the temple found in Luke 2:46.

I'm only twelve years old.
Of this little boy you have this to remember,
He was born the twenty-fifth of December,
The lawyers and the doctors were amazed,
All had to give this little boy praise.[39]

M. B. Buttler, The Blind Evangelist.

Has a state wide reputation in Revivals, Association and Conventions. He has been the means of thousands turning from the dark and broad way of sin into the clear and beautiful way of light and life. His songs arouses the inspirations and excites the emotions. His prayers pierces the hardest hearts and melts the eyes to tears.

It will pay any pastor to secure his aid in revivals.

He lost his sight while working at the Houston Infirmary on Aug. 26, 1895, inside of 24 hours. He did not enter the Evangelical Field until June, 1896.

M. B. BUTTLER, Hearne, Texas.

Figure 3. *Madkin Butler calling card. James Avery Lomax Family Papers, 1853–1986, Dolph Briscoe Center for American History, University of Texas at Austin.*

All along Butler's road were strewn the remnants of human souls. These were the forgotten, blinded, and disabled of his race left out in the cold due to discrimination, lack of opportunity, and the absence of resources that might otherwise fill in the gaps. Left to their own devices, few had little choice but to take to the streets, standing alone or with their family along the cruel sidewalks or street corners to sing religious songs, tin cups held firmly in hand or strung crudely to an inexpensive fiddle or guitar. They were the mendicant class, and although many sang religious songs or sold ballad sheets much like Butler to survive, they were not a part of the church in any substantial way. Instead, they were often regarded only as beggars, and it is this group who occupied the lowest rung of bard in American society. Most carried some variant of a single message that would frequently be scrawled on a cardboard sign that hung from their necks reading: "Please Don't Pass Me By. I Am Blind But You Can See."

It's a phrase derived from the parable of Bartimaeus, the blind beggar from the Bible, whose sight was restored as Jesus passed him near Jericho. And while Butler prided himself on the fact that he never had to put himself fully at the mercy of others, this was a song that he, and many that he would pass along the way, would sing.

Fanny Crosby, a white American mission worker and poet who was blinded as a child, composed the hymn "Pass Me Not, O Gentle Savior" in 1868 after she visited a prison and, upon leaving, heard one of the prisoners call out in a "pleading voice, 'Good Lord, do not pass me by.'"[40] The hymn was so popular that it was written and rearranged in ballad form several times and became a staple for many of the Black blind singers, including Isaac White, a religious street singer who could often be found wandering the streets of Hempstead, Texas, selling his ballad sheets. It was also a staple for Butler, who would often feature the song at the opening or closing of his appearances at revivals and association meetings.[41]

Crosby's version of the hymn contains no mention of the biblical Bartimaeus, but in the ballad circulated in Black circles the blind outcast is reinserted in his proper place as the main figure. This change was also reflected in the title, now reborn as "De Blin' Man Stood on de Road an' Cried." It's a song reassembled in the typical ballad and folk tradition to reflect the circumstances of the living Bartimaeus—out there hungry but still calling out, still hoping, still praying for a little mercy, and still singing:

O, de blin' man stood on de road an' cried,
O, de blin' man stood on de road an' cried.
Cryin' O, my Lord, save me,

CHRIST WENT ON MAN'S BOND.

Song By M. B. BUTLER, The Blind Man,
HEARNE, TEXAS.

I

My God said in Creation
    If we make man he will sin.
Christ said if he should break the Law
    I will bring him back again.

CHORUS.

    Jesus went on Man's bond,
    Went on Man's bond;
    Came all the way from Heaven down
    And went on Man's bond.

II

When Man had broken God's Holy Law
    Was on the sinking train;
Christ opened the Book of Seven Seals
    And in there wrote His name.

III

While writing in the Book of the Seven Seals,
    In writing the name down, said,
Four thousand and four years
    I will go on Man's bond.

IV

Father, prepare me a temporal bond
    That I may go down;
I promised Justice four thousand years
    I would go on Man's bond.

V

While he was hanging on the Cross.
    The blood was streaming down;
I promised Justice four thousand years
    I was going on Man's bond.

VI

Old John was taken captive,
    Placed in a kettle of oil;
The Angel from Heaven descended down
    And the oil refused to boil.

VII

You read in the Book of old Daniel
    Somewhere about the latter clause;
The Angels left for Glory
    And locked the lion's jaws.

VIII

You read about Paul and Silas;
    Those boys were prison bound,
And just before day when the cry was made
    The jail came easing down.

IX

While praying in the garden of Gethsemane
    The sweat was raining down;
I promised Justice four thousand years
    I was going on Man's bond.

X

He came to the River of Old Jordan,
    Baptized there by old John,
And now he is sitting in Old Glory
    And is yet on Man's bond.

Figure 4. An example of a ballad Butler would distribute. James Avery Lomax Family Papers, 1853–1986, Dolph Briscoe Center for American History, University of Texas at Austin.

M. B. BUTLER
The Blind Evangelist
Hearne, Texas   Box 303

Figure 5. Madkin Butler. Robert "Mack" McCormick Collection, Archives Center, National Museum of American History, Smithsonian Institution.

De blin' man stood on de road an' cried.
Cryin' what kind o' shoes am dose you wear,
Cryin' what kind o' shoes am dose you wear,
Cryin' O, my Lord,
Save me
De blin' man stood on de road an' cried.
Cryin' dat he might receib his sight,
Cryin' dat he might receib his sight,
Cryin' O, my Lord, save-a me,
De blin' man stood on de rod an' cried.
Cryin' dese shoes I wear am de Gospel shoes,
Cryin' dese shoes I wear am de Gospel shoes,
Cryin' O, my Lord,
Save me
De blin' man stood on de road an' cried.[42]

By the time the United States began drafting soldiers for the First World War, Butler and Ophelia were still residing in Hearne. Butler was in his mid-forties and listed his occupation as "Evangelist" and his address as "On the Road." And the road is where he spent his time for much of the decade. But when he wasn't away singing at the conventions or meetings, most often in the cooler months when the revivals were fewer, he could be found on Sundays at the Elam Missionary Baptist Church on the west side of Hearne. On other days, outside of church, he was fond of sitting alone on the steps of his front porch singing in the chilly evening breeze. After the train engines were far into the distance, and if you were out for a late stroll or just stepping out for a moment to hang clothes on the wire to dry, you may hear him, his booming, raspy voice traveling over a mile, sending out a message of hope for the saints and ringing out a warning to the sinners.[43]

But Butler was still of the old school, a class of singer that wasn't going to be around forever just due to the nature of things. Outside of the church, there were new sounds rising up from the streets of the expanding cities, the train depots, and the Saturday night jukes to meet the needs of a generation that yearned for an expression they could call their own. It had been boiling for years.

INTERLUDE 2

If I Had My Way I'd Tear the Building Down

The text origins for "If I Had My Way" can be found in the various interpretations of the spiritual "Wasn't That a Witness for My Lord" and was included as part of a collection titled *Calhoun Plantation Songs*, first published in 1901.[1] In this version, Samson's story is included along with that of Adam and Nicodemus as examples of the various witnesses "for my Lord":

> Wasn' that a witn-ness fo' my Lord,
> Wasn' that a witn-ness fo' my Lord.
> Read a-bout Samson from his birth,
> Stronges' man ev-er live' on earth.
> Read way back in de ancien' time,
> He kille' five thousan' ob de Phil-is-tine.[2]

Eight years later, in 1909, the folklorist Howard Odum included a version of the song in his collection of religious Black folk songs that closely resembled the one collected in 1901, both sharing its lines on Samson and the "witness" chorus.[3] The Fisk University Jubilee Singers recorded one of the earliest versions of the hymn in 1911 for the Victor label.[4] Up to this point, the song was strictly focused on the "witnesses," while biblical figures could be rearranged or inserted in the various verses around the chorus, and Samson was still limited to only a few verses. But in 1919, Scarborough, the folklorist, included what she described as a "hymn ballet" in her book *From a Southern Porch*. This version excised any reference to "witness" or other biblical figures to create a stand-alone ballad solely dedicated to Samson and Delilah.[5] Likely collected in the Central Texas region, it's unlike the other versions for this reason and because of its inclusion of the "If I had my way" chorus.[6] As Scarborough did not detail who relayed the ballad to her, we can never know if she may have come to this by hearing Johnson himself or another street singer. She described a musician who sang the song to her as he "twangled the strings of his ghostly guitar."[7] It is this adaptation that closely mirrors the version Johnson would go on to record in 1927.

The shift from "Wasn't That a Witness" to "If I Had My Way" is instructive because it shifts the focus away from Samson as merely a figure in the Bible and thrusts him into a tale of Old Testament vengeance: a warrior who was blinded, enslaved, and then, with his strength returned, able to tear down the temple of his captors. In this version, it is clearly a protest and was sung as such by the Pentecostal preacher Rev. T. T. Rose for a recording in 1927; in Rev. J. M. Gates's sermon recorded the same year; and by the character Slow Drag in August Wilson's play *Ma Rainey's Black Bottom* after his younger bandmate, Levee, describes the lynching of his father.[8]

James Baldwin, the author and civil rights activist, brought attention to the importance of the song's double meaning in a 1969 speech.

> The church has operated in the life of the American Negro, who was once a black African slave, as his only form, the only place where he was relatively free. And it is also the place in which he was able to act out, to sing out, to dance out, his pride, and his terrors, and his desire for revenge. All those sermons are bloodthirsty, and they're not talking about devils, and Samson and Delilah, or any of those things: they're talking about the master. And the song say it's about Samson, and the master thought it was supposed to be about Samson, only now he's beginning to think it was about something else. The man says, the slave says, "If I had my way—if I had my way—I'd tear this building down." That sounds like a very happy, innocent church song. It's lethal.[9]

IF I HAD MY WAY I'D TEAR THE BUILDING DOWN

Willie Johnson

Well, if I had my way
I had-a, a wicked world
If I had-Lord, tear this building down

Delilah was a woman fine an' fair
Her pleasant looks-a, her coal black hair
Delilah gained old Samson's mind
A-first saw the woman that looked so fine

A-well went to Timothy, I can't tell
A daughter of Timothy, a-pleased him well
A-Samson told his father to go an'
Help me Lord

(CHORUS)
If I had my way
Well, if a had-a, a wicked world
If I had, ah Lord, tear this building down

Samson's mother replied to him
'Can't you find a woman of your kind and kin
'Samson, will you please your mother's mind
Go' and marry that Philistine
Let me tell you what Sampson done.
He broke at de lion, an' de lion run.
Well, if I had-a, a wicked world
If I had, ah Lord, tear this building down

So many a thousand had formed a plot
Not many days 'fore Samson was caught
A-bind his hands whilst walkin' along
looked on the ground and found a lil' jawbone
He moved his arm ropes, a-pop like thread
Got through slaying, three thousand were dead

Poor Boy Long Ways From Home

It was just past eight in the evening when I decided to move outside the station to get some fresh air. That old hot sun had been beating on me all day, and I wanted to catch a glimpse of it finally going down. But what I wanted more than that was to just get home. I had arrived at the Yazoo & Mississippi Valley Railroad train depot at Tutwiler just about a quarter past noon, plenty early to watch the train—that I had caught almost a hundred times—pull into the station, hop on with my trumpet, and be on down the line. But it was not to be, and nothing had been explained. I was only told, "It was coming." In fact, I was told that so many times I just quit asking. Now all the other passengers had gone. To where, I have no idea. No one seemed to be going my way, and now the whole station appeared empty, as if in a dream. "That's what I get coming back down South," I whispered to myself as I stepped out onto the platform and set my suitcase down. There's no question that if I had packed up and left hours ago, I could have made it back to Clarksdale just by walking. The thought had definitely crossed my mind, but now it was too late. My whole body ached; I was hungry, and I was beat. So I sat and closed my eyes.

The next thing I remember is being jolted awake. There, suddenly beside me, sat a man of my same race and around my same age strumming a guitar, but in a manner unfamiliar yet utterly moving to me. He possessed rugged features common to the many wandering railway tramps I would frequently see in the depot stations, and he wore a look on his face that revealed a misery all too common in these parts. His clothes were ragged, and his toes were busting from the seams at the tips of his shoes, but none of it seemed to bother him. And that sound. I, at the time, could not find words to describe it. I had spent nearly my entire life in the music business and thought I heard everything, but here was this tone that seemed to penetrate right to my soul, and emanating from the most rudimentary of devices—one of the cheap guitars I had periodically seen advertised in some of the mail order catalogs, and a simple pocket-

knife being pressed against the strings. As to his origins, my initial assess-
ment seemed correct as the lines that accompanied this sound, which
he would repeat three times, were in reference to the crossing railway
lines in Moorhead, just south of where we were sitting: "Goin' where the
Southern cross' the Dog."

It was shortly after this that my train, long delayed, finally pulled
into the station. Prior to boarding I looked to say goodbye and get the
man's name, but he was nowhere to be found. Now, looking back, I can't
help but wonder about this mysterious experience. It was many things,
but mostly I thought about the decision of me declining that band leader
position in Michigan which led me to the South again, about me get-
ting stuck there in Tutwiler on that specific night, and then, out of all the
places, this brilliant musical drifter had chosen that exact spot beside me,
out of a whole empty station, to take his rest. Whatever it was, it seemed
like fate.[1]

It was a time of movement and change in the South and across the United States as cities were growing due to the expansion of railroads. In Texas, trains like the Missouri-Kansas-Texas Railroad (MKT or Katy) and the Atchison, Topeka and Santa Fe Railway (Santa Fe) became household names. The Houston and Texas Central spanned almost ten thousand miles of track from Houston to the Red River by the late 1890s, hitting all points in between, including Navasota, Hearne, Corsicana, and Dallas. This new transportation provided a way out of the South for some African Americans who were fed up with the discriminatory conditions in nearly every aspect of public and political life. In fact, the 1890s saw a massive flight of African Americans to the North, the first of what became several streams of migration over the ensuing decades.

The music in the Black communities was also quickly evolving. The religious songs were, for the most part, still being sung a cappella, but as people had more freedom to move and work became more transient, a different type of song was also being spread, developed, and expanded. Scott Joplin, a former railroad laborer from Northeast Texas, would propel ragtime into the mainstream.[2] Soon to follow would be boogie-woogie, a sound originating in the sawmill and railroad towns along the lines of the Santa Fe and the Texas and Pacific railways. This was enter-tainment music, a chance to let off steam and to express oneself after a day of grueling work, but it was also something more. It was an original musical language, one that expressed a more exuberant sense of wildness than would have been afforded the earlier generations. Oftentimes no words even had to be sung; and for those who played or stayed up in the all-night chock houses gambling and drinking, that rhythm was as much the truth as any they had heard from any sermon. Sunday may have been for church, but the nighttime and, especially on Saturday nights, the stage belonged to the itinerant solo performers who let it all out on the keys, fiddles, or banjos. Whether they were singing or just playing, what came out was the sound of the human condition carved deep in the soul from the same struggles that birthed the spirituals; and just like the spirituals, it was all about the feeling and about getting together and saying—"Ain't no system gonna take my soul!"

This was a world outside of the church, but its core function wasn't much different: to restore social bonds in a community pushed out from the greater society. If they could not be accepted, then one of the solutions was to lay a new foundation stone by stone. New heroes, like John Henry, were being born from the old, and forms of song like the field holler, now freed from the confinement of the slave plantation, evolved into a more direct critique of the labor conditions, the bosses who watched over them, and the existential alienation many felt. But there was also a joy in the music that had nothing to do with any of that; it was just a celebration of being alive, and a freedom to say it out loud in a way that would have been impossible a few decades prior.

It was an original language that had to be forged to get at what was going on *now*. For the individual now uprooted, it would take a new voice and a new sound to affirm a hopeful existence in the face of the harsh realities of modern life. Many in the younger generation—who felt the residual effects of slavery but did not bear the personal scars—needed their own mode of expression separate from the spirituals. Money trouble, fear of being locked up, drinking, lovers leaving, and the overall violence that came with the struggles of poverty were the themes that would make up this new American art form.

These were the secular bards who existed outside the order of the church. Some were sharecroppers who would play the country party circuit on the weekends, while others were full-time ramblers who whistled train songs as they rode the rails and sang murder ballads about real life incidents—crimes that would be difficult to believe if you weren't around when they happened. Many bards took on multiple aliases to cover their tracks from jealous husbands or the police, who were always never too far behind, ready to pick them up on trumped-up charges and send them straight to the bottoms. It was here where the call-and-response of the fields became solo, where one line was repeated not by the group but by the performers themselves, because there were many days when there were no groups to offer a response. It was self-reliance at its best and at its worst—a freedom of having nothing and being no one, but where home was wherever you could lay your head, and too often the cold ground your bed.

There was music everywhere if you were in the right places to find it. Scenes like the one recalled by a woman who had just moved into a neighborhood in New Orleans in 1892 were not uncommon.

> Every night I would see the Negroes going through the streets with their gui-
> tars, and they would stand under the galleries serenading. They sang sweet
> love songs, and I could hear their voices in the quiet. The first night I was in
> New Orleans my husband and I walked through the Vieux Carre together in
> the moonlight. It was a beautiful spring night. When we turned, the corner
> in front of the Cabildo, right across the street from our flat, there was a man
> under the arches with a hurdy gurdy playing very softly, *After the ball is over,*
> *after the dance is through.*[3]

On Saturdays, when the weather was good, many of the Black share-croppers from the cotton country would ride into town and hit the streets of the freedmen town districts. It was a day to cut loose, spend some money, and at night head to a "breakdown" or Saturday night supper where a solid meal could be had and dancing could extend until the early morning hours. It was here that the local string band, songster, "musicianer," or "music physicianer" (all terms that would eventually merge into the one word "songster") could be found playing instruments that had descended from slavery and were the most equipped to travel at short notice, including the banjo, fiddle, and harmonica.[4] And while the vast majority of the names of these performers will forever remain unknown in the written history of music, there were two such performers out of Texas who would have a far-reaching influence on the evolution of playing styles, folk songs, and the younger generations of performers who would carry on their legacies. They were the first type of songster—as opposed to the roustabout who was always on the move—who would set the stage for the coming of a musical revolution. But they did so in backyards and gin houses, not on the minstrel stage or in the recording studio. Most of them had families and made a living farming on shares

during the week, but who would play music in the evenings and especially on those high-spirited Saturday nights.

Lewis Shaw was a sharecropper born in 1872. He spent most of his
life in Brenham and Washington County area of Texas, and he would,
like Butler, sing the old a cappella spiritual songs and sell ballad sheets.
But on the nights of the picnics, fish fries, and breakdowns, he could
be found with an accordion, harmonica, and later a guitar entertaining
with the early ballads or rags common in Texas like "Ella Speed," "Take
Me Back Baby," and "Alabama Bound."[5] And in Navasota, an area of
Texas about twenty-five miles northeast from where Shaw would entertain, lived Charles Lipscomb. Born in 1868 with a father who was both
a banjo and fiddle player, Lipscomb would entertain on the party circuit
and at square dances around the area with his fiddle, or "box" as it was
often called. The instrument was possibly the most popular instrument
for the solo performer not only because of its inherent portability, but
also because it could replicate the human voice so well.[6] It was a quality that lent itself to vocal and instrumental antiphonal exchanges that
normally would have required a singing partner.[7] These were men who,
like Butler and Dock Johnson, were the first generation born out of the
institution of slavery but still under the thumb of racialized terror. They
grew up knowing all the forms of song that emerged from the fields and
the worship services, but they now had a little more latitude to explore
and improvise in ways that their parents never could. Theirs was a scene
that moved parallel to the circulating of the church songs, like two trains
running across the whole territory of East Texas at high speed, from the
port of Galveston heading west past Houston, through all the plantation
communities surrounding the Brazos, then all the way up to the Red
River, and then east out across the rest of the Deep South.

But one of the biggest shifts in Black secular music was still to emerge,
and it came in the 1890s with the introduction of a new "box" that
would eventually become the instrument of choice for many Black musicians in the South. The guitar had been around in some form for centuries, but by the end of the nineteenth century it was being mass produced
in factories, thus becoming readily available and inexpensive. Furthermore, it was relatively light and portable and could be carried from place
to place just as the banjo or fiddle. But it had a wider range of sound
and was particularly adept at adopting the syncopated ragtime rhythms
of piano players that would come to prominence near the turn of the
century without the musician ever needing to enter one of the sporting

places. But maybe the guitar's most appealing attribute was its superior ability over the fiddle to imitate the human voice, allowing the solo performer greater independence as they could utilize the strings to either accompany the lyrics to a song similar to the "basing" in the church, or as a response to their own call; a technique that could be further aided by sliding the back of a knife against the strings.

"Knife songs" were performed in open tunings under various nicknames that could be interchangeable: "Spanish," "Vastopol," and sometimes "Hawaiian."[9] This was the sound of the itinerant songster who, separate from the back porch musicians like Lipscomb and Shaw, were men who seemed to always be on the move. They were street musicians and hustlers who hung around train depots picking up whatever money they could before moving on to wherever the train was going next. These were the early masters of the instrument who, with the assistance of a knife or a piece of bone, could manipulate the pitch of their guitar and conjure the image of the railroad in the listener's imagination without singing a word, as in the case of "John Henry."[10] The singer could also accompany the running of the knife with their own voice or more often could just let the guitar "talk" or "sing" the lines in response to what the singer had already introduced.[11] One of the earliest examples of this style was written about in 1911 by the folk collector Howard W. Odum, who heard a guitar player utilize the technique in northern Mississippi on an early iteration of what would be later known as "Minglewood Blues."[12] Odum wrote of the song, "[T]wo lines are sung in harmony with the running of the knife over the strings . . . ; while the refrain, '*Lawd, lawd, lawd!*' wherever found, is sung to the 'talking' of the knife."[13]

The most traveled song played in the slide style though was "Po' Boy Long Ways From Home," a song also documented by Odum as he heard it in northern Mississippi well before any recordings were made.[14] It was a song that moved from mining camp to mining camp, from one station to the next, and was a secular take on the stranger theme that borrowed lines from the spiritual "Sometimes I Feel Like a Motherless Child." The sharecropper and jug band performer, Gus Cannon, heard the song near Clarksdale, Mississippi, around the turn of the twentieth century, and would end up recording it under the moniker Banjo Joe in 1927 for Paramount Records. Frank Hutchison, a white guitar player who learned slide from an itinerant Black musician making his rounds in the coal country of West Virginia, would take the "Poor Boy" sound and record the train standards *Train that Carried the Girl from Town* and *Cannon Ball Blues*.[15] Always on the move, the practitioners of this new sound would come to see themselves as secular preachers, going from town to town, learning new songs, devising new lyrics, and bringing them back home before hitting the road again.

> *Been a poor ol' boy an' a long ways from home*
> *Long way from home*
> *Been a poor ol' boy and a long ways from home*
> *I got 'rested, no money to buy my fine*
> *Money to buy my fine*
> *I got 'rested, no money to buy my fine*

This was all coming at a time when many of the first-generation African American artists born in the post-emancipation period began to have children. It would be this generation who would be exposed not only to the entire range of sounds spanning the past few decades—from the religious forms of song like the a cappella field holler, the ring shouts, the church moans, and the call-and-response rhythms—but nearly in equal measure to the secular sounds of the evening as well. Eventually new singers and new songs would arise, and it all would be a part of this thing that would be called the blues, but that was still a long way off. For now, the so-called blues was just a thing people lived. They were songs constructed from the lives of people who were in perpetual motion—songs built, like Van Gogh's paintings, not in a studio with perfect lighting, but with feeling and in conjunction with the sun, the wind, and the sweat. They didn't tiptoe around the truth of their experience, and as a result, within the spiritual community, the music was disdained by many for its seemingly blasphemous and selfish connotations, and the type of lifestyle that ran alongside it. But it could not be condemned for failing to be honest, both in lyrics and sound. "Every roof is agreeable to the eye until it is lifted; then we find tragedy and moaning women, and hard-eyed husbands," Ralph Waldo Emerson wrote."[16] In the blues the roof is ripped off, and the veneer is revealed for the sham it always was.

Janie Pratt, Charles Lipscomb's wife, never attended the out-of-town weekend functions with her fiddle playing husband and was often left alone caring for a houseful of children while Charles stayed out all night entertaining and picking up different women. And although she didn't play any instruments, she did sing, and one of her favorites was a version of the spiritual "What Yo' Gwine Do When Yo' Lamp Burn Down?" a song that centers around the admonishment of the sinner while also referencing the Crucifixion spiritual "Were You There." But instead of singing about the abstract "you" referenced in the original, she turned it inward, making herself the focus while the "lamp" in the original was no longer a biblical metaphor but a practical concern to keep the light in the coal oil lamp burning when you don't have electricity.

> *When my eyes git so' I can't see no mow,*
> *What you gonna do wit yo 'ligion*
> *When yo lamps gone out.*
> *[I'll just hang down my head and I'll cry]*[8]

These were lives lived. They were messy, and the ones who lived them didn't have the luxury to adopt certain popular stances or ideas and never have them challenged. Like the music, their lives were always in flux, and they always had to be ready to improvise at a moment's notice. There was a separating line, but it wasn't always as simple as staying on just one side of it when death was always close behind. What this music offered were routes for survival. In place of a physical home, a spiritual one was constructed, and by accepting death as part of the story, one embraced living. What the blues understood is that it's a mean old world to live in all by yourself, but that it's all temporary, that suffering doesn't last always, and that even in the darkest days the sun was gonna shine in the back door someday.

INTERLUDE 3

Lord, I Just Can't Keep From Crying

In March of 1927, the Reverend H. R. Tomlin recorded a sermon and song with congregational members for Columbia Records. In it we get a sense of how Johnson would have heard this in church, and we can also hear what was likely the theme from which the song was built. It is the same for both Reverend Tomlin and Johnson: the lost mother.

> *Our Blessed Savior was a compassionate friend.*
> *He fed the hungry, healed the sick, and raised the dead.*
> *When He stood at the grave of Lazarus with Mary and Martha,*
> *His humanity asserted itself and Jesus wept.*
> *So long as we tarry in this low ground of sorrow,*
> *. . . and we are forced to give up our loved ones,*
> *Go on through the world with a hung down head and aching heart,*
> *Oh, we just can't help from crying, sometimes.*
> *Oh some of you got a mother waving and watching around the great white throne,*
> *Ohhhhhh, didn't you promise her before she died that you would meet her in the glory land?*
> *My mother took a train, a mighty long time ago.*
> *I promised her I'd meet her on Canaan's happy shore,*
> *But the day my mother died, I just walked the floor and cried.*[1]

LORD I JUST CAN'T KEEP FROM CRYING

Willie Johnson

Lord, I just can't keep from crying sometimes
Lord, I just can't keep from crying sometimes
When my heart's full of sorrow and my eyes are filled with tears
Lord, I just can't keep from crying sometimes

My mother often told me, angels bonded your life away
She said I would accomplish, if I trust in God and pray
I'm on the King's Highway, I'm trusting him everyday

'Cause I just can't keep from crying sometimes
Well, I just can't keep from crying sometimes
When my heart's full of sorrow and my eyes are filled with tears
Lord, I just can't keep from crying sometimes

My mother, she's in glory, thank God I'm on my way
Father, he's gone too, and sister she could not stay
I'm trusting Him everyday, to bear my burdens away

'Cause I just can't keep from crying sometimes
Well, I just can't keep from crying sometimes
When my heart's full of sorrow and my eyes are filled with tears
Lord, I just can't keep from crying sometimes

I thought when she first left me, I'd pray for a little while
Soon it all would be over, and I'd journey on with a smile
But the thought as I get older, I think of what I told her

And I just can't keep from crying sometimes
Well, I just can't keep from crying sometimes
When my heart's full of sorrow and my eyes are filled with tears
Lord, I just can't keep from crying sometimes

WILLIE JOHNSON

The Birth of the Bard, Part I

Now death in 1900,
About 15 years ago,
You brought a storm ask my mother,
With you she had to go.
—"WASN'T THAT A MIGHTY STORM"

Most of the congregants had made their way inside and had taken their
seats. A woman in her fifties, after catching a glimpse of an old friend she
hadn't seen in a while, smiled and waved over at her and would make
it a point to meet up with her when services were over. For now, though,
a silence enveloped the cramped wooden church house. A child, with
shoelaces untied, coughs and it echoes throughout the building. At this
exact moment, two elders, who are standing near the left of the altar
begin to stir and one of them approaches the front of the pulpit and calls
the service to order before taking his seat again. Suddenly, breaking the
stillness, the song leader raises a line from an all-too familiar hymn in
the Dr. Watts' style. The first time he begins, his words are more spoken
than sung, and his voice is soft but audible. A chorus responds, drawing
out his words ever so faintly. The leader repeats the line again, this time
louder and with more confidence and clarity. In return the congregation
responds with a similar intensity, and with more members now joining
the chorus. This rhythm continues, intensifying with each intoned line; the
leader disclosing the lyrics in short bursts before pausing and allowing
the parishioners to affirm these same lines but stretching them out and all
in unison:

Leader: Dark was the night, and cold the ground.
Congregation: Daaark waaas theeee niiiight, aaaand collllld waaas theeee
grouuuund.

    As the moments pass, the energy deepens. Feet beneath the pews begin to pound out a pulse, like a drumbeat. Some cry out, and some groan; bodies lean forward and sway as they respond to the building emotion, which swells to a wondrous crescendo; the whole church on fire with the passion of souls calling out in one enduring moan before silence envelops the atmosphere once more as the clergy enter.

A solemn prayer commences before the song leader rises once more and with a heavy voice, he sings:

Pass me not, O gentle Savior, hear my humble cry.

This song arose in many a deep feeling of compassion, and money was given over to help the blind song leader as well as the church. During this temporary break some chatter could be heard among the members before a brief wave of calm once again took hold as the preacher made his entrance and approached the lectern. He began his sermon, which he titled "Crucifixion," with a tender voice as he brought to mind the image of Jesus in Gethsemane before contorting his voice to its fullest rasp when he spoke of Judas. "Oh, looook at black-hearted Judas," he roared. "Sneaking through the dark . . . leading his crucifying mob."[1] All the while, the sisters in Amen Corner and some of the congregation would release shouts. They yelled "Well," "Amen," and "Oh yes!"

The sermon concluded on the subject of the day of judgment, when He would be coming back again. Summoning all his power, the preacher began in a solemn tone before rising again into a mighty groan:

I find my text this evening at the sixth chapter,
And seventeenth verse of the book of the Revelation . . .

These words were spoken by John, who was exiled from Ephesus,
And kept on the Isle of Patmos, by the word of God.

"Ohhhhh John, I am the beginning and the ending,
I am he was dead in the hole I'm alive forevermore
Ohhhhh John, I want you to write my friends
And tell the churches, John, about me while you're on the island."
And John began to write, my friends. [2]

At his most intense, his voice obtained a hoarse quality, and his veins were visible as his neck strained to constrain the energy that seemed to *overflow from his body. At some moments he would clench his fists while at other times he held his arms outstretched as if to touch the congregants who aided him with their shouts. There were instances where he may pause but only to gather momentum as he surged forward, sweat dripping from his brow, sometimes speaking rapidly while at other times sweet, and there were moments where it seemed as if, together, all that fervent joy would be so much that it would tear this building down.*

It was September 1900 when the big storm struck Galveston. For fear of spreading panic on the island, warnings were sent out late, and even once they were, most disregarded them. Instead, many flocked to the shores to watch as the storm began to roll in, but as the wind and the rain began to sweep through the city, they began to realize this was no ordinary storm. Some attempted to move themselves and their belongings to upper floors, but the water began to rise, and it wasn't long before the entire island was submerged in a storm surge that was at least fifteen feet deep. Some who had just arrived by train sought refuge in a lighthouse and would survive the night, while others chose to try and escape by just turning back, but the tracks had all been covered in water.[3] Many others also had no escape, so they remained in their homes and prayed. When the sun rose in the morning, it was all over, and at least six thousand were dead. The bodies were spread over the island, an island now unrecognizable in the devastation. "I managed to find a raft of driftwood or wreckage, and got on it, going with the tide, I knew not where. I had not drifted far before I was struck with some wreckage and my niece was knocked out of my arms. I could not save her, and had to see her drown," a survivor recalled.[4] In the aftermath, the heat bore down on the island, and a stench occupied the city. Soldiers and the Black population were ordered to toss the dead into the sea. Many other African Americans were labeled as looters and were shot at gunpoint. "Every hour during the night a fresh negro shooting was reported at headquarters," one author wrote in the year of the storm.[5]

Death had come to Galveston.

The Storm

Willie Johnson was three when the storm hit. He was born in Pendleton, Texas, a farming community built around the Santa Fe railroad, on the twenty-fifth day of January in 1897 to Dock Johnson and Mary King.[6] The Santa Fe was the line Dock had been following for the past decade or so. The line connected the port of Galveston to cities deep in East Texas as well as Central Texas on up to Waco,

Dallas, and Fort Worth. But for Dock, the main stops that mattered were up in Bosque County, where he married Mary King in 1894; Moody, where Mary was likely from; and Pendleton, where Johnson was born in 1897. Pendleton was also where Johnson's three brothers—Wallace, Carl, and Robert—were born. Amanda Jettie, Johnson's only sister and the last of the children born to Dock and Mary, was born following the family's move just south, another ten miles down the Santa Fe line, in Bell County just outside of Temple proper in 1900, the year of the Galveston hurricane.[7]

Dock was still working as a farmer and likely raised his children in the Missionary Baptist Church, possibly attending Corinth Missionary in the very early days of the family's arrival in Temple. Corinth Missionary Baptist Church would have been located on the east side of the city and had the distinction of being a member of the Lincoln Association as well as the first Black Baptist church in Temple. It would have been here that Johnson may have first became acquainted with the prominent role the Black preacher played within his segregated community and the critical role song had within the Black church tradition. It was where he first would have listened to the soul-stirring sermons, heard the sustained moans of the line hymns, and become aware of the freedom of travel the best of the preachers and song leaders enjoyed. During the warm summer months he also would have likely attended church picnics, Juneteenth celebrations, and revival meetings where he and his siblings would have been introduced to some of the fiery sermons of the traveling preachers and witnessed as the flock cried out, fell down on their knees, and "got religion." Zora Neale Hurston, the author and folklorist born in 1891 whose father was a preacher and moderator of the South Florida Baptist Association, described the scenes as "stepped up by music and high drama," and even recalled instances in the services when her father would "stop preaching suddenly and walk down to the front edge of the pulpit and breathe into a whispered song . . . : *Run! Run! Run to the City of Refuge, children! Run! Oh, run! Or else you'll be consumed* [emphasis added]."[8] Scenes like this were particularly moving to her as she was growing up, and sermons such as these likely prompted Willie, even at a very young age, to confide in his father his desire to become a preacher. Hurston elaborated:

> I liked revival meetings particularly. During these meetings the preacher let himself go. . . . The scenery of heaven was described in detail. Hallelujah Avenue and Amen Street were paved with gold so fine. . . . Hallelujah Avenue ran north and south across heaven, and was tuned to alto and bass. Amen Street ran east to west and was tuned to "treble" and tenor. These streets crossed each other right in front of the throne and made harmony all the time.[9]

And hell, she wrote, "was described in dramatic fury."

Flames of fire leaped up a thousand miles from the furnaces of Hell, and raised blisters on a sinning man's back before he hardly got started downward. Hellhounds pursued their ever-dying souls. Everybody under the sound of the preacher's voice was warned.[10]

And while the church may have been the first big impact on Johnson's life, it was two successive personal tragedies in those first few years around Temple that would alter his route forever. The first occurred sometime between 1900 and 1904 when Mary, his mother, died.[11] This death certainly had a profound effect on the entire family, and it was only compounded when—shortly following his mother's death, either in 1904 or 1905—Johnson lost vision in both of eyes when he was around the age of seven.[12] There is much speculation regarding the cause of Johnson's blinding (all of which I have included in the footnotes), but it is not the source of his blinding that is the most important, but the impact the blinding had on him. After all, Johnson may well have had his path permanently altered if it was only his mother's death that occurred while still a child, but it was the blinding that would have the largest practical consequence—not only for evident reasons, like knowing what the world looks like and then for it all to disappear, but also because of what it would mean financially and spiritually. After all, all four of Johnson's siblings lost their mother at a very early age, but the impact of losing one's sight in an already precarious environment could mean the difference between living and dying. It meant a sharp turn away from most labor jobs that were typical for African American males at the time; with no government assistance available, the road ahead could be very bleak. It was precisely for this reason that Dock likely built Willie his first guitar, one made from some rudimentary materials and a cigar box—providing him a way to make a living for himself if anything should happen that left him alone with no other way of making it but for begging on the street. The guitar was a tool of survival. But there was something else the blinding likely did, and that was to push him more forcefully onto the spiritual path. It was a way, much like Butler believed about his own blinding, that offered the route out of the darkness and into the light. And also like Butler, he may have seen it as a calling.

In June of 1908 Dock married Catherine Garrett, and by 1911 the family had moved to a working-class neighborhood located on the south side of Temple in the shadow of the newly constructed Santa Fe railroad passenger station.[13] Dock's mother, Ellen, and his stepfather also moved to the neighborhood, and it was here, among various rent houses all within just eight square blocks—from

South Thirteenth to South Fifth bordered by West Avenue D and West Avenue E—that Dock and Catherine would live, and the kids would continually return over the next couple of decades. This was no longer farmland, and Dock made money with his son Wallace by securing odd jobs where they could find them.

The opportunity to get a proper education was still a major issue for the Black community at this time, and there are no records of Willie receiving any formal schooling, either in Temple or at the Blind Institute in Austin (which did enroll Black students); but early records do indicate that both his brother Robert and his sister, Jettie, attended school around 1910. The closest church, which was always within a short walking distance from their homes, was the Mount Zion Missionary Baptist on South Thirteenth and West Avenue E. Organized in 1906 by Rev. J. C. Curtis, the church served the community not only in religious matters but also in academic instruction, an offering among some early African American churches that saw it as one of their missions to secure educational self-determination for their communities. Mount Zion was certainly the church the Johnson family likely attended, and for years it doubled as an unofficial public school for Black children in the neighborhood.[14] So it is reasonable to assume that many of the children in the community, including Johnson's siblings, would attend class at the church. It's also possible that a young Willie Johnson may have accompanied his siblings to the church on occasions for study, but more likely his real education in the church was to immerse himself in the teachings, prophesy, and poetry of the Bible as well as the oratory perfection of the preacher.

⁚⁚

Meanwhile, Johnson was coming of age in a time of a struggle within his community to forge both an individual identity separate from whites and also to assert their legal equality among them. On the organizing front, the National Association for the Advancement of Colored People (NAACP) was formed in 1909 to advocate for political and social reform, while the number of Black universities in the South continued to grow to help support the mission of educating future Black leaders. And while institutional reform would be years in the making, Black businesses were being built in their segregated neighborhoods, while out in the streets, new art forms, including blues and jazz, were being born from the African American experience. In addition, new cultural symbols were arising that would soon rival the biblical narratives both in story and song. For example, a new folk hero emerged in the form of a young fighter from Galveston named Jack Johnson who not only became the first Black heavyweight champion but also an almost mythical figure when he knocked out the former champion James J. Jeffries, a white boxer, in 1910.

And, a couple of years later when the *Titanic* was swallowed by the Atlantic Ocean, the event immediately became a symbol not only of man's hubris at believing he could build something that could not sink, but also of the wrath the Old Testament God still could exert on a system that favored the rich over the poor or one race superior to another.[15] The response to the event by the street singers was swift, as almost immediately ballads were being circulated recounting the fate of the doomed ocean liner. Some focused on the class divide on the ship, while others, like the one popularized in Texas by Madkin Butler, "God Moves on the Water," were more existential, serving as a stark reminder that no one, regardless of race or wealth, could escape death, and only God would have the last word on the folly of man. Framing current events in terms of morality became symbolic of a Black resistance movement. The community Johnson grew up in may have been advancing intellectually, artistically, and spiritually, but just outside the lines that were drawn for them, there was another world that was always prepared to maintain the economic status quo and would use all the old-fashioned barbaric means to do so. Two such cases of terror were carried out in close proximity to where Johnson was living in his late teens; both would gain national attention, including from the NAACP, when photos began to circulate of the brazen brutality carried out by the mobs. Now there were images to accompany the stories, which too often before could be twisted against the victims of the public executions.

The Crucifixion at Temple

Three weeks after Jack Johnson's defeat of Jeffries on Independence Day in 1910, eighteen-year-old Henry Gentry was accused of murder, dragged through the streets by his neck, and set on fire upon a woodpile soaked with oil in Belton, Texas, some ten miles from Temple.[16] Five years later on July 30, 1915, in Temple, a Black man by the name of Will Stanley was pulled from Judge R. L. Cooper's office at the Wilkerson Building, dragged through the public square on West Adams and Main, about a mile north from where the Johnson family lived, and lynched. The *Crisis*, the official magazine of the NAACP, labeled the killing "The Crucifixion at Temple, Texas." In their report they described how Stanley's feet and hands were bound and how he was forced into a fire that had been lit on a pile of dry goods boxes as up to ten thousand people looked on and shouted.[17] A picture of Stanley's charred body, still suspended from chains and surrounded by the proud perpetrators, was taken and distributed on postcards. On the back of one of them, the message read, "This is the barbecue we had last night. My picture is to the left with a cross over it." It was signed, "Your son, Joe." The postcard of Stanley's murder is often confused with one of the most infamous lynching cases, that of a Black farmhand named Jesse Washington that occurred just north of Temple in Waco less than a year later.

Washington, after being convicted in an hour-long trial for the murder of Lucy Fryer, was pulled from the courtroom by a lynch mob, his clothes were stripped, his body was wrapped in chains, and he then was dragged to the suspension bridge over the Brazos to be hung.[18] When the mob learned that a fire was prepared back at City Hall, they returned to the town square with the intention of crucifying Washington in the same manner as Stanley. Along the route Washington's body was brutalized with knives, bricks, and shovels. Once reaching the square, Washington was strung up to a tree by chains, coal oil was poured on his body, and he was lowered repeatedly into the flames that sparked from dry good boxes and oil below, much in the same manner of Stanley's barbarous death.[19] Washington was only seventeen, just two years younger than Johnson was at the time, when he was executed in front of a mob of fifteen thousand. Shortly after Washington's death, the NAACP launched the organization's Anti-Lynching Fund as well as an investigation into the incident. They published their findings in the *Crisis* under the title "The Waco Horror," covering the disturbing details and running graphic images of Washington's charred body. The magazine's investigation was the delayed answer to Washington's final plea to the throng of onlookers as his life was taken: "Haven't I one friend in this crowd?"[20] These were the lynching deaths that occurred close to where Johnson was living in this period, of which he was surely aware of, but they were hardly isolated incidents in the state. From 1882 to 1968, only two states had more recorded lynchings than Texas.[21]

> *Dey whupped him up de hill,*
> *and he never said a mumbalin' word;*
> *Dey pierced him in de side,*
> *and he never said a mumbalin' word.*
> *An' de blood come a-twinklin' down,*
> *and he never said a mumbalin' word;*
> *Not a word, not a word, not a word.*
> —From the traditional hymn, "He Never Said
>   a Mumblin' Word"

The Beginnings of a Songster

Out of the flock, you I choose.

By as early as 1916, Johnson was already on his way to developing his own unique sound. He was certainly already acquainted with many of the best preachers of his day as well as the great song leader Madkin Butler, who would have been a familiar name for those families who attended a Baptist church within the Lincoln Association or were frequent visitors to the church picnics or conventions. He also would have likely crossed paths with Lemon Jefferson, a blind singer who was already gaining recognition as a songster who straddled the line between religious and secular music in and around the Central Texas neighborhoods. Jefferson was in his early twenties by this time, and being a few years older than Johnson, was someone of his same generation whose church picnic performances would likely have been an inspiration. Jefferson came out of the Baptist Buffalo Association, where Butler was a frequent guest and which likely gave Jefferson the confidence to believe he could make better money playing music than he could doing anything else.[22] While he began by singing church songs, Jefferson quickly gravitated more toward the secular, understanding the opportunity to expand his repertoire while not leaving him exclusively reliant on the church offerings for his meals.[23]

This new music termed "the blues" was also already gaining in popularity by this time, and the name itself—"blues"—had been solidified after sheet music with the word in the title was published by W. C. Handy ("The Memphis Blues") in 1912 and with "Jelly Roll Blues," an early jazz composition published by Ferdinand Joseph LaMothe (Jelly Roll Morton) in 1915. In addition to the church music and the original songs coming out of the blues singers, Johnson would have also likely been familiar with the medicine shows and Black vaudeville. Both employed traveling singers and musicians who were the precursors of this secular style of entertainment with entertainers moving from town to town similar to the way preachers and song leaders would. Though neither the names of the performers nor the emerging style of blues music were mentioned in the white newspapers of the segregated South, by Johnson's late teens, these wholly original musical expressions were developing everywhere around him.

Johnson had to be absorbing much of this new world, but while many of the young guitar players coming of age at this time were part of a lineage of musical families, Johnson seems to have had no mentor when it came to playing an instrument. He started teaching himself how to play very early on with his cigar box version of the guitar constructed by his father, but Johnson's main interest—and one likely only confirmed from his blinding—was to fully develop his own voice as a singer, an intuition sparked from his earliest childhood impulse to preach.[24] Likely understanding his blinding to be a conversion experience, much as Butler had, Johnson was pulled closer to the religious path, eschewing the direction of Jefferson and other performers who made a living in the places where drinking, gambling, and inevitably, violence were routine. Instead, by choosing to sing only religious music, he took the right-hand road and modeled himself on the preachers he admired. Thus, he began to develop, through his voice, the emotional intensity he would hear in the deliverance of impassioned sermons.

Butler and Jefferson shared the belief that the streets were an avenue predominantly reserved for the destitute, but Johnson felt this was where he had been called. This domain was off-limits to most performers in the segregated South, as they always had to navigate within the made-up rules of vigilante justice, but it was open to the blind musician. It was here he envisioned a path not to be pitied but one in the continuation of James Weldon Johnson's description of the celebrated bards, who were the true "makers of song." By doing so, Johnson naturally began to set himself up as a spiritual counterpoint to what he had been hearing from other rising secular performers like Jefferson.[25]

By the time Johnson decided to leave home, he had a guitar, a step up from the cigar box model his father first constructed for him years before, but it was still one that was full of holes and "rusty as a terrapin."[26] But, for Johnson at this time, his guitar was still secondary to his voice, and instead of relying on the instrument, he preferred to travel with a second singer who could contribute a human response in the antiphonal style he was accustomed to in the church. He would later seek to master the same pattern, when alone, through just his voice and guitar, by incorporating the second, congregational voice into his own with sustained moans or shouts of "well," or by allowing the guitar to complete lines for him. But this command of his own voice and skills, of his ability to bring together the sounds of the itinerant street musician with the preacher, would still be years away. In order to fully attain individuation and fulfill his destiny, Johnson would be forced to step out of familiar surroundings and into the wilderness, to venture out into that territory where he had witnessed the rulers of the day segregate, demean, and murder his race. The only way to attain transformation was to move. This also was a departure from many of the religious street singers who would routinely be found in the same city on the same street corners. By choosing to travel, Johnson was not only separating himself from the so-called beggar class of street singers, but also from familiarity. He would have to journey out and, in the words of the great spiritual, "walk that lonesome valley" for himself. It was the mandate for all those who wished to free themselves from the shackles of conformity and cultivate their own spiritual or artistic voice. "No one can build thee the bridge, over which thou must cross the river of life, save thyself alone," the philosopher Friedrich Nietzsche wrote, echoing the sentiment at the heart of every itinerant musician or anyone who feels their soul adrift, detached culturally or spiritually.[27] Johnson had been converted and answered the call. The time was here to "go into the world and preach the gospel to every creature." He had been called, and in this faith was explicit the assurance that even as he crossed over a land consumed in turmoil and murder, he had nothing to fear, that the world could do him no harm because there was a higher law ensuring the righteous would ultimately triumph over the wicked, and that, just as God had promised the prophet Jeremiah, Christ would be with him.[28]

::

Johnson left Temple and headed east for Houston on the H&TC sometime around 1917. It was a route the twenty-year-old Johnson would become intimately familiar with over the next fifteen years as he perfected his own style while riding the passenger train nearly every weekend and hitting every town along the track that had a depot from the Buffalo Bayou to Waco.

It's a rough, rocky road, but I'm trampin','
Tryin' to make heaven my home.
—from the spiritual "Trying to Make Heaven My Home"

INTERLUDE 4

Let Your Light Shine on Me

"Let Your Light Shine on Me" was sung as a line hymn, much like "Amazing Grace" and "Dark Was the Night." Its origins are uncertain, but because of the way it was sung, it may, in fact, date back to the days of slavery in an iteration known to the African American communities. It certainly is a religious song, as it references the biblical light, but the line "Let your light shine on me" was also used in the secular sense when it was sung by African American soldiers during the First World War.[1] Published in 1919 with words by Sgt. Allen Griggs and music by Lucie E. Campbell, the sheet music had a cover with a Black soldier standing alone in the shadows while a light from the Statue of Liberty shone brightly on white businessmen. The lyrics themselves highlight the racial injustice of the soldiers as they returned home from France asking for a "square deal" in their own country.[2]

In hymn books, there is a reference to "Let Your Light Shine" in the 1910s that again refers to the Gospel of Matthew and the light emanating through the individual, born from God, as the individual makes their way through the "darkness on [their] journey."[3] Then there is "Will the Lighthouse Shine on Me?" published in 1921 that uses the title posed as a question for the chorus.[4] The first recording, made in 1923 by the Wiseman Sextette, begins with an introduction telling of the song's popularity with Black soldiers before moving into a line hymn, distinct from the 1921 hymn except for its chorus, lined-out, of wondering if the lighthouse will shine on the singer.[5] Rev. E. D. Campbell's 1927 recording/sermon is of a preacher who does away with the question and gets us closer to Johnson's version as he growls at certain points, stretches the syllables as one would a line hymn, and summons, in all his strength, the lighthouse to "shine on me."[6] And in 1929, the same year Johnson recorded his version, Reverend Beaumont preached out of the book of John, chapter 9, telling of how Jesus came upon a blind man who was blinded at birth so that "the works of God might be displayed in him" before restoring his sight through placing clay over his eyes and sending him to wash them in the Pool of Siloam.[7]

In one of Johnson's most unique and artistic performances on record, "Let Your Light Shine on Me" is a journey through various tempos, voice changes, and styles. He began by lining-out the hymn and lightly strumming on his guitar before shifting into a somewhat faster pace and then deepening his voice into a false bass while using his guitar as a percussion instrument. Remaining in this vocal register, he stayed with the chorus until he returned to a falsetto as he concluded in the line hymn style. It is never a pleading or straining for the light to shine on him, nor is it a question if the light is, indeed, shining. Instead, it is a faith that he, the traveler, the stranger, is already walking in the light and therefore basking in this love.[8]

LET YOUR LIGHT SHINE ON ME
Willie Johnson

Let it shine on me, let it shine on me
Let your light, from the lighthouse, shine on me
Let it shine on me, let it shine on me
Let your light, from the lighthouse, shine on

My Lord, He done, just what He said
Let your light, from the lighthouse, shine on me
Healed the sick, and raised the dead
Let your light, from the lighthouse, shine on

Oh, let it shine on, oh, let it shine on
Let your light, from the lighthouse, shine on me
Shine on, oh, let it shine on
Let your light, from the lighthouse, shine on

I know I've got religion, and I ain't ashamed
Let your light, from the lighthouse, shine on me
Angels in the heavens, done wrote my name
Let your light, from the lighthouse, shine on

Oh, let it shine on, oh, let it shine on
Let your light, from the lighthouse, shine on me
Shine on, oh, let it shine on
Let your light, from the lighthouse, shine on

Oh, let it shine on, oh, let it shine on
Let your light, from the lighthouse, shine on me
Shine on, oh, let it shine on
Let your light, from the lighthouse, shine on me

Oh, let it shine on, oh, let it shine on
Let your light, from the lighthouse, shine on me
Shine on, oh, let it shine on
Let your light, shine on me

WILLIE JOHNSON

The Birth of the Bard, Part II

> As I descended impassable rivers,
> I no longer felt guided by the ferrymen.
> —*Arthur Rimbaud*, "LE BATEAU IVRE"

Following the 1900 storm in Galveston, the city of Houston naturally began to see migration from what had been, prior to the hurricane, Texas's largest city. Only a short train ride away from Galveston, it became a logical destination for those fleeing the island. Houston was already a landing-spot for African Americans looking to escape the farming life, and its population began to increase substantially in the new century. By the time of Johnson's arrival around 1917, it was on the verge of exploding. In fact, the next ten years would see the African American population in the city more than double, and by 1920 the Fourth Ward Freedmen's Town, where Johnson would end up settling for a few years, was home to one-third of Houston's Black population.[1]

⁞⁞

It was a time when the country was witnessing a furious outburst of Black expression both in terms of political activity and creativity. A new spirit was finding its outlet in the row houses of America. And even though this growing courage and mobilization also faced backlash in the form of terror—the awakening of the KKK and continued lynchings—voices were rising in protest that could be heard vocally and witnessed both financially and through migration. After all those years in the fields—being put down, messed up, and screwed over—a new Black working class was moving to the cities in search of better pay and hopefully a better life. The buildup to war was also producing defense industries in the North, which led to a mass exodus from the South for people who were eager to escape oppression and the rough work and low pay of the sawmills and lumber camps. For them, and for others like Johnson, just moving was in itself an act of resistance and activism. It is this type of experience Johnson must have been searching for when he made his way to the Fourth Ward. The area, born as Freedmen's Town following emancipation, was exploding with a sense of true independence that Johnson would not have found growing up in Temple. Here, there was a strong Black working and professional class building businesses during the day and enjoying a thriving entertainment scene at night. Everyone's separate voices fused together like the splendid miracle of jazz, and you could hear it. The bustling streets were alive, and there were few places in the country that buzzed with the sort of chaos and joy and beauty of these several blocks that intersected with downtown.

While Galveston may have been declining in population, it remained a vibrant city both musically, artistically, and spiritually within the Black community, and through its close proximity to Houston, the two cities became somewhat of a spiritual corridor for some of the area's best Baptist preachers and young musical talent. Rev. H. M. Williams, pastor of Avenue L in Galveston and "one of the world's greatest gospel preachers," was a frequent visitor to Houston and the Antioch Church in the Fourth Ward.[2] These were still the cornerstone churches within the Lincoln Association at the time, and the churches, as well as their leadership, were at the forefront of reform within Black communities in Texas. But the link between the two cities also was artistic. The route was a key artery traveled by many of Houston's best piano players, who would frequently navigate the rail lines between the Fourth Ward and the bustling Post Office Street district in Galveston.[3]

New Orleans was also a close enough ride on the Southern Pacific; it brought jazz across the state line to Texas, where it tangled with the blues—the real, hardcore blues, the genius born from the plantations and the loneliest solitude that sprang from *real life*. People were tired from work, but they knew complaining wasn't worth their time—they had to do it all again, and even if they ended up pushing a boulder up the hill, they were going to find a way to sing about it. These were the sounds that came pouring forth from the open windows of the boarding houses and from the street bars both in this district and just north where the red lights thrived for a time. It was the center of Black life and where almost all the early Texas blues and jazz performers could be seen at one time or another. It was where Jelly Roll Morton could entertain in the brothels and local theaters when he lived in a boarding house on Fuller Street in the district, and where musicians could perfect the ragtime on their guitars long before anybody came calling to record them. It was where the famous Santa Fe Group of barrelhouse piano players found a welcome home base, and where Geeshie Wiley found L. V. Thomas in the 1920s and later went on to record one of the most haunting blues masterpieces for Paramount Records in 1930. It was here, in what some would later refer to as the "Harlem of the South," where a new language was being invented by its Black residents—their own dialect spoken in their own businesses, churches, newspapers, and schools, and in back room dice and gambling games. The debates about politics and the struggles went on in a sociological sense, but so did life—in prayer, in work, and in song—because food had to be put on the table, and your spirit had to have meaning. It was the perfect atmosphere for someone like Johnson to walk into at that time in his life. So many movements seemed to be at the cusp of breaking out, and the Fourth Ward of Houston seemed to have a little bit of everything to offer at a time when he was really just beginning to find his own voice.

It was also a place where he would have been able to make a little money. By the time of Johnson's arrival, the district was home to at least four hundred Black-owned businesses ranging from saloons, barbers, grocers, and jewelers to physicians and attorneys, with most of them situated along the dividing line between the core of the Fourth Ward and the "Reservation," the former red light district that was just beginning to be dismantled as Johnson arrived.[4] The street, known to most of the residents as West Dallas Street, was the main drag where some of the best practitioners of the blues anywhere in the South could be found at any given time for the next forty years, drinking, working in shoeshine parlors, or playing a guitar out on the sidewalks. Lemon Jefferson strolled the street with "guitar in one hand, folding chair in the other," and Alger "Texas" Alexander, another singer out of the Madkin Butler vein, could often be found with L. V. Thomas or a young New Orleans guitarist named Lonnie Johnson. Thomas lived in the district and would join "Texas" for his excursions into the country to play for the Saturday night suppers.[5] The singer Bernice Edwards lived her whole life in the area and was undoubtedly a fixture on the street as well as in the jooks and brothels where she was frequently accompanying the boogie-woogie and barrel-house pianists.[6] And it was here that Johnson himself was often found "dangling a tin cup and shouting blues-patterned spirituals."[7]

The Houston and Texas Central

On the weekends, and especially in the late summer when church events were more frequent, Johnson would depart Houston on the H&TC and could be found outside the various Baptist associations, revivals, and conventions. On Saturdays, especially in the fall, when the harvest season brought in more money, he would seek out the best street corners in the various Central and East Texas towns dotting the railroad line and perform for the rural farm workers as they flooded into the towns to spend money after the long week. Frequently he would travel with a singing partner and enter a town, much like an ancient bard out of one of William Blake's Illuminated Books, with staff in hand inquiring about the best places to set up to play. It was through these excursions in East Texas that Johnson would be introduced to the lineage of musicians and ballad makers who were still working the farms in the country towns; many of them were around his age but, unlike him, had been raised on the fiddles and banjos of their parents.

One such musician was Emancipation "Mance" Lipscomb. "Mance," a young guitar player himself who was just two years older than Johnson, was the son of the fiddler Charlie Lipscomb and Janie Pratt. He had started out playing the fiddle at a young age with his father before switching to the guitar around age thirteen. By his early twenties he had taken up sharecropping in his hometown of Navasota and was a regular at various country suppers and dances.

Like many of the cities in East Texas, Navasota was a cotton town that had been transformed from slave plantation land to sharecropper territory. A stop on the H&TC line between Hearne to the north and Houston to the southeast, it was here in front of the two-story Texas Radio and Electric Company building at 202 West Washington Avenue where Lipscomb would frequently encounter Johnson playing his "rough old guitar" with a tin cup fastened with a wire loop around the guitar's neck to collect change. He was often accompanied by another blind singer who had a "lighter voice" to sing responses which contrasted with Johnson's already gravelly preacher's tone.[8] Johnson's guitar skills were minimal at the time, and he was still a model symbol of the original songster—a singer more than a musician—and often relied on Lipscomb to squeeze through the crowds to assist him in tuning his guitar into his preferred open, or "cross-note," tuning when he was in town.[9] But despite his lack of proficiency with the instrument, Johnson was already becoming well-respected for his voice and had a solid reper-toire of songs including "You'll Need Somebody on Your Bond," Butler's Titanic ballad "God Moves on the Water," and the Samson and Delilah hymn Johnson called "If I Had My Way I'd Tear the Building Down."[10] And even with his voice as the main draw, Johnson still managed to assemble a substantial crowd on his Saturday visits:

> He'd come right there on the corner, an he had people from here ta the high-way. Jest hunnuds a people standin right there on the streets. White an black. Old colored folks an young ones an all. Listenin at his voice.[11]

When he wasn't in Navasota, Johnson would often spend his Saturdays attracting new audiences in other cities nearby like Hempstead and around the Prairie View Normal Black College, just a couple stops south on the H&TC

line. He also made trips to Madisonville—just north of Navasota on the I&GN line—where Dennis Gainus, a young musician from Crockett, Texas, remembered several street singers, including Johnson, passing through.[12] The Santa Fe also crossed through Navasota, and it's probable Johnson hopped the train and headed about thirty-five miles west to Somerville where Walter James Dixon (aka Arvella Gray), was born in 1906. Dixon likely saw Johnson while picking cotton on a local plantation before Dixon left town for a traveling labor job with the Ringling Brothers circus. A trip to Somerville certainly wouldn't be a stretch for Johnson, as the depot just south of the city in Brenham, in Washington County, would be a major stopping point for him.

Brenham sits at the lower end of an inverted triangle at the center of cotton country encompassing Navasota to its northeast and Somerville to the northwest, and it was here that Johnson first made the acquaintance of the Shaw family of musicians, including musician and ballad maker Lewis Shaw and his young son Thomas. Even though the elder Shaw was close to Johnson's father's age, the two became close in the few years before Shaw died in 1918, as Johnson assisted him with ballad compositions, which Shaw would print and sell for fifteen cents a copy at the Sunday church services.[13] It is also possible that it was through Johnson's friendship with Shaw that he also became friendly with another family of musicians who lived on a farm nearby. The Robinson family, headed by Asa (A. C.) and Mary Jane Robinson, also lived in Brenham and would frequently host country dances that would have been a meeting place for any number of musicians on Saturday nights. Johnson's level of participation in the dances is unclear, but what is certain is that by the late 1910s to early 1920s Johnson was a frequent guest and would routinely stay overnight and "play that guitar, religious songs" with a bottle for a slide for the two young sons, Louis Charles (L. C.) Robinson and Arthur Clay (A. C.) Robinson.[14]

It was a time when many musical influences were intersecting at once in Johnson's life, and it was a pivotal learning period when he would have been introduced to a number of musicians who frequented the country musical circuit, all bringing with them a number of different styles that Johnson would have to measure himself against. Everywhere he went, Johnson was being introduced to a confluence of several generations of singers, from the a cappella church styles of Shaw and Butler to the old-time songsters who entertained on fiddles and banjos. And the track stretched farther. To the west, rumbling northward on the H&TC, Johnson would have found a supportive community and possibly more money than he would have managed in the smaller towns as he made his way to the famous Bridge Street district in Waco. With a similar atmosphere to the West Dallas district of Houston, Bridge Street was lined with many Black- and minority-owned businesses, and on the weekends the street filled with throngs of shoppers who flocked to the district to spend money at the restaurants, barbershops, and retail shops.

Heading back southeast, halfway between Waco and Navasota, Butler's hometown of Hearne was also likely one of Johnson's most influential stopping points for collecting ballads. He undoubtedly first heard Butler sing "Everybody Ought to Treat a Stranger Right" on one of these weekend trips. The song, which Butler could often be heard singing outside of New Elam, was a favorite to solicit ballad sales and would have certainly resonated with Johnson as it encompassed the words of the street song, "Poor Boy" as well as the spiritual "Motherless Children." With its refrain of "long ways from home," "Motherless Children" was centered on a similar theme of the stranger from Exodus, the same role Johnson would consistently play as he made his way from town to town.[15]

> *Everybody ought to treat a stranger right, long ways from home,*
> *Everybody ought to treat a stranger right, a long ways from home.*
> *All of us down here are strangers, none of us have no home,*
> *Don't ever hurt your brother and cause him to feel alone.*
> **"Everybody Ought to Treat a Stranger Right,"**
> *"Blind" Willie Johnson, 1930*

If You Ever Go to Houston, You Better Walk Right

Johnson's journey to Houston not only coincided with burgeoning financial and artistic freedom, but also with a sense of political resistance that was coming to life in the city and around the South. Tensions were boiling as the country poured its resources into a foreign war, while the battle that had been raging at home was hitting its breaking point; all that energy was about to erupt in the fight to stop African Americans from being summarily executed, exploited for labor, and intimidated by the law.

On June 25, 1917, rumors of a race war spread throughout Galveston when a group of several hundreds of Black citizens met to discuss how to respond when a Black man named Chester Sawyer was shot and hanged by an armed mob after being accused of assaulting a white woman in the city.[16] In Houston, three days later, an op-ed ran in the *Houston Daily Post* decrying the living conditions for far too many of its Black citizens. The author outlined a number of explanations to address the concerns of the business community, which was witnessing the exodus of many Black workers to the North, a migration that many Black preachers supported and even helped to facilitate through relief organizations and loans.[17]

"They are not disturbed about politics or social equality, but the insanitary surroundings amid which circumstances compel them to exist are unsatisfactory," it read.[18] The author described the people "huddled in miserable shacks . . . without sewerage, without water service, and without ordinary comforts and conveniences which are really essential to community health."[19] Schools, both in rural communities and the cities, designed for the Black community were described as a "joke." The author also railed against the discrepancies in treatment between African Americans and whites in the legal system, both in terms of the "heavy penalties assessed against negroes for petty offenses" and calling for whites to "stamp out lynching by punishing lynchers."[20] A few weeks later, Rev. H. M. Williams responded optimistically to the *Post* article, mainly for the purpose of agreeing and thanking the paper for giving a voice to the plight of the Black community for a mostly white audience that did not read the Black newspapers.[21] But without real action, it was inevitable that the strain would lead to an eventual break. That's what arrived in the Fourth Ward a month later when the 24th Infantry Regiment, an all-Black battalion that was not accustomed to the strict Jim Crow segregation of the South, was sent to guard the construction of Camp Logan, a military base about four miles outside of the ward.

It all began when two white police officers, who were known in the area for harassment of the community, broke up a dice game in the district. While pursuing a suspect, one of the officers, Lee Sparks, entered the home of Sara Travers as she was washing her clothes. Sparks failed to locate his suspect, but some words were exchanged with Travers leading to her being forcefully removed from her home in her bathrobe and arrested. At that exact moment, Pvt. Alonzo Edwards, a member of the 24th Regiment, witnessed the assault as he passed by the home and took issue with Sparks's treatment of Travers. A confrontation ensued, ending in Private Edwards being beaten and arrested.

Later in the afternoon, when Cpl. Charles Baltimore, a military policeman for the 24th, went to inquire about Edwards's arrest, he himself was beaten, shot at, and arrested. Rumors immediately circulated around the base that Baltimore had been killed, and a plot for revenge began to take shape. Baltimore, though, was released the same day and returned to the base where he informed his fellow soldiers of his treatment. The regiment, already set on their plan, began seizing ammunition and rifles to march toward the police station starting at nine o'clock that night and "burn the town as they went." By the end of the night, fifteen whites, including four police officers, had been killed by the soldiers.[22] The next morning, the city of Houston was placed under martial law, and eventually 118 members of the 24th were tried for mutiny. The NAACP once again sent a correspondent from the *Crisis* to investigate, and in its November 1917 issue, concluded "the primary cause of the Houston riot was the habitual brutality of the white police officers in Houston in their treatment of colored people."[23]

Nevertheless, at trial, 110 people were convicted.[24] Forty-one were given sentences of life, and thirteen were condemned to be hung. The executions were carried out in secret just a few months later at dawn at Fort Sam Houston in San Antonio on December 11, 1917. A white infantry soldier, who was part of the team responsible for guarding the prisoners, later described the scene as it unfolded in the early morning hours:

> The unlucky thirteen were lined up. The conductors took their places and the men for the last time heard the command, "March." Thirteen ropes dangled from the crossbeam of the scaffold, a chair in front of every rope. . . . As the ropes were being fastened about the mens' necks, big [Pvt. Frank] Johnson's voice suddenly broke into a hymn, "Lord, I'm comin' home." And the others joined him. The eyes of even the hardest of us were wet.[25]

> *Coming home, Coming home,*
> *never more to roam.*
> *Open wide your arms of love,*
> *Lord, I'm coming home.*
> "Coming Home," *William J. Kirkpatrick, 1892*

The 1918 Influenza Epidemic

Johnson, who turned twenty-one in January of 1918, was called in the summer of that year to register for the draft, a requirement of the recently passed Selective Service Act. The United States had been at war for over a year, and at the time he was renting a room in the home of the thirty-two-year-old Narcissa Waters at 912 Fuller Street in the Fourth Ward, blocks from Antioch Baptist Church. Registering on June 5, Johnson's draft card listed him as "tall" with a "medium" build, and in the section asking if he was "physically disqualified" it read, "He is blind, states was blind 13 years."[26]

Johnson would never have to serve in the military, but he was certainly aware of many of the effects the war was having at home, both socially and financially. One was the conscription of Blacks into segregated units during the war effort. In fact, there was much discussion within the African American community at the time, especially in Black churches, about the inherent conflict of morality and war and also the irony of forcing southern Black citizens to fight for a country where they themselves were not afforded many basic liberties.[27] In addition, taxes were drastically increased to support the war effort: first with the 1916 Revenue Act and a year later with the War Revenue Act, which increased the highest income tax rate from 15 percent to 67 percent in the first year and all the way to 77 percent by 1918. Closer to home, the US Food Administration, created in 1917, funded a campaign to convince Americans to cut down on certain foods so that they may be shipped to the troops overseas. And although there were no official rations, the USFA coined terms like "Meatless Mondays" and "Wheatless Wednesdays," and encouraged citizens to conserve white sugar to support the cause.[28]

To make matters more complicated, in the spring of 1918, a novel and deadly flu virus was beginning to spread rapidly among soldiers at several military camps within the United States, and although the first wave of the virus was relatively mild, the second wave, appearing as early as August of that year, proved to be devastating. There were few control efforts that could be put into effect except those of personal isolation, mask wearing, and limitations on public gatherings, which many cities were slow to enforce. And while the Spanish Flu, as it came to be named, affected people of all ages and social class, for those low-income communities where basic services were already lacking, measures such as isolation were nearly impossible to follow, making them particularly vulnerable as the flu rapidly spread among households. By late September, in Houston, it was reported that there were between six hundred and seven hundred cases at Camp Logan. And even though Houston was still resisting closures in early October, by the ninth of that month, the city had relented and shut down public gatherings. That same day the front page of the *Houston Chronicle* urged all citizens to comply with the stay-at-home order:

> There is no need to discuss whether it was necessary to close the public schools and places of amusement in Houston. Since this has been done by those in authority, acting under high medical advice, let us abide by the decision without complaint or criticism.[29]

The war would come to a close in early November of 1918, but it wouldn't be until the next year that cases of the Spanish Flu began dropping, eventually taking the lives of fifty million worldwide and an estimated 675,000 in the United States.[30] In the next few years, both the war, with its natural newsworthy elements, and the modern-day plague, with its inherent biblical allusions, would be ample material for the preacher's sermons and the street singer's broadsheets, thus ripe for a singer such as Johnson.

::

Meanwhile, it was around this time that another faith was gaining momentum in the African American community. It was one that would serve as "a protest against the high-brow tendency in Negro Protestant congregations," which some saw as leaving behind the "rhythm of sound and motion" in religion.[31] This new church distinguished itself in many ways from the Baptists and Methodists, but one of the major distinctions was its emphasis on music as a central component in the worship service, welcoming "dancing" and instruments, such as the guitar, into service. The services demanded a more vigorous mode of expression that was more physical in nature, and music that made the body move. It was a message that Johnson would find himself gravitating toward, and it would become his main devotion—absorbing its teachings, its songs, and its stricter way of living.

By the early 1920s, Johnson departed Houston and made his way closer to home in Temple, settling halfway between Waco and Hearne on the H&TC in Marlin, a bustling city known for its healing waters. It was here where he found himself among a thriving community who practiced this more exuberant form of worship. And while still on the fringes, the Pentecostal Church of God in Christ (COGIC) church may have been just what Johnson needed, both spiritually and artistically.

Glossolalia

They hung him on a cross,
they hung him on a cross for me.
They speared him in the side,
they speared him in the side for me.
And the blood came streaming down,
and the blood came streaming down for me.

It was March 1907 when Charles Harrison (C. H.) Mason, a Black preacher in his forties, ventured to Los Angeles, California, to "investigate" what was happening at a two-story "tumble down shack" and former African Methodist Episcopal Church on Azusa Street.[32] He had been trained as a minister in the Missionary Baptist Church but was forced to split to form his own church in 1895 after he and a few other members, including Charles Price (C. P.) Jones, began conducting revivals based on the doctrine of Sanctification, a belief in a "second blessing" whereby the converted are "set apart" and cleansed of original sin—a doctrine rejected by the Baptist Church. They had since been preaching from a deserted cotton gin in Lexington, Mississippi, but when they heard of a great revival taking place in Los Angeles, led by a Black Holiness preacher, where illnesses were being cured without medicine, the blind were having their eyesight restored, and where congregants could be heard shouting, singing, and testifying at all hours of the day and night, they felt they had to witness it for themselves.[33] What was most intriguing to Mason—and the many others who flocked to the church to see what was happening—were the accounts filtering out of Azusa Street describing crowds of worshippers "work[ing] themselves into a state of mad excitement" and claiming to have the "gift of tongues" as a result of their sanctification.[34] While Mason's church believed in sanctification, this was the first account they had heard of there being proof that sanctification could be physically evident. These were accounts of biblical proportions echoing the details described in the second chapter of the book of Acts when a "mighty rushing wind" descended on the apostles on the day of Pentecost:

> The power of God now has this city agitated as never before. Pentecost has surely come and with it the Bible evidences are following, many converted and sanctified and filled with the Holy Ghost, speaking in tongues as they did on the day of Pentecost.[35]

The Azusa Street Revival had already been in progress since just before the devastating San Francisco earthquake in 1906 when William James Seymour, an African American preacher born in Louisiana, had been called to preach in the city early that year. Seymour had arrived in Los Angeles as a preacher who had learned his brand of Holiness, called the Apostolic Faith Movement, under the teaching of the white preacher and evangelist Charles Fox Parham in Houston. Parham was an itinerant pastor who had split from the Methodist Church and moved to Houston, where he quickly set up a Bible school and held tent revivals and camp meetings in the city. Parham's Holiness differed from other sects in that Parham's preaching embraced the healing practice of laying on of hands to invoke the Holy Spirit, and baptism by the Holy Ghost and fire. It was a teaching that followed the lead of John the Baptist, who, in Matthew 3:11, preached that the Holy Spirit was evidenced through glossolalia, or speaking in tongues, referencing the day of Pentecost when "tongues as of fire" appear.[36]

Seymour's involvement with Parham and the Apostolic Faith Movement came not long after Seymour moved from Cincinnati to settle in Houston in 1903 on a mission to fulfill his call to join the ministry, a call he accepted after suffering a severe bout of smallpox that left him blinded in one eye.[37] The introduction was made through Lucy Farrow, a former slave and fellow Holiness preacher who ran her own church and who was convinced of Parham's teachings after experiencing glossolalia herself while working for him in Kansas. Upon her insistence, and despite segregation, Seymour began attending Parham's Bible school and quickly became a convert and began ministering to Black citizens in Houston.

In 1906, Seymour experienced his second "divine call" when he was invited to minister at a Holiness church in Los Angeles.[38] Arriving by train in late February, Seymour began preaching on the baptism by the spirit learned from Parham's Bible school. It was a doctrine the elders roundly rejected—especially considering Seymour had not, himself, experienced glossolalia—forcing him from the church and into several private homes to continue his preaching. Temporarily lost, he reached out to Farrow in Houston to join and assist him. Farrow agreed, and within weeks of her arrival they had a breakthrough. Following days of fasting at a home Seymour and Farrow had set up, one of the congregants began speaking in tongues, and suddenly it was as if the dam had been broken, as others in the prayer meetings began getting baptized by the spirit, including Seymour himself. Word quickly spread about what was happening at this home on North Bonnie Brae Street, and within days the meetings were growing so large they were forced to find another venue, which they found a couple miles away at 312 Azusa Street. It was the beginning of Pentecostalism.

⁘

Inside the building at Azusa, Mason found a "barn-like room" on the lower floor and makeshift pews set up in a rectangular pattern. He took a seat by himself and "began to thank God in [his] heart for all things."[39] When he witnessed some of the people around him speaking in tongues, he didn't understand it, but in the days that followed he had a vision and returned to pray at the altar to "ask for the baptism of the Holy Ghost."[40] Then, suddenly around him someone, one of the saints, called out for a song, and rising to his feet he began to shout:

He brought me out of the miry clay,
He set my feet on the Rock to stay;
I'll sing my new song, the glad story of love,
Then join in the chorus with the saints above!

"The Spirit came upon me," Mason recalled. And "[w]hen I opened my mouth to say Glory, a flame touched my tongue which ran down me. My language changed. . . . My soul was then satisfied."[41]

Mason returned to Mississippi a convert, but soon found himself expelled from his own church over his adoption of the teachings of glossolalia. So he returned to Memphis, near the city of his birth, and began his own church which he named the Church of God in Christ. It would be one of many Pentecostal churches that was spawned from Azusa Street, and one that would appeal to many nonprofessional, working-class Blacks in the years to come. They were drawn to it for many reasons, including its emphasis on being sanctified or "called" to preach over ordination, and its belief that women should play a larger role in leadership positions of the church—two ideas the Baptist Church did not share. In fact, in support of Mason's determination to secure a more critical role for women in the church, in 1911 he established the Women's Department, which over the years saw many women take on vital roles as mothers of the church, evangelists, and missionaries, all of whom would work to reshape not only the sanctified, inner lives of women but also their social and political lives as well.[42] In addition, the COGIC encouraged a more spirited approach to music making, a rebuke to the concert stage spirituals that were being performed by groups like the Fisk Jubilee Singers. Being baptized in the Holy Ghost meant a greater freedom of physical expression with the body and with instruments, as words alone were insufficient to convey what was going on inside. Members were free to speak with "new tongues," and to "make a joyful noise unto the Lord" both vocally and with tambourines, guitars, and the piano.[43] Furthermore, the rhythm of singing and playing was even further intensified in comparison with the Baptist service, giving the impression that all participants were on fire with the word of God.

∷

The church grew through the power of Reverend Mason's sermons as well as with the assistance of numerous evangelists.[44] Defined as those who had "no fixed place of residence," the evangelists would spread the word on street corners and in empty commercial spaces (often in low-income communities), which the church rented and converted. These storefront churches became the setting of improvised revival meetings led by a charismatic preacher as well as several members with tambourines and guitars to try and attract members.[45] In his short story "Sonny's Blues," the author James Baldwin describes the effect such a scene would have on passersby as they stopped and witnessed such a spontaneous revival before them on the street. "[The] faces underwent a change, the eyes focusing on something within; the music seemed to soothe a poison out of them; and time seemed, nearly, to fall away," he wrote. [46]

For many, especially the blind singer or street preacher who otherwise may be seen as a beggar, as well as for many others who had little education or felt resigned to the lower rungs of society, the pull was irresistible. The church grew, becoming one of the largest independent Black denominations in the world, reporting 425,000 members and 4,100 congregations by 1964.[47] But with growth also came ridicule, backlash, and surveillance. Often members in the community were seen as outcasts and referred to by derogatory slurs such as "holy rollers." Moreover, the churches, mostly set up in rural communities, would be subject to harassment in the form of noise complaints, and especially in the early days, many were burned to try and force them out of town.[48] And during the First World War, while the church was preaching pacifism, the Bureau of Investigation investigated C. H. Mason and other preachers on suspicion that they were dissuading Black men from registering for the draft.[49]

But the church and its members were not dissuaded. For them, the world was divided between sinners and saints, where the "saints" had been saved, and the sinners were worldly people who were walking the path of sin. There was a clear dividing line. The saints had been baptized in water, and again by the spirit.[50] They abstained from the secular world of entertainment like movie theaters or juke joints. They fasted as part of the sanctification process, and while "the whole movement of the Sanctified Church is a rebirth of song-making," the blues was sure to lead to the sinner's road and therefore fully opposed.[51] "The blues we play in our homes is a club to beat up Jesus," Rev. C. C. Lovelace exhorted from a sanctified church in Florida in 1929. Instead, this was music meant to be shouted out loud, and contrary to the blues, it was not a solo music but one that gained strength through participation. Their songs also had their own language; it was a vocabulary centered on a few themes including the "blood of Jesus," through which one becomes sanctified and cleansed from sins; and the "latter rain," which they believe will fall in the end times when there is an outpouring of the Holy Spirit similar to the "early rain" that fell upon the apostles in Acts 2. The saints believe that the rapture is imminent, and many of the early songs carried warnings drawn from natural disasters and epidemics, and they frequently advised sinners to "get your business straight" for when God comes again. They even adopted the hymn "When the Saints Go Marching In," which was inspired by the book of Acts, as an unofficial anthem, remaking the apocalyptic song in their style as a joyous occasion to be celebrated.[52] For the COGIC saints, this "world was not their home," Jesus was going to make up their dying bed, and one day soon they would be called back home. Until that day the saints would march forward, for they were soldiers in the army of the Lord bathed in the yellow light that only they could see; but which, through them, shone outward, and was visible through their dance and praise, illuminating the dark road out of the wilderness.

> Preach the word, preach the word
> If I never, never see you anymore!
> Preach the word, preach the word
> I'll meet you on that other shore.[53]

The Songster

How did you feel when you come out of the wilderness?
How did you feel when you...
—"Come Out the Wilderness," *traditional spiritual*

The people who knew Johnson during these early years referred to him as a "songster."[54] It was a term that took on many definitions from the mid-eighteenth to the twentieth century. First it was used as a description for an anthology of various secular ballads and popular songs (most often without musical notation) compiled into pocket-size collections. Later, "songster" was used as a reference to the Black entertainer who could both sing and was proficient with their instrument of choice. This new iteration of songster had to possess not only an impeccable memory for a wide variety of songs, but more importantly he had to have the knowledge and improvisational skill to make those songs his own—a tradition that dates back to the earliest of the Black preachers and musicians. These were the figures who, prior to radio and the widespread recording of Black artists, functioned in a similar fashion to the African griot. He was a keeper of heritage through poetry and music, and also the originator of new forms that were, much like him, continually in motion. The "songster" designation most often applied to a secular singer who had the ability to entertain with any number of ballads, blues, religious songs, or rags that the occasion demanded. But Johnson, whose prior focus had been concentrated on mastering the tone and customs of the experienced Black preacher, was about to embark on a journey that would lead to an evolution of the term centered strictly on the spiritual interpretation of the African American songbook. The Pentecostal church, for Johnson, revealed an unchartered territory imbued with its own rich vocabulary and rhythm, and that seemed to speak the language of the poor, though not of pity. It was also centered on fire, but this fire was not destruction for destruction's sake—it was a renewal of the spirit. In it, he must have seen himself and all the spiritual and artistic possibilities it offered, if only he was willing to wrestle with the depths of what it all meant.

The COGIC arrived in Texas when Elder David (D. J.) Young, a founding member and minister of the church who had been with Reverend Mason at Azusa Street, became the first representative of the church to be sent to the state. Beginning with success in Beaumont, he moved on to Dallas where, in 1910, the church quickly ran into a storm of backlash resulting in an early iteration of their worship space being set on fire. Threats of violence were made against Young himself, and petitions were drafted in the hopes of declaring the church a public nuisance.[55] But within a few years, a pastor who was also one of the early adherents of Reverend Mason and the church in Memphis, would be called to Texas and begin to turn things around.

Rev. Emmet (E. M.) Page was asked by Mason to venture to Texas in 1914, and after quickly gaining the trust of the neighborhood in Dallas, he was appointed overseer of Texas at the convocation in Houston the same year.[56] In the next five years Page was responsible for the acceleration in growth of the COGIC in Texas, developing a steady following and expanding worship locations from "22 small stations" in his first year to just over one hundred churches by 1920.[57] In addition to the construction of churches, Page oversaw the purchase of 268 acres of land in Hearne in 1918 for the purpose of establishing the Page Normal Industrial and Bible Institute where students were "trained . . . in the principles of holiness and the fundamentals of education through activities on and off campus."[58] Although still facing backlash from some communities, Page and the COGIC were having enormous success in Texas by the early 1920s, and the next decade would prove even more successful. In Sherman, just north of Dallas, a thriving congregation, often frequented by Page and home to a blind piano player by the name of Arizona Dranes, constructed the King Street COGIC at the start of the decade. Page himself also oversaw the purchase of land to build his own temple in the North Dallas Freedmantown district. Moreover, after seeing the progress he had made in the state, Page pushed north into Oklahoma beginning in 1917 and organized churches in Muskogee, Tulsa, and Oklahoma City, where he established the state headquarters. Page envisioned vast potential for the church's growth in Oklahoma, and he spent much of his time there when he wasn't in Dallas, frequently making trips with the piano player from Sherman, Ms. Dranes, as early as 1919.[59] Oklahoma was also where a young teacher turned preacher named Ford Washington (F. W.) McGee moved to teach in 1918. Washington had been raised north of Waco in the town of Hillsboro and graduated from the all-Black Paul Quinn College. By 1920, he was overseeing his own COGIC congregation in Oklahoma City. While Page and the saints still had to contend with some who were determined to "get holiness out of town," the movement was showing no signs of slowing, prompting Page to write in his letter for the 1926 COGIC Yearbook: "Watch Oklahoma."

Johnson was just settling into Marlin at a time when the city was on the rise, attracting tens of thousands of visitors nationwide who sought health and healing from the city's hot mineral water bathhouses. Newspaper advertisements promised the waters as a cure for a number of ailments from rheumatism to malaria.[60] Johnson himself may have been drawn to the city for just this reason while also recognizing the opportunity for a potential revenue source from receptive audiences who came and went from the city. In addition, Marlin's location, situated just east of the Brazos River, put Johnson closer to his hometown of Temple to the west, where his father still lived and was making a living as a dray driver. It was also a short train ride away from the deep cotton country towns he was used to frequenting like Navasota, Hempstead, and Hearne. It was around this time that Johnson was, most likely, introduced to the COGIC church for the first time. Johnson seemed to have no interest in pursuing any official role within the church, but considering its tenants—the healing of the blind and sick through the "the laying on of hands," a message of sanctification over ordination in order to preach the gospel, and the use of musical instruments to express praise—the church had obvious appeal. It seems as though it was also at this time that Johnson's skills on the guitar began to take a turn—from the rudimentary form of his very early beginnings into his playing as a fierce emotional tool with its own expressive voice. This came, most likely, for two reasons. The first is that traveling greater distances forced him to rely more and more on performing alone as opposed to having a singing partner. The second was his spiritual conversion with the COGIC, which he'd fully embraced by 1922, the same year a newspaper mentioned his frequent trips from Marlin to Oklahoma City and Okmulgee, two of the cities in Oklahoma that Elder Page and members of the church were in the process of building up at the time.[61] And, although we will never be certain, it's possible that Johnson even made trips to Memphis where Bishop C. H. Mason had established the headquarters of the COGIC.

Memphis is a city geographically equidistant from both Tutwiler, where W. C. Handy first heard slide guitar, and Lafayette County, where Howard Odum collected all of his examples of "knife songs." This sliding of a knife against the strings was a style, in conjunction with open tunings, that was more popular among itinerant secular musicians in the region, and while there may have been musicians who played with a slide in Texas, the state did not have a discernible history of slide guitar players the way northern Mississippi or the surrounding area did.[62] It is a style Johnson would have heard from the secular street performers who wandered the train depots or street corners. He would have recognized the inherent spiritual vocal qualities of this way of playing, adopted it, and set about perfecting the style to make it easier to perform without a singing partner, if needed. With the new found freedom of expression encouraged by the Church of God in Christ, and by embracing the language of the slide guitar with as equal a ferocity and passion to the manner in which he had trained his preacher's voice, Johnson was truly developing a style that was completely his own.[63] He was part African American preacher, well-versed in the old-time lyrics and vocal expressions, and part elite musician who adopted the language of the street guitar. And by doing so, Johnson came to stand, nearly peerless, as this new incarnation—the religious songster.

> *Lord, I ain't no stranger now,*
> *Lord, I ain't no stranger now,*
> *Since I've been introduced to the father and the son,*
> *Lord, I ain't no stranger now.*
> —**"I Ain't No Stranger Now,"** *traditional spiritual*

The COGIC was also making an impression on Madkin Butler. Although he would never stray from the Missionary Baptist Church, some of his surviving ballads suggest an unmistakable influence from the Pentecostals, including "I Am Working in the Lord," with its references to having a "right to shout" and to being "Holy sanctified," and one simply titled "A Song," in which the singer declares, "I ain't going to live in my sins no longer . . . the lamb's blood done washed me clean."[64] In fact, in addition to cities like Dallas, Fort Worth, and Sherman, Hearne was steadily becoming a focal point for the Pentecostal sect in Texas. It was home to Emma Stepnay, a prominent "mother" and traveling evangelist of the church, and it was a routine stop for leaders within the church including Bishop C. H. Mason, who was a frequent guest following the construction of the Page Normal School.

Butler, by the early part of the 1920s, began to slow down, limiting his travel to distances closer to home in Hearne. Some reports referring to him as Reverend Butler suggest he was doing some preaching, even if informally.[65] The reluctance to travel may have been due in part to his age (in his late 40s), but also because he and Ophelia were now raising their daughter, Martha Ozelle, who had been born in June 1920. Whatever the cause, the travel Madkin was so accustomed to nearly ceased altogether by the mid-1920s as his health began to steadily decline, so much so that he began to lose the use of his legs and would often have to resort to a wheelchair to assist him in getting around.[66]

::

Johnson, meanwhile, was a constant presence in Hearne by the mid-1920s. Taking the train from Marlin, he'd make the thirty mile trip nearly every Saturday to set up on a corner across from a myriad of other blind street singers, including Lemon Jefferson, to perform and make a living from the sharecroppers who moved through the streets to spend a little money.[67] He'd also stick around on Sundays to attend church, either at Butler's church or at that of Adam Booker, a blind piano player and preacher who lived in the town. And while there some efforts by some African American sectors within city departments to financially assist the blind who made a living panhandling on the streets, those who were true songsters (and not merely destitute playing music) kept traveling and performing the way they had always done; for them it was a life that was more enriching and profitable than the lure of a sedentary existence in charity housing and a twenty dollar a month "pension."[68] But there was also something else happening. Beginning in the early 1920s, a line was being drawn that would connect the Black vaudeville stages with record companies, which saw in the Black middle class a new source for revenue. Although the line was as segregated as the music was in the real world, suddenly Black performers were being recorded. Record companies were producing their phonograph records, "race records" as they were called, marketing them in Black newspapers, and selling them in pharmacies and furniture stores on the Black side of town.

Soon, that line would connect record companies with the Black preachers of both the Baptist and Pentecostal churches, and with rural musicians whose new sound had been building for years in the tent shows, train depots, and all-night backyard picnics and rent parties. It would all now be able to be heard, for a small price, in the comfort of one's own home. This revolution was occurring at just the same historical moment when many of the guitar players of the blues generation were truly coming into their own, with years of developing their skills firmly behind them. By 1927, when one of the field recording units traveled to Texas to record, that line was headed straight for Johnson.

INTERLUDE 5

Bye and Bye, I'm Goin' to See the King

The big wheel runs by faith,
little wheel runs by the grace of God.
—"EZEKIEL SAW THE WHEEL," traditional spiritual

Howard Washington Odum, who published the religious folk song "Bye and Bye We'll Go and See Them" in a 1909 collection, wrote of the song:

One who has heard the song . . . rendered in an effective way must recognize its power and beauty. It is pre-eminently a song for the emotions, and suggests scenes of the past and future; it brings back memories that have been forgotten and forms emotions and conceptions that have not before existed.[1]

In the version Odum collected the theme of the song is about reaching relatives who have passed over and now are "on de oder shore."[2] Also in Odum's collection was a variant of a song best known as "'Zekiel Saw De Wheel," which references the exiled prophet who had a vision of God approaching him on a chariot made of four wheels, each with a "wheel in the middle of a wheel."[3] It is the vision given to Ezekiel so that he may warn the people that they have turned away from God, and that destruction was to follow. Newman Ivey White collected a version in 1919 under the title "The Wheel," and in the text preceding the song, he mentioned several instances where the lyrics had been transcribed dating back as early as 1901.[4] The prophecy associated with "the wheel within a wheel" was also frequently transferred to another exiled prophet, John of Patmos, in the song "John Saw the Holy Number" with the line "way in the middle of the air."[5]

Roland Hayes, the great tenor who trained at Fisk University and recorded for Columbia Records, included "Ezekiel Saw de Wheel" as one of his favorite spirituals and wrote that in it "the power of the symbol . . . [is] barely hidden under the saving grace of light."[6]

Johnson's version paired these two songs, "Bye and Bye" and "'Zekiel Saw De Wheel," with the voice of the religious street singer who sang that they "wouldn't mind dying, but I got to go by myself." It incorporated the vision of the prophet

Ezekiel, who is tasked with warning the people about worshiping false idols, but it is also firmly rooted in the vision of the prophet Isaiah, who witnesses God's punishment of the corrupt as he returns from battle with garments dyed red in blood. It's a subject that recalls Johnson's last lines of "Jesus Is Coming Soon" and his reference to the prophet Zechariah while singing about the deaths during the Spanish Flu.

> *Read the Book of Zechariah, Bible plainly say*
> *The people in cities dying on account of their wicked ways.*

It's a song centered around God's judgment, but also the promise of the New Jerusalem as told by both Ezekiel and John of Patmos. For Johnson, "Bye and Bye" was a song about death, but not of dying. In the song he seems always at peace, the relaxed traveler who lives, who is on the road alone, knowing that like Ezekiel's, his warnings to the people to start living right will go unheeded, but that he will be protected when God comes back again.

BYE AND BYE I'M GOIN' TO SEE THE KING

Willie Johnson

(CHORUS)
Bye and bye goin' to see the King
Bye and bye I'm goin' to see a King
Bye and bye goin' to see a King
Wouldn't mind dyin' if dyin' was...

Wouldn't mind dyin' got to go by myself
Wouldn't mind dyin'...
Wouldn't mind dyin' got to go by myself
Wouldn't mind dyin' if dyin' was...

Ezekiel saw a wheel, wheel in the middle of
the wheel
Lord, he saw a wheel...
Ezekiel saw a wheel, wheel in the middle of
the wheel
Wouldn't mind dyin' if dyin' was...

Said he saw him comin' with his dying
garments on
Said he saw him comin'...
Said he saw him comin', dying garments on
Wouldn't mind dyin' if dyin was...

Lord, it's bye and bye goin' see the King
Bye and bye I'm goin' to see a King
Bye and bye goin' to see a King
Wouldn't mind dyin' if dyin' was...

After death you've got to stand the test Lord,
it's after death...
Well, it's after death you've got to stand the
test
Wouldn't mind dying if dying was all

THE MARRIAGE OF HEAVEN AND HELL

The Recordings of "Blind" Willie Johnson

"The highest praise that a guitarist can win in the South is—'He can make that box talk!'"[3]
—ALAN LOMAX

Dallas: Early December 1927—This wasn't either one of their first times to record. Frank Buckley Walker, in addition to being Bessie Smith's manager, was best known as a premier scout for Columbia Records, and the forty-nine-year-old William Frederick Frieberg was one of the best engineers Columbia had. He was used to recording in makeshift studios going back to at least 1915 when he helped to record the local German, Polish, and Italian music in the Athenaeum Building in Chicago during World War I.[1] So they knew how to make the artists feel more at home. It wasn't much. They picked a place that wasn't too luxurious, usually an inexpensive hotel room, hung some curtains, and to finish it off, Frank would place a bottle of bootleg moonshine on a table to help ease any performance anxiety. After all, many of these artists they were recording weren't the vaudeville stars they had recorded in the past; they were street singers, brothel pianists, and church singers answering the open call for artists from an ad they had placed in some of the local Black newspapers. It read something like: "Can you sing or play Old-Time Music? This is an actual try-out for the purpose of making Columbia Records."

They had been with the first artist they were going to record the night before when they were trying to decide what songs they would want to have him play on record. He played a number of songs for them: one about motherless children, a Samson ballad, an instrumental number he played with a knife, and a parable of the blind man who stood on the road and cried. Walker wrote down a few that he thought would be good, and they rehearsed those together early the next morning after breakfast, with Walker making sure the artist understood how the whole process would unfold, informing him he had to keep the songs to about three minutes and that he'd be there to help him know when to start, stop, etc. This was going to be their second day in Dallas and they felt good. They had the piano setup and extra guitars, and they were impressed with the kind of sound they were getting out of the modern "electric" recording equipment they had been utilizing for the past year. It gave them an edge over Paramount and the others, they both thought. Everything was in its place.

Later that afternoon Walker and Frieberg were sitting around discussing various things—from the acoustics of the room to the warmth of Texas in December—when they heard a knock on the door. It was the first recording artist of the day. He entered the room holding his guitar and was sharply dressed in a gray suit and tie. On the neck of the guitar was a sizable cup, nearly the size of a coffee mug. Walker made small talk with him while leading him to the seat at the piano. Frieberg also said a brief hello, shook his hand, and began testing the equipment one last time to make sure there would be no delays. Walker snapped a quick picture of the artist as he sat, and they went immediately into a final rehearsal of the first song. Frieberg kneeled in front of the musician to position the microphone just right. "Are you ready?" Walker asked him. There were two lights to signal to the artist—one for when to start and one for when to stop. But since the artist was blind, Walker told him he would tap him on the shoulder when it was time to begin and once more after the three minutes was up. The artist nodded that he understood, positioned his guitar, and cleared his throat. Frieberg signaled to Walker that they were ready and with that, the artist received a tap on the shoulder. Without even a moment to pause, he positioned the knife over the strings and began. After about twenty seconds of the guitar singing the lines, this growl arose from within him and the first line burst forth: "I know his blood can . . . ."[2]

It was the winter of 1868 when Mark Twain, almost by accident, first crossed paths with the great Blind Tom. He was in the middle of a lecture tour in Illinois and, while riding the train on his path from one destination to the next, sought solace by retreating to the smoking car where he thought he would not be disturbed. It was here that he witnessed "a burly negro man on the opposite side of the car [begin] to sway his body violently forward and back, and mimic with his mouth the hiss and clatter of the train."[4] When he inquired of this man's name, he was informed that he was the celebrated pianist Thomas Bethune "Blind Tom" Wiggins. A short time after this encounter, Twain attended several concerts given by "Blind Tom," after which writing that for Wiggins "all sounds were music, and the imitation of them an unceasing delight. Even discord had a charm for his exquisite ear. Even the groaning and clattering and hissing of a railway train was harmony to him."[5]

Wiggins was born blind in 1849 and was sold, along with his parents, onto a Georgia plantation. It was here that, at a very early age and at all hours of the night, he began imitating the animal noises he encountered. By the age of four his affinity and talent for piano was discovered by the slave-owning Bethune family when they overheard him imitating a terse musical piece the daughters of the home had been practicing. This talent was nurtured and in less than ten years' time, he was being marketed as "Blind Tom" and touring the Southern states. Wiggins' inspiration for his music was similar to those initial imitations, arising from the natural world that surrounded him. This is evidenced not only by Twain's recollection but also by his early compositions: "What the Wind, Rain and Thunder Said to Tom" and the more elaborate "Rain Storm." The latter integrated all the elements of a punishing thunderstorm—interpreted through sound—from the first moments of calm and moving through the ferocious wind and lightning before settling again in the clearing of daylight after the storm has passed.[6]

Following on the heels of Wiggins, another early blind pianist and composer, John William Boone, emerged on the stage. Unlike Wiggins, Boone was not born blind but had his eyes surgically removed when he was six months old to try and reduce swelling in his brain. Also unlike Wiggins, who, despite his indisputable skill, was advertised as more of a sideshow attraction highlighting his blindness, Boone and the people around him developed the slogan "Merit Wins, Not Sympathy" approach to advertising his talent.[7]

Boone was born in Miami, Missouri, just east of St. Louis, where he would end up attending the Missouri School for the Blind. Boone played piano and also formed a string band that would play on the streets before he was "discovered."[8] He undertook additional piano training and soon was taken on the road with a troupe consisting of a singer, a banjo and violin player, and Boone, who was initially billed as "Blind John" on piano.[9] Boone's piano style differed from Wiggins. Even though he also played the compositions of Beethoven or Brahms, Boone blended "European concert music . . . with black folk traditions."[10] He employed the vernacular found on the white and Black minstrel stage and also incorporated the syncopated rhythms and stride bass of the left hand in what came to be

Figure 6. Tom "Blind Tom" Wiggins, Oliver Gallop sheet music, 1860, 13¼ x 10¼. The Columbus Museum, Columbus, Georgia (Museum purchase made possible by Daniel P. and Kathelen V. Amos, Julie and Mizell Alexander, Friends of the Museum, and Gift by Exchange of Jim and Marge Krum G.2015.14.10).

known as "ragged" or ragtime style. He composed topical songs like his popular "Marshfield Tornado" after a tornado devastated the Missouri town and killed over one hundred people. He would also routinely perform songs as part of medleys that illuminated the road to where Black music would soon be headed. Pieces like "Alabama Bound" and "Make Me a Pallet on the Floor," along with Boone's frequent compositions incorporating call-and-response patterns, anticipated a whole new era of Black music that was forming organically far from the concert hall stages. The tremors from Boone's vigorous piano playing could be felt all the way through the Kansas City nightclubs, empty railroad cars, and streets of New Orleans. One day the levee was gonna break, and everyone knew it.

Crazy Blues, recorded by the vaudeville performer Mamie Smith and her Jazz Hounds for OKeh Records in August 1920, was the thing that would break it all wide open. It wasn't the first "blues" recorded or even the first time Smith stepped into a studio to record, but its popularity and sales among Black record buyers (an estimated seventy-five thousand copies in the first month) made it clear to the record executives that they had untapped financial potential just waiting to be excavated, and that's exactly what was about to occur.[11] Less than three years after the release of *Crazy Blues*, Frank Buckley Walker, a thirty-three-year-old Columbia Records talent scout from New York, together with Clarence Williams, a vaudeville piano player and businessman who had overseen recordings at OKeh, brought Bessie Smith into the studio for the first time. Smith would go on to become one of Columbia Records' biggest sellers, and she was the first, with her recording of *Cemetery Blues*, to record for the label's "race records" series in September 1923.[12] Clarence Williams also had a hand in getting the first slide guitar instrumentals—*Guitar Blues* and *Guitar Rag*—on record when Sylvester Weaver recorded for OKeh in October 1923. Weaver was a performer and guitar player based in Louisville, Kentucky, and was most likely recognized by Sara Martin, a blues singer from the same area who had already been recording with the likes of W. C. Handy and various piano players including Williams and Fats Waller prior to her session with Weaver for the label in 1923. Martin would also be present in Chicago in 1926 when OKeh recorded Arizona Dranes, the COGIC piano player from Sherman, Texas, for the first time.

Dranes made her first recordings in June of that year. At the time she was living just a couple doors down from Rev. E. M. Page and was a fixture at the piano in his North Dallas church. Dranes, in many ways, shared similar musical instincts with Johnson: using secular forms of music to express religious convictions. But instead of the guitar, she, like Boone, chose the piano, pounding out ragtime and barrelhouse rhythms familiar to northern and eastern Texas while shouting church songs in place of the suggestive drinking and sexual lyrics common to the "Classic Blues" sung by popular women at the time like Bessie Smith and Ma Rainey. Dranes sat for two sessions that year and in the first recorded lively COGIC-style iterations of the spirituals *My Soul is a Witness for the Lord* and *John Said He Saw a Number* complete with singers who answered Dranes's lines in congregational call-and-response church patterns.[13] She also recorded two solo instrumentals including *Crucifixion*, likely a take on the spiritual "Were You

There When They Crucified My Lord," but instead of it being more of a lament, in Dranes's hands it came through as a playful, joyous ragtime.[14] On her second session she was joined by the COGIC preacher F. W. McGee, who was now serving as an overseer for the church in Iowa, and recorded four additional sides including *Bye and Bye We're Going to See the King* and *Lamb's Blood Has Washed Me Clean*, the latter of which was a model COGIC song and one that Butler had sold as a ballad sheet under the title "A Song." In addition to recording, Dranes was also getting many of the songs she was performing copyrighted. This included "He's Got Better Things For You," a song that Dranes herself never recorded but that would find life through another adherent and singer of the sanctified church within a few years.[15]

> *I wouldn't mind dyin' got to go by myself,*
> *Wouldn't mind dyin' got to go by myself*
> *Wouldn't mind dyin' got to go by myself,*
> *Wouldn't mind dyin' if dyin' was all.*

Unlike the theater and church performers, the rural musicians and street singers were not so easily scouted. They moved too fast and lacked the kind of connections that came with performing with various groups. In 1924, OKeh recorded Ed Andrews for a couple of sides in Atlanta, and the minstrel and medicine show performer Papa Charlie Jackson recorded for Paramount in Chicago. But it wouldn't really be until late 1925, when the Black businessman Robert Thomas (R. T.) Ashford suggested Paramount record a blind busking songster he had frequently seen strolling the Central Avenue streets in Dallas, that interest for the solo blues musician began to grow. Ashford ran a record shop and shoeshine store in the center of the Black entertainment district on the Central tracks where Lemon Jefferson was often seen following the "Central Track north to Elm Street each morning with a walking stick and a guitar over his shoulder."[16] Jefferson traveled to Chicago to record for the first time in late December 1925 or January '26, when he recorded two religious songs under the pseudonym Deacon L. J. Bates. On one of them, *All I Want Is That Pure Religion*, Jefferson sang of the need to get religion as death's train nears, and while he didn't employ slide on the song, he did have responses in the form of the repeated, subtle "hallelu" and occasionally inferred the second response with only his guitar. But it wouldn't be Jefferson's religious material that would be the most popular. In fact, his first recordings wouldn't even be released until later in 1926. Instead, it was his next sessions, beginning in March of that year—when he recorded the traveling train songs *Booster Blues* and *Dry Southern Blues*—and later with the recordings of *Got the Blues* and *Long Lonesome Blues*, that would propel Jefferson from well-known Texas blues songster to a record-ing star selling records in the hundreds of thousands. Suddenly, everything had been accelerated. Just as Mamie Smith had opened the door for other prominent female artists, Jefferson had done the same for the rural blues. It was the start of something new. The record companies would begin venturing into select South-ern cities on field trips to search for talent, and Jefferson, although he would end up recording a couple more religious sides under the L. J. Bates alias, stuck almost exclusively to the blues and would become forever known through the name on the records: "Blind" Lemon Jefferson.

1927

A servant presently led in the famous bard, whom the muse had dearly loved . . . for though she had endowed him with a divine gift of song, she had robbed him of his eyesight.
—Homer, *Odyssey*

The Houston and Texas Central sped furiously north, rumbling through the flat land of the Texas prairie towns from Marlin to Corsicana and on into the station in Dallas where the brakes whistled and squealed to a halt. It seemed like a million thoughts and a thousand sounds were run-ning through his head all at once. It was the sound of the congested train platform that he himself had strolled through on and off for the past decade, the sound of Lemon's voice when he first heard him in person and then after someone played one of his records for him; the same thing for Arizona, whom he was introduced to at Page's church just a few years ago and who was now herself making records like the big travel-ing stars like Bessie Smith. There were a few others too, preachers, that put out records that he was familiar with. Rev. James (J. M.) Gates, the Atlanta preacher who had put out "Death's Black Train is Coming." He didn't know him personally, but the reverend possessed that voice that was immediately familiar, taking him back to the old-time preachers in the Baptist church when he was a boy. He was the type of preacher who could pick out almost any line in the Good Book and sing it like that was always the way it was meant to be heard. Gates had also been recorded by Columbia, and he figured if Columbia was good enough for Gates, it was good enough for him. And the sound of Rev. J. C. Burnett was there too, another preacher who was with Columbia and who he thought most resembled his own voice with his blend of gentle tones and harsh fire all in the same record. He had seen Reverend Burnett one year on the tent circuit as it made a swing through Texas years ago, and he remembered what it felt like when he began moaning those line hymn spirituals, like "The Downfall of Nebuchadnezzar" and "Daniel in the Lions' Den," as all the good Christians followed along feeling it all deep down like a wave of love washing right over the whole crowd. It was also that night when he first heard "Jesus is Going to Make Up My Dying Bed," in only the way Burnett could do it justice. It was a feeling he had been trying to get ever since on his own version.[17] He also thought of Rev. F. W. McGee, who he knew from the sanctified church and had seen all over Oklahoma and in Texas preaching and singing all those songs with Arizona on the piano, and the Jubilee singers shouting while others were playing guitars and trumpets and stomping around dispelling any tension that you had been carrying around in your mind and spirit. He had just heard the record Reverend McGee put out of "Lonesome Valley," and it was just like they had sung in church but without the preaching parts. Instead, it was just everybody singing those lines: "Oh, Sinner when the roll is called up yonder/ you've got to answer for yourself/ there's no one here who can answer for you/ you got to answer for yourself." As he sat there, he could feel that rhythm pounding in his brain while the words, "You've got to walk that lonesome valley/ you've got to walk it by yourself" kept repeating over and over as if they'd always been there from the day he was born, like he had known them before they were ever sung out loud, and they were meant for him.[18] "They had the congregations to assist with responses, while all this time it has always been me, trying to figure out how to make it all come together," he thought to himself. It was that idea of no one being able to answer for you and walking that lonesome valley for yourself that actually gave him reassurance. That's why he also felt connected to the sanctified preachers like McGee and Page and Rev. O. T. Jones.[19] There was something about that sound he heard in church that possessed the same natural, rapturous joy he heard when he sat all alone. It was like a thread that had been unraveling since those early days when he stood outside the Santa Fe station in his old backyard in Temple. He just had been going wherever it led. That's where his mind took him back to now—to when he had to find his place among the sinners and thieves, grasping for a song to pull from the air.

Suddenly, he heard the sound of the train car doors opening, interrupting the rhythm beating in his head, and it was time to go again. A woman's dress brushed up against his knee on her way through the aisle. A baby

*who had been fast asleep for the whole trip let out a lonesome cry as he
rose to exit. It was just him and his guitar. The way it had always been.*

Johnson recorded six songs for Walker and Freiberg on that first Saturday in
December of 1927. He sang the language of the slave in the voice of one who
had never be one, uniting the worlds of the solo blues performer with the group
power of the Black meeting houses and congregations. The first song he recorded,
I Know His Blood Can Make Me Whole, had been recorded before, but never like
this. The Reverend E. D. Campbell recorded a version of the hymn combined
with a sermon he titled *Faith* alongside three congregational voices for Victor
Records in Memphis in February. And Robert Hicks (aka Barbecue Bob), a cook
and musician who played with Curley Weaver in Atlanta, cut a version that was
paired with *When the Saints Go Marching In* for Columbia in June of '27. But
compare Hicks's version recorded just six months prior with Johnson's. Where
Hicks employed a more blues guitar style of playing, Johnson used the slide for
a call-and-response pattern making the guitar "talk" as if there are other voices
in the room answering Johnson's call of "Jesus' blood has . . . ," with "made me
whole" all in unison. And where Hicks used one style of voice to sing, Johnson
roared with the best of the Black preachers. The whole song becomes a shout, the
voice that once had to climb out over a crowd of people now amplified in front
of a microphone. Johnson was a master at using his voice to convey the greatest
ferocity and, even from these first recordings, was an artist showing no signs of
timidness or confusion as to what he was there to do.[20] Through him one can hear
not so much the singing that begins Reverend Campbell's version, but only the
shouts that conclude his sermon while the members of his assembled congregants
respond affirmatively with their own utterances of "well" and "all right now"
before the guitar finally trails off just after the three minute mark.

Johnson's next recording, *Jesus Make Up My Dying Bed*, was a song that had
been sung since slavery times in Texas. It was "a song us servants used to sing,"
recalled Lou Austin, a former slave from Crockett, Texas.[21] Rev. J. C. Burnett
had recorded it for Columbia in 1926, but it was never issued, and in June of
1927, a Baptist preacher and religious street singer out of Pittsburgh, Pennsylva-
nia, Edward W. Clayborn (Edward William Clayborn), who went by the moniker
"The Guitar Evangelist," recorded it for Vocalion under the title *Then We'll Need
That True Religion*.[22] It's a tough song, one that references "dyin' easy" instead of
the hard way of dying caused by the sinner's life. Sometimes the process of dying
could be difficult just due to the nature of pain or illness, and in order to help
relieve some of the suffering, one could assist the person by positioning their

bed in an "east-and-west position, with [the] patient's head to the west," and by removing the pillow from underneath the dying one's head.[23] It's a ritual that Clayborn references immediately in his version, which resembles Lemon Jefferson's *All I Want is That Pure Religion* released in the fall of 1926, but with the added lyrical content of the spiritual concerning Jesus making up the dying bed. While Clayborn may have used slide guitar on his recordings, and often used the technique to complete lines or act as a response in the antiphonal exchange—such as on *Death is Only a Dream* and *The Gospel Train is Coming*—what Johnson did in these first recordings goes much further. He set new rules for how a performer could sound vocally as a religious singer, and also for how the guitar could act as an extension of the Black preacher's voice by becoming just as demanding and fiery as the one who was holding it. To illustrate this point, one needs to look no further than to a comparison between the Clayborn and Johnson recordings. While Clayborn employed a steady bass line and the slide guitar in a predictable fashion, almost to the point of no discernible uniqueness musically between his works, Johnson's sound bears none of these hallmarks. Instead, as he had done on the recording *I Know His Blood Can Make Me Whole*, Johnson immediately launched into the deep slide sound that was more alive and varied than Clayborn's interpretation. So, while it may take a listener some time, as Clayborn begins singing, to distinguish which song he may be playing, with Johnson, the difference of one song to the next is unmistakable even before he utters a word. Moreover, when it comes to the vocal style, where Clayborn seems to be more *singing* on his recording, Johnson's sound comes pouring forth from the deep well of his forefathers; it is a roaring voice that one could have heard not only singing on a street corner but also coming out of an old church house, like a preacher in the middle of a frenzied sermon, no microphone, just shouting while the congregation moaned and cried out "well" or "oh" at regular intervals. But in this case, in the absence of separate passionate vocal expressions, Johnson responded for them, bringing the church members into the studio and transforming himself into both the impassioned preacher and the jubilant congregants. Seamlessly flowing from picking to slide on the guitar, from moans to singing, and to call-and-response patterns with guitar and voice, Johnson's delivery was varied, leaping from one expression to the next and making it clear from just these first two recordings that what was going on here was something different.[24]

Johnson's third song, *It's Nobody's Fault but Mine*, was different from the first two in the sense that it seemed to have no recorded precedent. Mamie Smith had recorded a similar title labeled *It's Right Here for You (If you don't get it—'tain't no fault of mine)* with her Jazz Hounds for OKeh in 1920, with the description "Popular blue song" included in the notes. Clara Smith, another of the classic blues singers, had also recorded a song under the title *T'ain't Nobody's Fault but Yours* in 1925, but these were not religious songs. It is with Rev. H. C. Gatewood, a Baptist preacher likely from the Kansas City area, and his song and sermon *Regeneration* for the Meritt Label in 1927 that one can begin to peer into the formation of what Johnson was doing on his version.[25] In his sermon, Reverend Gatewood references Nicodemus and his conversation with Jesus in which Jesus imparts to him that he must be "born again" to see the light and opens by singing the line, "It's nobody's fault but mine, It's nobody's fault but mine, If my soul gets lost in hell," and finishes with the congregation completing the last line.[26] It is a similar theme conjured in Rev. F. W. McGee's June 1927 recording of *Jonah In the Belly*, when he preaches of the failure of the prophet Jonah to answer his call to preach in the city of Nineveh. The result is Jonah being caught in a mighty storm that only ceases when he admits he is to blame for the turbulence and is thrown overboard to put a halt to the relentless disturbance. In McGee and the sanctified congregation's rendition, they sing of Jonah begging to be thrown overboard as he exclaims, "I've got the fault in me."[27] This is the version that Johnson likely connected to the most and probably heard on and off through his visits to McGee's church. It was the blood that flowed through his veins, as it did for Madkin Butler and all the preachers who do not choose but are called. As prophets. And although so many refuse at first, as can be seen in the case of Jonah, the consequences are severe, and the only way to make it right again is to give in to the mission that lies ahead.

The recording of *Mother's Children Have a Hard Time* followed, its origins dating back to the slave plantations before being picked up in later years for what would become the secular "Poor Boy Long Ways from Home." And while both share the same theme of the child (or boy) alone out in the world and the lyrical content of "long ways from home," (although not in Johnson's rendition) the spiritual is distinct from the secular version in that the focus is centered not on the "I" of the secular but on the motherless children as a group, now and forever, at its center. It's a subtle divergence, but one with clear contrasts, especially in the hands of Johnson, who could have brought truth to either of the versions as his connection to the lyrics was a personal one as well as a spiritual one.[28]

The recording session concluded with two last songs that couldn't be more different in tone: the Samson ballad "If I Had My Way I'd Tear the Building Down" and Johnson's wholly unique iteration of the Missionary Baptist lined-out hymn "Dark Was the Night." In Johnson's version of the hymn, under the title *Dark Was the Night, Cold Was the Ground*, the ferocity of tempo and voice of the other five performances are completely gone, and in their place resides this piece that, although quieter than the preceding songs, plunges the listener into a world that, if one was not prepared, could be even less comfortable—one where thoughts are not as simply converted to words to express true emotions as we'd like to assume, and where the sound itself is confrontational to the soul. This was accomplished by Johnson eliminating the linguistic elements of the original hymn and returning us to the scene of the cross where Jesus "never said a mumbalin' word" as Johnson used his guitar first as preacher and then as a congregational response where the moan was pronounced both vocally and with his slide. The effect of distilling the song to its most pure emotional language guides us even deeper to a place that becomes larger than one particular death and eventual redemption, and into a chasm of depth where we all become part of one universal moan.[29]

Johnson had no idea at the time whether he would ever record again, and by choosing the protest-themed "If I Had My Way I'd Tear the Building Down," he made a decision to return to the fire that defined the songs prior to "Dark Was the Night" and to the voice of the preacher who built his reputation not in front of microphones but through shouts and roars that were necessary to pierce through the noise and the chatter of the passing crowds on Saturday afternoons.[30] These were the songs of his tortured forbearers whose voices growled and hummed and shouted and now were exploding within this one soul. So, when he sang "If I Had My Way I'd Tear the Building Down," a song that had been around Texas and elsewhere in religious circles for decades, he brought a strength that collided with the subversive lyrics and removed the veil once and for all to reveal that this always was, as much as its spiritual cousin "Joshua Fit the Battle of Jericho," a protest song. And in this revolt Johnson did not just sing the song as its vocal preacher, but like a blues man, he also placed himself in the role of Samson, as the one who had his eyes gouged and was ready to tear the building down. Throughout the three minutes, he seamlessly fluctuated between tones, playing with the antiphonal response patterns to conjure an emotional intensity that no longer made any sense to remain constrained.

After the session was complete, Johnson was paid a flat fee with no promise of royalties and said goodbye, heading back down to the streets of the Deep Elm district to do it all again, but without all the equipment. He had recorded a total of six songs, actually a high number of songs for a session considering most artists were lucky if they were able to record two.[31] But it was over now. Tomorrow would be Sunday, a new day, and a chance to attend Page's church nearby.

⁙

James Weldon Johnson wrote of his affection and appreciation for those whose "spirit must have floated free, [t]hough still about his hands in chains," in his 1908 ode to the "black and unknown bards."[32] He described the creators of the spirituals as the "black slave singers, gone forgot, unfamed," but who "sang a race from wood and stone to Christ."[33] It is this tradition from which Johnson sprang, and even if he were to only have these six recordings as his musical legacy, it would be enough to prove it to be true. Here, in 1927, stood the modern bard who had come to "know [t]he power and beauty of the minstrel's lyre," and who was the living embodiment of "the maker of songs" and the "leaders of singing" who J. W. Johnson and many others knew so well.[34] It was the musician and artist Johnson who, on both *It's Nobody's Fault But Mine*, and *Dark Was the Night*, articulated so clearly the ancestral moan as both protest and prayer as it had been over the centuries. And it was on the spirituals, *Jesus Make Up My Dying Bed* and *Mother's Children Have A Hard Time* that he summoned the "tense, . . . hoarse-sounding vocal techniques" of the old-time preachers who risked their very lives to evangelize in the brush arbor services.[35] He was in full command of a past, but also of the future as he assembled the various slavery-era song structures and integrated them in the present through the incorporation of his guitar and own voice, which served to function as both accompaniment and accomplice in the antiphonal exchanges.

For Johnson, as it was in the slave minister's sermons on the pulpit or at the burial grounds, it was the *feeling* rather than the lyrics that conveys the *meaning*, as the lines stood to be improvised and changed at a moment's notice. That is why on *Jesus Make Up My Dying Bed* as well as on *If I Had My Way I'd Tear The Building Down*, some words may seem indecipherable, as Johnson was not attempting to perform a song in the exact manner of another, but to capture what he felt and to lay bare the emotional intensity of the song. It was not about repeating the written text memorized from a hymn book, which Johnson, like those enslaved, never had access to, but instead it was a spiritual literacy he was concerned with. This point is made even more plain in songs like "If I Had My Way" when words are rushed over quietly, but quickly followed with roaring intensity.[36] This all translates to the main mission, which is a pursuit toward freedom in Johnson's expression that is both of the past, in the form of the collectively produced spirituals, but also squarely in the present as he confidently asserted his own voice, which now, unconstrained from the necessity for subversiveness, was able to give full emotional expression to the so-called "sorrow songs," interpreting some with pure joy and others with the once only implied threat now out in the open, something that would have been unthinkable for their originators. It was an internal emancipation, shared by his ancestors, that arose from an understanding that one is born into systems but not of them and that to truly be liberated means not strictly toppling external structures that could easily be replaced with even more dangerous imaginations, but struggling and eventually untangling oneself from the internal bondage that can be far more complex and mysterious. This way, as it was for Johnson, is often revealed through faith, and while the individual names who "sang a race from wood and stone to Christ" may be forever lost, their voices were now resounding through the modern bards: the writers, the poets, and the songsters who were continuing the journey and would steadfastly refuse to be unknown any longer.

> *Motherless Children have a hard time*
> *Motherless Children have a hard time, mother's dead*
> *They'll not have anywhere to go, wanderin' around from door to door*
> *Have a hard time.*

1928

As early as January 1928, Columbia Records was advertising Johnson as a "new sensation."[37] In fact, for his first release they described him as someone who "sings sacred selections in a way you have never heard before" and his guitar playing as "nothing like it anywhere else." It was a description that the buying public must have agreed with, as his records were big sellers. The first record, *I Know His Blood Can Make Me Whole*, sold over fifteen thousand copies, such a high number that by the time *Mother's Children Have a Hard Time* was released, Columbia was already labeling him as a "very popular artist" and mentioning that the "demand for his recordings, places him in the front rank of Race artists."[38] Although there were few reviews, Edward "Abbe" Niles, a leading music critic of the day, wrote in his monthly column that Johnson was an "extraordinary guitarist" who possessed "violent, tortured . . . shouts and groans."[39]

Meanwhile, back in Marlin at this time, Johnson had met Willie B. Harris, a widowed farmer with two young kids also living in the city. Her husband, Ross, had died a few years earlier from tuberculosis, and she likely met Johnson at the Marlin Church of God in Christ Pentecostal Church located adjacent to the H&TC tracks on Commerce Street. They both attended the church, and she sang while Johnson played piano in addition to the guitar.[40] Marlin, at the time, was alive with energy due to its nationwide attraction as a wellness city. In a year, Conrad Hilton would begin construction on the Falls Hotel, only his eighth to date, to accommodate the thousands of visitors who came to bathe and be healed in the mineral waters of the town. The centers of attraction were the Marlin Sanitorium and Bathhouse and the Mineral Water Pavilion, just a four-minute walk north on the railroad line from where Johnson would set up, often accompanied by Harris, near the H&TC depot and the "Negro Bath" on the notorious

Figure 7. *Columbia Records publicity photo of "Blind" Willie Johnson, 1927.*

Wood Street.[41] Johnson was also still traveling, spending time playing at church meetings as well as revivals, but he could also frequently be found in nearby Waco and Hearne, near Harris's birthplace of Franklin, to sing alongside Madkin Butler.[42] He also had an association with some of the musicians working on the blues side of the line including Thomas Shaw, the son of Lewis Shaw out of Brenham, as well as Bob Jackson, a local Marlin pianist who was known for his extraordinary rendition of "Troublesome Mind" that included lyrics like "never drive a stranger from your door" and "Sometimes I feel like dyin'/ I'm gonna lay my head /On the lonesome railroad line."[43] But as the year was coming to a close, Johnson was again contacted by Columbia, which was planning another trip to Dallas in early winter, to see if he would be interested in making a few more records. It was rare that artists would be asked back in consecutive years. It was more likely that only a couple of sides would be recorded in one outing, and that would be it. But with Johnson's success came the call to do it again, and by December 5, he and Willie B. Harris were booked into the Delmonico, one of the more prestigious Black-owned hotels in Dallas, located at 302½ North Central near the corner of Pacific Avenue in the heart of the Black business district.[44] It would be here, in Dallas over the next couple of days, where Johnson and Harris would complete Johnson's second recording session for Columbia, spend time carefully selecting new guitars for Johnson to purchase, and—likely right on the Central Tracks near R. T. Ashford's music shop located on the same side of the street as the Delmonico just on the other side of Swiss Avenue—have a run-in with Lemon Jefferson.[45]

::

Harris and Johnson began the session by performing two songs that were much in the same vein as the last song Johnson recorded in 1927, *If I Had My Way I'd*

Tear the Building Down, in that they were more in the ballad structure as opposed to a more typical religious call-and-response pattern. Thus, as with *If I Had My Way*, Johnson did not employ the slide guitar, but instead allowed his voice, more than anything, to take over the song. This is true even when Harris assisted in the singing of the chorus, as it was not her voice alone responding to Johnson, but instead always in combination with Johnson and his guitar. The first song they recorded that afternoon, *I'm Gonna Run to the City of Refuge*, was a song that one could still hear being sung along the highways by the men laboring in chain gangs where "the basses would go to impressive depths, while the tenors and baritones would curl all around the heavier tones in improvised runs and quavers."[46] Johnson and Harris's version functions in much the same way with Johnson singing in the full-throated raspy false bass of the preacher while Harris matches his lyrics, especially in the chorus, in a more angelic fashion hovering just above him.[47] The next song they recorded was a religious warning ballad that took shape around the devastating 1918 Spanish Flu pandemic, and one that Johnson had likely been singing ever since: *Jesus is Coming Soon*. It's an apocalyptic song, but one that's not vague in specifics like *He's Coming Soon* recorded by Laura Henton, another sanctified singer earlier the same day in Dallas, nor did it resemble the one recorded by the evangelist R. H. Harris with her Pentecostal Sisters in Chicago in 1927.[48] Instead, Johnson and Harris focused on a specific event that they had actually lived through, and one that could have easily been pulled directly from Revelation.[49] With their main theme being the democratization of death, Johnson sang of the people who ordinarily would be in charge, those serving in upper classes in society like doctors and high-ranking military personnel, being just as confused and vulnerable as anyone in the face of the absurdity of a modern-day plague. And this was, in fact, the prevailing view of the Black community within the churches while the flu was spreading so rapidly in 1918. One of the leading African American preachers of the day, Rev. Francis J. Grimke, gave a sermon in November of that year, at a time when the country was still being ravaged by the second wave of infections, that encapsulated many of the themes that constructed the ballad being sung on the streets—the death of health care workers despite their high level of education, the powers afforded governments that in normal times would never be accepted by the citizens like closing schools or churches, and that no man is immune from death so one must "mend his evil" ways before it is too late.[50]

The final two songs recorded for the day (that would be released) were *Lord I Just Can't Keep from Crying* and *Keep Your Lamp Trimmed and Burning*. Being more directly related to the spirituals, they are the only two sides of the session for which Johnson decided to use the slide on his guitar with the latter being the sole recording of the session in which Harris was free to sing the response without being hidden by Johnson's own voice, providing insight into what may have been a common sound heard by the passersby on Commerce Street in Marlin at the time.[51]

Two additional songs were recorded following the spirituals, but Columbia didn't name or release them. They were filed under the moniker of "Blind Texas Marlin." While we will never know with certainty, considering there were only four recordings released from the session, it is very likely these were two unreleased Johnson selections. With Johnson's popularity, it is highly unlikely that Walker would have wanted Johnson to record less than he had the year previously, especially considering it probably would be another year before he would be able to record him again.[52]

1929

It was December on Canal Street in New Orleans, and the streetcars once again glided down the street following the end of the strikes in October that saw cars burned and a few deaths as thousands rallied to support the workers. Columbia Records and its subsidiary OKeh had just moved their recording unit from Dallas where they recorded the pianist Alex Moore, the vaudeville and spiritual singer Lillian Glinn, and a young T-Bone Walker (Aaron Thibeaux Walker). Rev. Arthur Armstead (A. A.) Gundy, the pastor of New Elam Baptist Church in Hearne that Madkin Butler attended, also recorded four sides. He was the same pastor whom the folklorist Mary Virginia Bales likely saw with his congregation singing "When the Saints Go Marching In," on her visit in the late 1920s.[53] Columbia had set up in a makeshift studio on Canal, possibly in the top room of the popular music store Werlein's, recording Cajun, jazz, and country music.[54] The duo of the Black accordion player Amédé Ardoin and white fiddler Dennis McGee even made their first beautiful Cajun recordings together on December 9 in the city. Music was everywhere. It was the birthplace of jazz. Louis Armstrong, who possessed that deep growl of a voice and improvisational techniques on his trumpet that were so favored in the spiritual Black idiom, was born only blocks away in a rough section of town dubbed James Alley. It's the same James Alley that the ballad and street singer Richard "Rabbit" Brown sang about in his song of the same name recorded for Victor in March 1927 in the city.[55] And Storyville, the red-light district that mirrored Houston's Reservation (and was dismantled the same year as Houston's) could be located *by heading straight up Canal walking the opposite direction from the Mississippi.*

Somewhere, among the chaos and laughter, Willie Johnson strolled down the sidewalk with his guitar, passing along the way the various street vendors and singers like Dave Ross who, like Johnson, was both blind and a member of the Pentecostal Church and would play on the streets singing strictly religious songs. Ross was one of many who would encounter Johnson throughout his weeks-long stay in New Orleans.

Finally, Johnson arrived at 605 Canal. The date was Tuesday, December 10, and it was the first day of his third recording session for Columbia.

The 1929 session was divided into two distinct parts: Tuesday, December 10, when Johnson recorded alone; and Wednesday, December 11, when he sang with a partner who, at many times, although familiar with the songs Johnson was performing, was consistently out of sync with Johnson's rhythm and interpretation of them.

Tuesday, December 10

Johnson's first recorded song of the day, *Let Your Light Shine on Me*, references a few sections in the Bible, but none more related to Johnson than in John, chapter 9, when Jesus and his disciples pass a beggar on the street who has been blind since birth. When asked what kind of sin was committed to allow this man to live in such a way, Jesus responds, "Neither this man nor his parents sinned, but this happened so that the works of God would be displayed in him. . . . While I am in the world, I am the light of the world."[56] Jesus cures his blindness and later remarks on the separation from the blind who can see "the light of the world" through faith, and those who suffer from spiritual blindness although their physical eyesight may be unscathed. The song itself was sung in the Baptist Church as a long-meter line hymn, not dissimilar from "Amazing Grace" and "Dark Was the Night." Johnson both opened and closed the song in this tradition while also employing an ever-quickening rhythm through the guitar and by using the instrument as a percussive device in successive verses. His voice also moved with the pulse of the song itself, gaining momentum and emotion as he went from his natural tenor voice to false bass, where he remained for the bulk of the song before settling back again in the voice of the tenor as he lined out "shine on me."[57] In *God Don't Never Change*, his second song of the afternoon, Johnson once again returned to the slide, but in both singing and playing, the tone is in stark contrast to the fiery protest approach of his first recordings like *I Know His Blood Can Make Me Whole* or *Jesus Make Up My Dying Bed*. Instead, here both his slide and voice were slowed in more of an appeal to tenderness as he referenced the Missionary Baptist Amen Corner, where women would sit and moan out those line hymns of his youth. He also referenced the Spanish Flu when he stated, "In the time of the influenza/ He truly was a God to you," before resolving the piece with a sequence solely spoken by the guitar that recalls his own *It's Nobody's Fault But Mine*.[58] Johnson ended the four song session by returning to the slide guitar on *Bye and Bye I'm Goin' to See the King* and *Sweeter as the Years Roll By* a rendition of the hymn "Sweeter as the Years Go By," published by the composer Leila Morris in 1912.[59] And while the latter was scarcely recorded, "Bye and Bye" was well known in the COGIC circles and was recorded by Arizona Dranes with F. W. McGee in 1926 and—under the title *Wouldn't Mind Dying if Dying Was All*—by blind Pentecostal street singers A. C. and "Blind" Mamie Forehand for Victor in Memphis in 1927.[60]

Wednesday, December 11

Johnson's preference to perform with a singer is once again evident on his second consecutive day of recording, but without Willie B. Harris on the trip, he was forced to rely on the aid of an unknown female voice for five of the six additional sides.[61] But the vast gap between what Johnson was doing and what the singer was prepared for becomes glaringly obvious from their first recording together, *You'll Need Somebody on Your Bond*. Listening to the song, a version of a Baptist song/sermon, brings to life James Weldon Johnson's example of "Singing" Johnson's interplay with the congregation. James Weldon Johnson wrote that, as the church members listened to the new songs being introduced, they would "hang on his voice," and would "[sing] at first hesitantly, but seizing the song quickly, made up for hesitation by added gusto in the response."[62] This sort of "hesitancy" becomes even more clear when comparing Johnson's recording to the antiphonal exchanges Rev. J. M. Gates had with his assembled members on their interpretation, titled *You Gonna Need This Man Jesus on Your Bond*, recorded less than a week later. Gates's recording of *Bond* is performed in the conventional fashion of the Black church with Gates preaching a short sermon while his assembled singers, knowing exactly where to come in, respond with shouts of "well" and "oh." On Johnson's recording, on the other hand, his partner appears tentative in some instances, while at other times, almost too bold, resisting the softer counterpoint Harris provided a year earlier. There are moments when this singer attempted to almost match Johnson in his intensity, making it apparent that she never seemed to know where Johnson could be heading in the constantly shifting territory where he resided. The result is a contrast almost so evident that one could easily believe, especially as the pair progressed, that Johnson and his partner were recorded in separate rooms and the voices paired only later through editing.[63]

This balance was slightly improved on *When the War Was On*, Johnson's interpretation of a popular World War I broadside ballad that shares a similar nature with "Jesus Is Coming Soon" in that both served as news and commentary on what were, at the time they were occurring, current events.[64] But they differ in the respect that "When the War Was On" is essentially secular in nature and focuses more on the social predicaments facing the citizens of a country at war. And while Johnson's recording shares many lyrical similarities with the street singing couple William and Versey Smith's *Everybody Help The Boys Come Home*, recorded in 1927, there are crucial differences, and none more important than the subversive second verse of Johnson's when he sang of President Wilson "sitting on his throne / making laws for everyone" and following with the line "Didn't call the Black man to lay with the white" before allowing his guitar to "speak" the last line and, by doing so, announcing that something has clearly been removed from the recording that he would have been accustomed to singing on the streets for a Black audience. So, while William and Versey Smith's version shares the same first two lines of the verse, on their version they went directly into lines concerning laws regarding taxes versus commenting on the segregation of the battalions during the war. The significance of this is that the song, at its core, alludes to the sacrifices that citizens had to make including tax increases, registering for the draft, and food rations on items like sugar. Johnson was clearly pointing out the hypocrisy of a government that insisted, through advertising, on unity while at the same time legally and institutionally ensuring division. But Johnson's tone was never cutting, never accusatory. Instead, it was playful, as if to say, "what else would you expect," before quickly moving on. He continued that tone on *Praise God I'm Satisfied*, a reworking of an old hymn that likely, in its original conception upon publication, would have been sung in white churches with less jubilation than the version Johnson performed on the streets.[65] Here, Johnson and his partner raised their voices in praise, pairing their inner joy with jubilant lyrics equating Christ's Crucifixion not with something to be mourned, but to be celebrated. It is a song that, in their hands, referenced back to the great spirituals of the Crucifixion, "Were You There When They Crucified My Lord" and "He Never Said a Mumblin' Word," in that Johnson placed himself beside Jesus, the one who was executed on that "cruel tree." While in the 1923 version of the hymn, the author "hope[s] to meet Him in the air" after death, in Johnson's version God is already with him as God has already "placed His arms about me and . . . drawed me to His side." As was becoming more common as Johnson performed with a singing partner, Johnson did not play slide on this song, but it is easy to see that this is certainly one he may have performed on the street alone in that form, as there are moments at the end of a line where his voice would suddenly drop out, allowing his partner to complete it the same way that his guitar may have done if solo.

"Take Your Burden to the Lord and Leave It There," the Charles A. Tindley hymn, was popular among the Baptist street singers and preachers, and Johnson's iteration is the only one recorded at the time that fiercely combined the two styles, as he employed his deep bass voice while also at ease in his antiphonal exchanges with his partner.[66] While "Take Your Burden to the Lord" could more easily be molded to suit the style of any singer, a song like "Take Your Stand" is far more difficult to pull off, as it achieves its strength, more than anything, from the collective power of the group. It's a song that gains momentum as the singers are roused, consumed in spirit and natural energy from the lyrical content of the song—themes of movement and of loss—but more so from the way it is felt in those that are preaching and singing it. With its demand on the listener (but clearly instilled in the singer as well) to "take a stand," it's a song of protest. But it's also a message of love, imparting to the one they are leaving behind to "preach the word," and in the event that they should not return, they will "meet [them] on the other shore," assuring them that death is not the end. It's not a song to be sung by the timid, and one could easily imagine it being confused for an overt call for revolt on the streets in Johnson's time, which could lead to arrest or worse. This is further evidenced by the most affecting recorded renditions sung by the Pentecostal preacher Rev. Shy (E. S.) Moore, Rev. J. C. Burnett, and Charley Patton—all three being the most spiritually and vocally related to Johnson himself.[67] And while it is a song resolute in its demand for "taking a stand," the stand always seems far more internal than external. It is a call to arms in the name of "truth" and to live unencumbered by fear and to never be afraid either for oneself or for the singer, because no matter how the world may judge, there is something higher that connects you to that which is greater than the earthly terrors of fallible men. Thus, once one is freed, the joy arises. The theme for the song itself arises from the promise following the Resurrection that there are worse things than death if one did not have faith, a warning Jesus imparts to his disciples who could not believe that he had risen.

> Whoever believes and is baptized will be saved, but whoever does not believe will be condemned. And these signs will accompany those who believe: In my name they will drive out demons; they will speak in new tongues; they will pick up snakes with their hands; and when they drink deadly poison, it will

not hurt them at all; they will place their hands on sick people, and they will get well.[68]

It is fitting that Johnson recorded a song like "Take Your Stand" because it is the anthem of those who are *called to preach*, who are unafraid to leave everyone behind knowing that they may not be there when they return. It's a song signaling departure, not with sorrow; but a message of earthly perseverance and heavenly reassurance that if the worst should pass, they will meet once more on Canaan's shore.[69] The recording also seemed to carry a sort of cosmic fate as it also served as a sort of farewell to both his singing companion on the session and to the world, for even though Johnson had yet to record a third of, what would be his overall output, *Take Your Stand* would the last record of his that Columbia would release in 1930.

There was one last song Johnson would perform before walking out onto Canal and leaving New Orleans behind. So even as he said goodbye to his partner, Johnson prepared himself once more, this time with his slide at the ready, to perform solo. Within a few moments, he felt a hand tap him on the shoulder signaling it was time to begin. Johnson then, the way he had done a thousand times on the streets, placed his slide over the strings to finally get on record the broadside, likely composed by Madkin Butler, he had been carrying around in his head with him almost since the beginning—the one that relays the tragic tale of the Great Ship that got swallowed by the ocean in 1912—*God Moves on the Water*.[70]

::

A week following Johnson's recordings, "Blind" Lemon Jefferson was found dead in the Chicago streets, and his body was shipped back to Texas. As for Johnson, there was still no way of knowing what kind of effect the stock market crash would have on his life, much less his ability to record. But it would turn out to be his shortest wait between sessions when, only four months later, in April of 1930, Johnson was on his way again, this time to the city of Reverend Gates— who would also record three days after Johnson for OKeh in 1930—in Atlanta to lay down his last recordings. And with him this time a more assured companion was by his side.

1930

It was on the Marlin city sidewalks, as the travelers sought their cures from the healing waters, where Johnson sang "Jesus Met the Woman at the Well," a ballad that recalls when Jesus revealed himself as being the true

giver of eternal life to the Samaritan woman at Jacob's well.[71] It's a song that
not only speaks of the outcast being accepted despite their race or faults,
but also of faith being the only path of true salvation. It was this faith that led
Johnson to his current path and the Pentecostal Church, where its believers
pursued a similar wish as those who visited the bathhouses—that they too be
made whole and healed from their earthly wounds.[72]

Johnson's last session took place on Sunday, April 20, 1930, in Atlanta, Georgia. It would end up being, probably, the most significant and productive session of his entire recording career for several reasons. The first is that he was once again united with his companion, Willie B. Harris. It had been a year and a half since they had recorded in Dallas, and since that time their relationship obviously deepened. According to the 1930 census, conducted only six days prior to their recording date in Atlanta, they were sharing a house together in Marlin with two of Harris's children from her previous marriage.[73] And while Johnson was listed only as a "boarder" on the document, their pairing on what would be their last records reveals a much more intimate balance than the official record could ever explain. Another aspect the 1930 sessions lays bare was Johnson's maturity with the act of recording itself. It had only been two and a half years since his first recordings, and while those first songs displayed both the technical and spiritual accomplishment of a master artist of the street, in this final session one can feel his confidence strengthened as he allowed his voice to be more subtle and vulnerable. While this was mostly due to his having Harris by his side, there can be no doubt that his familiarity with the process of recording itself was a significant factor.

The 1930 session was also Johnson's longest for a single day as he recorded a third of his total output for Columbia Records, and again, likely because of his and Harris's personal connection as well as their involvement with the Church of God in Christ in Marlin, these recordings also exhibit the deepest influence from the Pentecostal Church. Mainly, what the 1930 recordings represent is Johnson, at the age of only thirty-three (Harris was twenty-eight), at the height of his artistic prowess, neither leaning solely on his voice or his slide guitar—he only used the slide once out of the final ten recordings—but perfectly at ease as he favored the response patterns of Harris. Here it is obvious that, although he could present these songs in a number of different ways, displaying the myriad of skills he had developed over the years, it was actually with a partner with whom he was most comfortable. But not just any partner. For, unlike with his improvised companion in New Orleans, these recordings reveal a pair that had sung together many times—in the streets, in church, and at home. It is a critical difference and something that he had been searching for since the beginning. Now, he finally had found it. What these last recordings illustrate so plainly is Johnson's assuredness—not only with Harris but with himself, his own humanity and what he had endured. There was still a defiance, but it was now balanced with a tenderness, with love. And it is evident from the very first song the couple collaborated on, *Can't Nobody Hide from God.*

The session commenced with the voice of Willie B. Harris singing in her own rhythm just before Johnson entered, not roaring but joining her, as his guitar softly fluttered underneath them. The song, one that was likely performed with overwhelming exuberance by members in both the white and Black Pentecostal churches, was now more muted, more solemn, not threatening as the lyrics may suggest, but instead confident and beautiful. One could easily envision a younger Johnson performing the same lyrics with a vengeful slide paired with his equally fierce and prophetic sermon vocals as he did in 1927. It was also not a street version with tambourines jangling in the hands of the Sisters on the sidewalk, or even a fall-down-on-your-knees shout as it would be in the church on Commerce Street in Marlin. Instead, the musicians displayed a delicate polyphonic texture in perfect sync. Even compared to their last two songs recorded together in 1928, *Lord, I Just Can't Keep from Crying* and *Keep Your Lamp Trimmed and Burning*, on *Can't Nobody Hide* they achieved a deeper level of intimacy that can only be gained through a close knowingness, one brought about by lazy evenings sitting around the living room or on the early Sunday mornings as one dresses for church. It is a confidence that continued on *If It Had Not Been for Jesus* and *Go with Me to That Land.* Harris took the lead on both songs, and if they'd been labeled as Willie B. Harris songs, no one would question it at all.[74]

The impression that we are not listening to two people recording, but rather eavesdropping on a couple performing only for themselves continues on the Pentecostal favorite *The Rain Don't Fall on Me.* It's a song well-known to the members of the Church of God in Christ (and really should be titled "Rain Done Fell on Me") that references the future end time revival through the biblical "latter rain," as opposed to the "former rain" when the Holy Ghost visited the apostles during the first Pentecost. It is a shout most exemplified on record in the COGIC tradition by Elders McIntorsh and Edwards and the Sisters Bessie Johnson and Melinda Taylor on their recording *The Latter Rain is Fall* for OKeh in 1928.[75] But through Johnson and Harris, the song was disguised and transfigured. Their version, like many from this session, displayed the vulnerable all-too-human imperfections that shouts or cries could mask.

Trouble Soon Be Over, taken from a number of spirituals, originated as a communal song, but through Johnson it became both a collective and more personal trouble, making it more of a *blues* if it were not so rooted in Black religious history and imagery.[76] Most likely a song Johnson had sung for years on the streets, in it he sang that "Christ is *his* burden bearer/ *his* only friend" and one day *he* will have rest. It's part of a pair of songs he recorded during this session that illuminate the struggle of the one that stands outside of established society, a refugee in his own land. The other record, *Everybody Ought to Treat a Stranger Right*, a take on Madkin Butler's ballad, functions in the same way.[77] On both these recordings, Johnson returned to his roaring false bass familiar in the early recordings and was able to balance the intensity with a tenderness in his natural singing voice. And with his voice, always in flux, he was able to emphasize areas where the emotion was more raw and uncompromising. This command over both his voice and the material was a distinctive characteristic of Johnson's that was lacking in other performers who came out of a similar religious tradition like Edward W. Clayborn or "Blind" Joe Taggart. Willing to put all of his internal defiance and skills of the preacher on display, Johnson, much like he had done on other early songs like *If I Had My Way*, pulls us gently forward into *Everybody Ought to Treat a Stranger Right* before suddenly rattling us with the intense storm of emotion, only to then allow it to subside just as quickly as it began. One can tell by hearing him that, although the lines "trouble soon be over" may have originated around an entire people's bondage, and "Everybody Ought to Treat a Stranger Right" may have been printed and sold by Butler, Johnson had lived these truths and from that moment on they would become *his* songs.

Church I'm Fully Saved To-Day is derived from a COGIC hymn that would lean more toward a shout in public, but with Harris and Johnson we hear a more private performance; their voices are softer, more endearing and open to each other in ways that only time provides.[78] We are, essentially, invited in once more to witness something far more intimate, both between the pair singing as well as their love for their spiritual place in the world. It is also an ideal song to demonstrate how comfortable Johnson was, not only with Harris as his partner, but also as a performer compared to his first recording, *I Know His Blood Can Make Me Whole*, a song that was based around a similar theme and used some of the same lyrics. Johnson, with his strained vocals, took on the ministerial role in both songs, but on "Church I'm Fully Saved" he had the luxury of a partner who could move with him and read where he was going, allowing him to depart from the slide and solely rely on Harris for the response patterns. This trust also opened up space for Johnson to explore a variety of diverse expressions, including when, for a few exchanges in the chorus, he abandoned the guitar as a stringed instrument completely in favor of using it as a percussive tool, tapping on the wood while Harris and he engaged in an a cappella exchange.[79] On the lyrical side, it is a song, much like "Were You There When They Crucified My Lord," that placed the singers beside Jesus, a device Johnson would use again on the more personal *The Soul of a Man* when he placed himself inside the temple with the young Jesus and became a witness himself as Jesus questioned the scholars.[80]

The session concluded with Johnson's last unique recording as well as an alternative version of *You'll Need Somebody on Your Bond*, which he originally recorded in 1929. The first, *John the Revelator*, is a song concerning the rebel, evangelist, and prophet John who was exiled to the island of Patmos for posing a threat to Roman rule. Coming once again out of the Church of God in Christ Church and with its subject being the book of Revelation, and specifically, the apocalyptic vision associated with the seven seals, the song had the potential to be far more aggressive and accusatory than the way Johnson approached it. But instead of outlining the prophecy laid out with the unrolling of the seals with an inclination toward vengeance, Johnson and Harris chose to rest in the comfort of being among the saints who'd already been redeemed. With Johnson there is no requirement to spell out the details of mankind's ending in words, as he seemed acutely aware that the truth resided within him, as if he had been here before and has returned with it all in his veins. It was all apparent through his artistry and especially his voice, a tone, which through its rough growl, was able to convey where it all ends and how. This is what was meant by the *experienced* voice dating back to slavery, and what both Courlander and Amiri Baraka emphasized when they spoke of the power of the voice. As we already are aware of the details of John's Revelation, Johnson's mission, like the prophets he sang about, was to show us the way through it, his inflection the evidence of the hard trials from which he had emerged. So instead of the fire and brimstone spoken through language, what we get is the compassionate preacher, the evangelist set up with Harris in some alcove of an abandoned storefront who confronts us with the feeling of the moon turning to blood and the stars falling from the sky, but also of the trumpets as they sound the coming of what will be.[81]

The very last song Johnson recorded was a remaking of his *You'll Need Somebody on Your Bond*, cut only four months earlier and now retitled *You're Gonna Need Somebody on Your Bond*. This time Willie B. Harris was his partner, and the difference is remarkable. Returning to the slide one last time on record, Johnson slowed down the rhythm, and where his partner in 1929 attempted to follow Johnson's lead and almost shouted rather than sang, Harris stayed with him the whole way, as if they'd performed the song a hundred times, allowing Johnson to play with the tempo and phrasing.

But as the last tap came to Johnson's shoulder, it signaled not only the end to the recording, but also Johnson's association with Columbia Records. On the way out of the makeshift studio, they met Pillie Bolling, a performer from Alabama who had rode into Atlanta on the train with Edward Bell ("Barfoot Bill"). The three of them had a brief exchange after which Johnson lent Bolling his Washburn guitar for his own session, the last of the afternoon for Columbia. Bolling used the guitar to record *Brown Skin Woman* and *Shake Me Like a Dog*.[82]

::

As for Harris and Johnson, they stayed a total of two weeks in Atlanta before making their way back home to Marlin, and by Christmas they were anticipating the birth of their first child together, a daughter who they named Ora Sam Faye.[83] Yet, so many things were uncertain. Not only had the Depression had a negative impact on the economic viability of "race records," but with money tight all around, the days of being able to make a living strictly by playing on the streets appeared, at least at the moment, to be over. Even with the hard times, it would have helped if Johnson received some royalty checks from his record sales, but Columbia had a bad habit of not paying royalties to many of its Black artists. Bessie Smith, another one of the label's top performers, was paid on average a $200 flat fee for her records with no royalty.[84] The same was true for many rural recording artists across the spectrum of labels and race.[85] Frank Walker's assertion that, for many of the artists, "[making a record] was the next thing to being President of the United States in their mind" may have been true, but this thinking is how exploitation continues to this day while someone is always profiting from the labor of others. What Walker was really doing was taking advantage of the artists' lack of business sophistication and their educational deficiencies while telling himself it was *he* who was doing them a favor. From the start, but even more so as the Depression worsened, it was the poorer musicians who suffered the most as they faced not only inadequate job opportunities, but with money scarce everywhere, they could no longer depend on their music to earn a living as local performance circuits dried up. For Johnson, the bottom seemed to be dropping out just as he was entering his prime, and it wouldn't be long before it would be time to go again.

INTERLUDE 6

God Moves on the Water

A week after the *Titanic* sank on April 15, 1912, A. E. Perkins sat aboard a train and noticed a blind Black preacher already selling a ballad on the disaster titled "Didn't That Ship Go Down?"[1]

Few events captured the symbolism of the race and power dynamic in America at this time like the fights of Jack Johnson and the sinking of the *Titanic*.[2] In the *Chicago Defender,* editorials were running within five days of the event shedding light on the way the Black community interpreted the *Titanic* going down. The phrase, "In the midst of life we are in death [was] truly exemplified in the sinking of the *Titanic*," one wrote. And in another, the concept of the democracy of death is expressed in the lines: "The horror of the *Titanic* becomes a triumph, if we learn these lessons of sacrifice and the equality of men and the supremacy of God."[3] In another piece titled "The Awakening," the author once again pointed to the doomed fate of the *Titanic* as a lesson in the "equality of man." The author also made a statement on the power of God and nature in comparison to the arrogance of man with his dependence on wealth when he wrote that "the lesson comes home to us in the tragedies of the times that Nature after all is long and will endure, notwithstanding the conquests of science and gold. The greatest achievements of the day are but toys in comparison with God's own handiwork."[4]

The paper even printed an early ballad, composed by Mrs. Mattye E. Anderson, that included many verses on man's hubris, this being one:

Bravely those men lingered with pride,
Bravely those men fought death and died;
Poor souls so desolate.
Great wealth, the powerful and the
Strong.
Cruelly death sweeps them all along;
To a sorrowful fate.[5]

And while there were expressions of sympathy for the dead in several African American outlets, they were only to bring home the point that "one touch of nature makes the world kin."[6]

⁚⁚

In the days and weeks that followed many ballads were composed, mostly by Black street singers, and were sung on street corners all over the South. The broadside ballad circulated in Texas, "God Moves on the Water," was likely composed by Madkin Butler around the time the *Chicago Defender* was first printing commentary on the incident.[7] It would later be published as part of Dorothy Scarborough's *From a Southern Porch* in 1919, and bore an unmistakable likeness to Johnson's recorded version.

The moral message of the songs born from the sinking of the *Titanic* were just as relevant twenty-one years later when, in 1933, John and Alan Lomax visited the Darrington State Prison Farm in Texas and captured, with their recording equipment, "Lightning" Washington and his group still singing that original Texas ballad, sending out the same timeless warning that had still gone unheeded.[8]

GOD MOVES ON THE WATER

Willie Johnson

Year of nineteen hundred and twelve
April the fourteenth day
Great Titanic struck an iceberg
People had to run and pray

(CHORUS)
God moves, moves. God moves,
And the people had to run and pray

The guards who had been a-watching
Asleep 'cause they were tired
When they heard the great excitement
Many gunshots was fired

Captain Smith gave orders
Women and children first
Many of the lifeboats was let down
Many of the lives were crushed

Oh many had to leave their happy home
All that they possess
Lord Jesus, will you hear us now
Help us in our distress

Women had to leave their loving ones
And flee for the safest place
But when they seen their loved ones drown
They hearts did almost break

A.G. Smith, mighty man, built a boat
That he couldn't understand
Named it a name of God in a tin
In the middle of the sea, Lord, he pulled it in

THE SUN WILL
NEVER GO DOWN

The Arms of God, stretched out.

Equally as capable of giving life as taking one, The River runs ceaselessly, unconcerned with its banks' inhabitants. Its turbid surface permits neither reflection nor excavation. The tracks have all been covered. Deep; the bones carried away in the flood. Some have passed over, while others, lacking silver to pay Charon, still roam.

This is where the ghosts are singing. This is where the ghosts are singing.

It was mid-February 1934 when John Lomax received a promising letter from the general manager of the Texas Prison System in Huntsville, Lee Simmons. Lomax had already visited a string of prison farms throughout East Texas in December, but he was planning a return in the coming months, and Simmons was hoping to further accommodate him:

> As I am on the go so much [I] would like for you to try to let me know a few days before hand when you will come down, so I can try to arrange to make the trip with you as I believe we could get better results. I might get Elder Griffin, our colored Chaplain, to come to Huntsville and lead the singing . . . as he is a past master in this regard. . . . so just let me know as near as possible and I will try to be here.[1]

By this point, Lomax had been on the road since the summer of 1933 traveling to the various prison farms that spread out all over the South. He was searching for "songs that, in musical phrasing and in poetic content, [were] most unlike those of the white race, the least contaminated by white influence or by modern Negro jazz."[2] It was a sound that predated the recent recordings distributed by the major record labels. They were the voices he had heard himself, as a child, in the period immediately following the end of the American Civil War. Essentially what Lomax desired to capture on record were the voices and songs of a people who were still living in a form of perpetual slavery, where the field hollers and work songs were still being sung in their most raw and unadulterated form, almost as if they had been preserved in amber. And it was, in the new slavery of the agricultural prison farms spread out over the South, that he found not only the system of subjugation entirely intact but also the sound of a people who were still protesting it the way their ancestors had done over a half-century before.

∷

In a way, John Lomax was always trying to get back to the songs he had heard growing up in Bosque County. He had published a collection of cowboy songs in 1910 and had assembled a number of folk ballads he had hoped to one day return to but never found the time. Then, suddenly, with the onset of the Depression, his job working for a bank in Dallas quickly evaporated, and a short time later, his wife, Bess Brown, died.[3] Finding himself broke and alone at age sixty-three with two kids still to support, Lomax returned to song collecting, this time armed with a recording machine that weighed nearly 350 pounds, which he had built into the back of his Model A Ford. His first recording took place about thirty miles east of Dallas in Terrell, Texas. Accompanied by his eighteen-year-old son, Alan, the pair located an older Black woman as she rested from her work as a laundress who agreed to sing for them. After changing into a fresh white apron and with the machine recording, her voice began in "shakes and quivers" to sing out before them, first in a "slow and sweet" tone before picking up the tempo and incorporating her body in the rhythm, both her and the song moving "faster with more drive, clapping her hands and tapping out drum rhythm with her heel and toe of her bare feet" while she sang of the river:

> Wade in de water, wade in the water,
> Wade in the water, childrens;
> God's gonna trouble the water.
> Healin' water done move,
> Healin' water done move,
> Soul so happy now,
> Healin water done move.
> O Lord Have Mercy.[4]

For Alan Lomax, the moment was both life affirming and course altering. It was the beginning of a summer that would see him take a break from his schooling and join his father as they journeyed ever further into the backroads of America. It was here where they were to discover the places that time forgot and return with the evidence of the rebels who still inhabited them.

::

It was nearing Easter when John and Alan pulled their Ford sedan into the parking lot of the Darrington Prison Farm, a cotton and sugar plantation renamed after it was sold to the Texas Prison Commission in 1918.[5] Located on Oyster Creek, just east of the Brazos in Sandy Point, Darrington was one of a series of former plantations owned by Abner Jackson, a Virginia-born planter who had relocated to Texas following the Texas Revolution in 1836. But there was no mistaking what was going on in 1934. For all intents and purposes, what was happening at Darrington was, in both motive and music, not much different than the Darrington of 1854.

On their last swing through the farm in December, John and Alan met and recorded "Lightning" Washington, a leader of singing who used his voice as a way of keeping time as he and his fellow prisoners chopped wood. These were work songs, and just like in the church or in the fields of yesterday, it was the strongest voice that would take the lead. At Darrington in the early 1930s, that role belonged to Lightning. John and Alan watched and recorded as he would, at the top of his voice, call out lines while the prisoners raised their axes over their shoulders before lowering them down again, shouting, with the blades and their voices all swinging in unison. "Lightning" and his men sang songs of the loneliness of being in prison, of their yearning to escape, and of being worked to the point of death under the punishing sun they referred to as "Hannah." And in the winter of 1933, the Lomaxes' recording device also captured the men as they sat singing, not in the mode of the work song but something more equivalent to a jubilee quartet as "Lightning" led the men in the singing of a four-minute interpretation of the Titanic ballad that was familiar in Texas. It was a version of "God Moves on the Water" that closely mirrored Johnson's recording of the song in 1929, sharing lines while also inserting new ones concerning the devastation brought to Galveston by the 1900 hurricane as well as the aftermath of the Crucifixion. In this setting, free from any time constraints inherent in commercial recording, the song was able to be as open to possibility and improvisation as the singer's imagination could create. So, while they all joined in on the chorus, it was the leader, "Lightning," who sang the verses as the men moaned behind him, only stopping when they heard that bell from the big house toll:

Captain Smith was lying down,
Asleep because he was tired.
Well he woke up in a great fright,
As many gunshots were fired.
Galveston with her sea wall,
To keep the water down.
But the high tide from the ocean lord,
Put the water all over the town.[6]

On their return to Darrington in April 1934, John and Alan recorded "Lightning" again, but the highlight of this specific trip was their ability to witness and record a full Missionary Baptist service in celebration of Easter. Facilitated by Lee Simmons, the prison system's general manager, the sermon was to be led by the current chaplain to the Black inmates of the Texas Prison System, Elder Griffin, better known as "Sin-Killer" Griffin.[7]

∷

Three hundred convicts, lying in their cots and state-issued clothes, gathered in the spacious dormitory as John and Alan set up their recording equipment near the front of the makeshift pulpit and altar.[8] Once all was set, the song leader approached the center of the podium very near to where Alan sat positioned with his recording device.[9] Silence. With a signal from Griffin, the song leader began what John Lomax would later describe as a "swinging spiritual"; it was a line hymn, a moaning incantation. It lasted for only a short while though before he paused and a separate voice addressed the men, "You know the master said, 'Blessed he that moans.' . . . Let's moan.'" At this moment, the song leader began to do just that joined by a cast of three hundred imprisoned men, and:

> Something swept through the crowd, something powerful and poignant. No words were uttered, only waves of sound, deep and pregnant, moans of unutterable woe. The silence grew deeper and deeper.[10]

It is the collective moan that begins the line hymn, followed by singing. The first line was sung in haste, followed by the collective moan or lining-out of the same. It was Isaac Watts's Psalm 116:

I love the Lord; he heard my cries,
And pitied every groan;
Long as I live, when troubles rise,

I'll hasten to his throne.
I love the Lord; he bowed his ear,
And chased my griefs away;
O let my heart no more despair,
While I have breath to pray![11]

The leader then lead them in prayer:

Take care of them, my Father,
And guide them;
And, then, my Father,
When they all is standing in glory,
And Thou art satisfied at my staying here,
O meet me at the river, I ask in Thy name.
Amen![12]

A song now erupted as the song leader moved into the ballad of the tragedy on Galveston Island. And as the feet pounded and hands clapped, he sang:

Galveston with her sea wall,
To keep the water down.
But the high tide from the ocean,
Put water over the town.
Wasn't that a mighty storm,
Wasn't that a mighty storm, great water.
Wasn't that a mighty storm,
That blew the people all away.
Their trumpets gave them warning,
"You'd better leave this place."
They never thought of leaving,
'Till death looked them in the face.

All of this was merely a lead-in for the appearance of Reverend Griffin, who now approached the pulpit, "dignified and solemn," to begin to preach on the subject of "The Man of Calvary," his Easter sermon.[13] With gray hair and sporting what John Lomax described as a "Prince Albert coat which almost touched his shoe tops," he looked out over the sea of men spread out in the large prison sleeping quarters and called out to his "brothers and sisters" and "sinner friends":

Something was bringing a disturbance—
That was the wind,
The water was jumpin' in the vessel.[14]

Immediately capturing the room with his presence, Griffin launched into his sermon, the deep gravel of his voice painting the scene of Jesus' capture and execution; at some points it lingered low almost in a speaking tone, but it never stayed still, instead always moving at breakneck speed guided only by the emotion of the words themselves, which would every so often incite a long exclamatory "ohhhhh" before falling right back down again, his breath regained to continue the exhortation. All the while, Alan furiously tried to keep pace with the recording equipment, flipping sides every seven minutes as the men shouted "Yes!" and "All right!" as Griffin paced just feet from where he sat. Griffin, sometimes extolling in speech and at other times pushing forward in song, placed himself at the scene of the Crucifixion:

Roman soldiers come riding in full speed on their horses,
And splunged him in the side,
We seen the blood and water come out.
Ohhhhhh! God a'mighty placed it in the minds of the people
Why water is for baptism
And blood is for the cleansin.'
I seen while he was hangin' the mounting began to tremble
On which Jesus was hangin' on;
The blood was dropping from the mounting,
Holy blood, dropping on the mounting, my friends,
Corrupting the mounting;
I seen about that time while the blood was dropping down,
One drop after another . . .
Ohhhhhh! The dyin' thief on the cross
Seen the moon going down in blood . . .
It got so dark
Until the men who was putting' Jesus to death
They said they could feel the darkness in their fingers.[15]

At the end of nearly an hour, Griffin concluded with the image of Jesus rising from the grave and then, like a storm, his voice rose to usher in a closing hymn, a line hymn soaked in both rage and redemption, recalling the many calamities of those washed away by the literal and spiritual sea:

How can I sink with such a prop
As my eternal God.

And for those who wish to oppress, either by prison or through death, in defiance the men sang:

How can I die while Jesus lives,
Who rose and left the dead?
Pardon and grace my soul receives
From mine exalted Head.[16]

At the end of the evening, as they were preparing to leave, John and Alan played the recording back for Griffin, who responded, "Mr. Lomax, for a long time I've been hearing that I'm a good preacher. Now I know it."[17] It would be the Lomaxes only encounter with Griffin, but not their last with the prisons for, just as these discs were completed, it was on up the trail of the winding Brazos to the next farm, the next song. But Griffin was certainly not forgotten by the Lomaxes, who later wrote that "his sermon is at once poetry and song and must be chanted and sung in a highly dramatic manner."[18]

⁘

In the summer of 1934, a historical moment had been forged. Alan Lomax did not see the world in the same way his father did. The segregated narrative had now been exposed, another lie pried wide open, and there was no going back. He would later write of his nineteen-year-old self:

> That summer about all I heard was "yassuh boss . . . thank you kindly boss,"
> but I knew this was all a sham. By then I knew that this music was the best art,
> the strongest and most vital thing I had ever come across in my life, something
> worth working for. I knew that the people who made it must be the most
> important people I had ever met.[19]

"These are my brothers," he repeated to himself. "Out of their pain they have made a river of song. How can I repay them for this hard-won beauty?"[20]

Interlude 7

John the Revelator

In a night session held at the 1925 annual COGIC Holy Convocation, requests for prayers were offered, an offering was taken up by Elder E. M. Page, believers were saved, and twin sisters Rhetha and Letha Morris "sang so sweetly, 'Who is That Writing John, the Revelator?'"[1]

Johnson was the first to record "John the Revelator," the song that tells of the persecuted and exiled John of Patmos, whose prophetic visions inspired the book of Revelation. It's a song that primarily focuses on God's judgment as revealed to both John and Moses. Johnson used the song, though, not to illustrate all the horrors revealed in the seven seals, but to celebrate this prophecy that is to come; one that promises to right the wrongs for those who have been enslaved by others and punish the persecutors.[2] But it is also the song of the visionary who is chosen by God—either to warn the people of what is to come, through John, or be an active participant in freeing those who are in bondage, through Moses. In it, one can hear the message, coming across time, of protest heard in the one who sang "If I Had My Way" and "God Moves on the Water," and shared the vision of those who are chosen, of divine justice.

> *Well Moses to Moses, watchin' the flock*
> *Saw the bush where they had to stop*
> *God told Moses, "Pull off your shoes"*
> *Out of the flock, well you I choose.*

JOHN THE REVELATOR
Willie Johnson

(CHORUS)
Well who's that writin' John the Revelator
Who's that writin' John the Revelator
Who's that writin' John the Revelator
A book of the seven seals

Tell me what's John writin' Ask the
Revelator What's John writin' Ask the
Revelator What's John writin' Ask the
Revelator
A book of the seven seals

Well who are worthy, cried holy
Bountiful, Son of our God
Daughter of Zion, Judah the Lion
He redeemeth, and bought us with his blood

John the Revelator, great advocator
Get's 'em on the battle of Zion
Was tellin' the story, risin' in glory
Cried, "Lord, don't you love some I"

Well Moses to Moses, watchin' the flock Saw
the bush where they had to stop
God told Moses, "Pull off your shoes
Out of the flock, well you I choose"

Tell me what's John writin' Ask the
Revelator What's John writin' Ask the
Revelator What's John writin' Ask the
Revelator
A book of the seven seals

BROTHER
WILLIE JOHNSON

The Alamo Special thunders out of Houston heading west, passing the construction of what would become Central State Farm on the bones of the old Imperial in Sugar Land about twenty minutes after midnight. Some of the men in their bunks, used to the sound of the rattling of the rails, remained fast asleep, while others stared, wide awake, as the light from the headlamp came flooding in, like that same old dream: of jumping on board and heading out to California and never coming back. But just like every night, the sound of the engine just gets farther and farther away. To Richmond, Rosenberg, East Bernard, Eagle Lake, Columbus, Weimar, Schulenburg, Flatonia, Waelder, Seguin, and by sunrise arriving at the Spanish mission disguised as a depot on San Antonio's east side. Without them.

It's May 29, 1932, the beginning of summer and the height of the Depression. People everywhere are suddenly being turned into migrants: suffering, losing their jobs and homes. Shantytowns, nicknamed Hoovervilles after the current president, Herbert Hoover, are springing up all over the country. Just a week ago, Franklin Roosevelt, governor of New York, gave a commencement speech calling out the "small group of men whose chief outlook upon the social welfare is tinctured by the fact that they can make huge profits from the lending of money and the marketing of securities."[1] But the people around here didn't need to hear any speech. They already knew all about it. So they shuffle among the departing passengers, make small talk, and go about their business.

And this morning on Center Street, less than a mile from the depot, the Union Missionary Baptist Church will be having their service, the way they've done every Sunday. And with today being the last Sunday of the month, the service would be in the hands of the Missionary Society, and if you were able to arrive early enough you may be able to catch this morning's selections, which are to be delivered by "Brother Johnson, the blind evangelist."[2]

By the early months of 1932, Johnson had landed in San Antonio. It was a city that, after the storm in Galveston, had been the most populated in Texas until 1930. It was also a popular recording location for labels such as OKeh, which just in the past few years had recorded everything from *corridos* (ballads) of the Mexican Revolution to "Texas" Alexander as he moaned out the *Death Bed Blues* with Lonnie Johnson on guitar. The Mississippi Sheiks spent four days recording for the label in San Antonio in June of 1930. They also met up with Alexander and recorded several sides with him, including one about the tornado that ripped through the city of Frost, a little town that sits just west of Corsicana, just a month earlier, and one they called *Seen Better Days* in which Alexander recalled "when times wasn't so hard." And it would be just five days later that a songster named "Little Hat" Jones (George Jones) recorded the song *Cherry Street Blues* and sang, "I've got a woman in San Antone, I declares, really sweet to me."[3] Cherry Street runs north and south straight through East Commerce, where, if you stood and looked to the west, you could see the passenger trains pull in from Houston at the SP Depot. Cherry Street was also familiar to Johnson, as it was a road that passed just east through the neighborhood where he was living near the corner of Center and Pine, practically next door to the Union Missionary Baptist Church, where he could be found giving selections on that last Sunday in May.

Likely due to the hardships thrust upon him during the Depression, Johnson was beginning to look to the church much in the same way "Singing" Johnson or Madkin Butler had done exclusively: as a way to help supplement his income from singing on the streets. And although he didn't seem to be confined to any specific denomination, there seems to have been a clear shift in the early 1930s away from the Pentecostal tradition that influenced him so greatly in the previous decade and back toward the Missionary Baptist Church of his youth. This is evidenced by his participation both at the Union Missionary Baptist Church but also through his close relationship with the Olive Street Christian Methodist Episcopal Church and its prominent members, Maggie and John Fields, a couple who had deep ties to the east side community where Johnson was living, and at whose home he would be married on the last Sunday of November 1932.[4]

But despite his marriage and developing ties within the community, Johnson didn't settle in the city for long; instead, throughout the 1930s, he was constantly on the move. He found a new singing partner and traveled throughout Central and East Texas, including in Columbus, Eagle Lake, Rockdale, Chapel Hill, Shiner, and as far south as Goliad. Not limited to a particular area, he even made his way out of state and crossed paths with William Samuel McTier, a street-singing songster from Georgia better known as "Blind" Willie McTell.[5] Their first meeting may have come in Atlanta in 1930 when they both were recording for

Columbia days apart, but with the Depression and with both constantly on the move, their roads were converging more often, because even though he was one of the few Black blues artists able to maintain a recording schedule, McTell, like Johnson, began performing at churches to help make up for some of the lost income he otherwise would have made on the streets.[6]

All this time Johnson was getting assistance like train fare, when he needed it, from the Lighthouse for the Blind, an organization on the rise during the 1930s that trained those without sight in various marketable skills like sewing and broom making.[7] He was also frequently returning home to Temple where his family still resided, even staying long enough in 1935 to be included in the city directory alongside his siblings Carl, Wallace, Robert, and Jettie.[8] Temple, along with nearby Waco, at the time, were hotbeds for musicians both white and Black. Bob Wills was just forming his new band the Texas Playboys there, and people Johnson only knew as children, like L. C. Robinson and his brother A. C., moved there in 1934 to try and make it in music, performing as the Hot Brown Boys around town and on the local radio station KTEM.[9] Meanwhile, Johnson's brother Carl, who was farming land out near Moody during the 1930s, reintroduced Johnson to Thomas Shaw, the guitar player and son of his old ballad writing partner Lewis Shaw. Carl had befriended Shaw while farming in the fields and would frequently invite him to stay at the Johnson house in Temple on the weekends when he was playing for dances in the area.[10] The two would play together, but even as recordings began to pick up steadily again in the mid-1930s, Johnson would never record again.

::

Charley Patton, Johnson's closest contemporary style-wise, made his first records since 1929 for the Vocalion label in the early part of 1934, including a pair of religious songs that he sang with his wife, Bertha Lee. They would be Patton's last recordings, as just three months later he would be gone. Gussie Nesbitt, a blind singer from the Carolinas who only recorded religious music and shared similarities both musically and vocally to Johnson, recorded *Motherless Children* and *Nobody's Fault but Mine* in his first session in almost five years for the Decca label in 1935. And even though Johnson was no longer recording, his records were still in high demand, and it would be the Dallas-based record producer Don Law and Vocalion who would re-release several of his Columbia recordings in the mid-1930s including *Dark Was the Night, Mother's Children Have a Hard Time*, and *Keep Your Lamp Trimmed and Burning*.

∷

Johnson also began losing people close to him at this time. Madkin Butler passed away from inflammation of the kidneys in February 1936. Butler's widow, Ophelia, listed his final occupation as minister, and he was buried at the Greater Riverside Cemetery in Hearne, the same location where his previous wife, Hannah, was buried in 1911. Butler had influenced many of the early greats of Black music in Texas including Lemon Jefferson, Willie Johnson, "Texas" Alexander, and a thousand now anonymous bards—and then he was gone. Johnson's old running partner, the piano player Bob Jackson, in an incident that recalled the lyrics from his most famous song, "Troublesome Mind," died a short time later when his body was torn to pieces by a Missouri Pacific train in September 1936.[11] He was only in his mid-thirties. And in the early part of 1937, almost a year to the day after Butler's death, Johnson's brother Carl died in Temple from pneumonia with the "Spanish Flu" listed as a contributing factor. Carl, who was close in age to Willie, left behind his wife Elfreda and their two-year-old child, James, when he was buried in the White Hall cemetery, located just west of Pendleton.[12]

∷

By the end of the decade, people had been through a lot, but there was optimism as economic situations were steadily improving. Franklin Roosevelt was elected to the presidency in November 1932 and reelected four years later. He oversaw the passage of the Social Security Act and the establishment of the Works Progress Administration, a New Deal agency that put millions of people—from artists to those in construction—back to work. There were still issues, but things looked to be getting better. Hard times songs of the early part of the decade had faded, and Roosevelt had even made inroads with the African American community the way no president had done before. But these weren't the only changes. Music in the Black church had also shifted in this period. Thomas A. Dorsey, a bluesman who had worked with "Ma" Rainey (Gertrude Rainey) and Tampa Red (Hudson Whittaker), made a full switch to the religious side beginning in the latter part of the 1920s and injected new compositions as well as some of the raw vocal energy of the blues directly into the Baptist tradition, both of which would be fully integrated into the church by the late 1930s. And although the term had been around, it would be people like Dorsey, the singer and businesswoman Sallie Martin, and Mahalia Jackson who would clear the way into the future of the style that would become forever known as gospel music. It was the sound for a new generation of younger churchgoers who had grown up with the blues and who had left the South to forge a new future in Chicago. But the musicians and street preachers who were combining the secular with the sacred were still to be found predominantly in the Pentecostal Church. Guys like the traveling evangelist Elder Utah Smith assumed the role Johnson may have taken himself if he had remained with the Pentecostal Church. Based out of the Shreveport, Louisiana, area in his early days, Smith was about a decade younger than Johnson and was called to preach in 1923.[13] Smith would often perform with two large, white-feathered wings attached to his back as he accompanied himself on guitar. He played in the same tuning as Johnson but without a slide; and he likely knew Johnson, as even by the early 1930s he was a frequent visitor both to New Orleans as well as Bishop Page's church in Dallas.[14] Then there was Sister Rosetta Tharpe, who grew up in the Church of God in Christ and would make her first recordings in November 1938, including a version of "Blind Man Sit in the Way and Cried" under the title "Saviour Don't Pass Me By" in January 1939. And Ola Mae Long, who was born in the same Summerhill neighborhood of Atlanta that Rev. J. M. Gates had his church, had been composing songs on her guitar in open D tuning and with a slide since her conversion in 1923 at the age of twelve thanks to the Fire Baptized Holiness Church of God of the Americas.[15] During the decade, performers were also frequently being heard on the radio, spreading songs and styles of singing faster than at any time before. The outlet provided new audiences beyond the performers' records.

Meanwhile, Johnson, throughout much of the decade, remained elusive, always on the road. For others, those records and that name, "Blind" Willie Johnson, may define him, but for Johnson himself there had always been a higher calling. Just as a new war was starting in Europe, one could feel the winds shifting once again, and with them, Johnson was being blown back to one of his earliest stomping grounds.

INTERLUDE 8

The Soul of a Man

Johnson's spiritual inquiry at the root of "The Soul of a Man" stands in stark opposition to Ivan's purely rational intellectualism and eventual madness in Dostoevsky's *The Brothers Karamazov*. The song, likely a version of a broadside ballad in Johnson's time, pulls from "Lit'l Boy, How Old Are You," a "solo-type folk song" that recounts the story of Jesus as a boy in the temple and reflects Johnson's searing question regarding the soul of man.[1]

Roland Hayes learned "Lit'l Boy," a song he posited was "decidedly African" in origin due to its rhythm, from a friend who was introduced to it through a "traveling Aframerican evangelist."[2] Its lyrics convey the story of Jesus in the temple at the age of twelve as he listens to the scholars and poses questions in response to their teachings that seem to surprise the elders, so much so that they turn to him and want to know "Little Boy, how old are you?"

> *This little boy had them to remember,*
> *He was born the twenty-fifth of December,*
> *Lawyers and Doctors were amazed,*
> *They had to give the little boy praise.*

In Johnson's version, the song is turned into more of an existential blues through which Johnson inserted himself in the temple and reframed the narrative from one about the age of the child into more of what was arguably at the core of the section of the chapter in Luke from which the drama originates—one of searching. Mirroring the timeline of the Crucifixion and Resurrection, Jesus becomes "lost" after he is left behind by his parents in Jerusalem. When his parents return, after three days, they locate him in the temple with the scholars and ask why he had caused them so much anxiety, to which he replies that they had been searching needlessly because, confounding his parents, he was never lost at all.[3]

Here, Johnson placed himself, uneducated in terms of formalized schooling, in the role of the young Christ as he entered the temple and sat among the scholars and turned the question back toward them, begging to know, *what is the soul of a man?* But unlike in "Little Boy," where Christ responded with his age, the scholars in Johnson's song have no reply. The answer, Johnson seemed to suggest, is spiritual and not intellectual. In fact, in Johnson's view, it is possible that there are no words sufficient as a universal response to the question he asked, but possibly only a personal one, which, at least for Johnson himself, he may have answered already. The first instance was in "Jesus Make Up My Dying Bed" where, like in "The Soul of a Man," he also placed himself as the one who is thought to be lost when he referenced Christ's empty tomb, and declares that he is not among the dead, that death is merely a transition, and that he is going on, with the saints, who are living.

> *I'm dead and buried,*
> *Somebody said that I was lost.*
> *When you get down to Jordan,*
> *Ask the ferryman, hired there, to cross.*

In "The Soul of a Man," Johnson gave us a hint that if there is an answer to the question, then it lies not in the pages of dead books studied by the scholars, but in the act of living; and we know this for certain, both lyrically and from the pure emotion he put forth while singing, when he thundered out the cry of "*nothing but a burning light.*"[4]

THE SOUL OF A MAN
Willie Johnson

Well, want somebody tell me, answer if you can
Want somebody to tell me, just what is the soul of a
man

I'm going to ask the question, please answer if you can
If anybody surely can tell me, just what is the soul of a
man

Well, want somebody tell me, answer if you can
I want somebody tell me, just what is the soul of a man

I've traveled in different countries, I've traveled in
foreign lands
I've found nobody could tell me, just what about the
soul of a man

Well, I want somebody tell me, answer if you can
I Want somebody to tell me, just what is the soul of a
man

I saw a crowd stand talking, I just came up in time
Was teaching the lawyers, the doctors, that a man ain't
nothing but his mind

I read the bible often, I try to read it right
As far as I could understand, nothing but a burning light

When Christ had entered the temple, the people all stood
amazed
Was teaching the lawyer and the doctors how to raise a
man from the grave

Coming Home

Reverend Willie Johnson

Someday I'll rest with Jesus and wear a starry crown.
— *"Blind" Willie Johnson*, TROUBLE SOON BE OVER

My house shall be called a House of Prayer.
Elder Otis Jones, HOLY MOUNTAIN

Even in the distance, across the stretch of the long field we still had to cross, I could hear it. And with each step toward that old wooden church, what sounded at first just like a low hum grew louder and louder. It is like yesterday to me, watching my father, in his good suit, march out ahead as I followed a few steps behind; the dew from the grass finding its way through my shoes and into my socks weighing down each step. And I can still feel that immediate rush of emotions pulsing through me as we finally got closer, those voices that moments ago had been but a murmur now were raised up in a full sustained roar. They were moaning, but it was not from sorrow. It was at this moment that something new had entered me, something that existed beyond anything that could be processed by the mind. I couldn't articulate it, but at this moment I knew that I had been changed. All the sadness I had been carrying was suddenly taken away.

I sped up now, racing to make up the distance between me and my father, and just as we reached the front steps, the most beautiful and vivid butterfly painted blue and yellow landed on the handle of the door. My father, who had spent the past week trying to hold it all together, turned toward me, his face undergoing an obvious shift, and he smiled. No words were exchanged, but I could feel his love unlike at any time before. And as soon as we went to look again at the butterfly, it had flown away. But the singing continued, and just as my father reached down to take hold of my hand, the pace of the voices inside had quickened, feet began to stomp, the moans had turned to words, and as we entered, I let them overwhelm me.

By and By when the morning comes
When all the saints of God are gathered home
We will tell the story how we've overcome
And we'll understand it better by and by.

On this first Sunday following my mother's death, I found out where I belonged and that she was with me.

"I think 'Blind' Willie Johnson is dead, according to a letter . . . I got from his wife," the songster Willie McTell answered as he sat in an Atlanta hotel room speaking to John and Ruby Lomax in November of 1940.[1]

The impromptu session arose by chance when Ruby, university professor and John's wife since 1934, had noticed McTell playing for tips outside the Pig & Whistle, one of his usual hangouts in the city. The following morning they all sat in a hotel room as McTell answered their questions by taking them on a journey through his life and a brief history of Black song as he hummed and sang, most all of which John recorded for the Library of Congress. And at one point, the conversation turned to his thoughts on Willie Johnson, who McTell referred to as a "very good friend of mine," a "notable singer in his type of singing," and someone he had played with "in many parts of the state, different parts of the country."[2]

"What do you consider his best music?" John asked.

"Well, sacred music. He has a heavy voice. Almost sound like a preacher," McTell responded.

The hotel window was open, and with the sounds of car horns blaring every so often from the street below, McTell punctured through the perceived barriers of song that to him were so embedded in his youth and life, but which seemed so foreign and mysterious to those to whom the world had been closed. He weaved in and out of the history of Black music talking some, but mostly playing through the entire evolution of blues and spirituals as he heard it growing up over the past four decades. He sang about gamblers, about losing the people you love because of one terrible thing that you can never take back, and of the chain gang he'd sentenced himself to in "Murderer's Home Blues." But every time he turned inward, toward the spirituals, that's when he reached for the slide, a sound absent on all the secular numbers in the session. He tenderly recounted the hymns he had learned from his parents or in church and played Lomax the lined-hymn "Amazing Grace," but with barely a line of singing. Instead, he performed it in what he described as the "colored form," letting his instrument moan and hum the response lines with the use of the slide just as Johnson had done on "Dark Was the Night." And as further evidence of their bond both as friends, but also as musical peers, McTell introduced "I Got to Cross That River of Jordan" as a song he and Johnson would play together.[3] It's a song that would have fit right in with all the other songs Johnson recorded, but especially "Bye and Bye I'm Goin' to See the King" and "Nobody's Fault but Mine," two of his songs along the same theme in that they emphasize the ultimate universal truth—that no one can cross that spiritual boundary for you, and that the road that must be walked toward the light, must be walked alone. And just as he had done on "Amazing Grace," McTell dropped his voice as an instrument to let the guitar sing.

> *I got to cross that . . .*
> *I got to cross, well for myself*
> *There's nobody here can cross it for me*
> *For I got to . . .*
> *There for my . . .*
> *And I got to meet my dear old mother*
> *I got to meet her for my . . .*

Any thought that John Lomax may have had at finding Johnson likely died in that Atlanta hotel room in the approaching winter of 1940. But unbeknownst to McTell, his friend was very much alive. Still, only in his early forties, Johnson had remained on the streets playing many of the same songs that he had been playing for decades. It was all he knew, even after the troubles of the '30s and losing Madkin Butler, his partner Bob Jackson, his brother Carl, and in the early months of 1940, his baby sister Jettie.[4] He had even returned to Houston's Fourth Ward, and it would be on the redbrick roads of the district, in the fall of 1941, that his Samson ballad would catch the attention of a passerby.

Angelina and Reverend Willie Johnson

Until this writing, there has been much confusion as to who Angelina was or even if she and Johnson had an official marriage. In the complete recording Sam Charters made with Angelina, she said they were married on June 22 before hesitating and naming the year as 1922. The "1922" was excised from the Folkways release, and Charters would report that they were married in 1927, leaving many to wonder if Johnson was married to multiple women at the same time—something the complete audio and marriage records finally are able to dismiss.

Angelina Broussard was born in Lafayette, Louisiana, and likely had made her way to Texas sometime in the 1920s.[5] Both of her parents died when she was young, leaving her to be raised by the white family her mother was working for as a cook. She sang in church, but her introduction to Johnson was in the early 1940s on a sidewalk in Houston when she noticed him playing on the streets. After catching his attention, she followed in with him as he sang: "Oh, if I had my way. . . ." After introducing herself, she invited Johnson to her house where she cooked him lunch and played piano for him before returning to the streets. They were officially wed on September 15, 1941, and on the marriage certificate, Johnson listed himself as Rev. Willie Johnson.[6] A few months later, the couple departed Houston and headed east, landing closer to the Louisiana border.

∷

Just outside the window of their furnished room in the St. Charles Hotel, a boarding house in the heart of the Black business and entertainment district of Beaumont, one could listen to all the signs of life that still pulsated in these sorts of districts before the money and the highways would come and strip them all away. There was the Gem Theatre (the Black movie house), the Sweet Dream barber shop, the Long Edwards BBQ joint, and a shoe repair shop run by Charles Smith. The taxi station was close by, as were churches including East Mount Olive, the Missionary Baptist Church on Wall Street where Johnson and Angelina were members. And outside Fowler's, the pharmacy and drug store just two doors down from the entrance of where they were staying, was where Johnson would set up and play among the energetic whirlwind that blew in on Saturdays from the men who worked the oil refineries and shipyards Monday through Friday.[7]

Johnson, despite the state beginning to take over support for the vulnerable population who had for too many years been pushed onto the streets, stayed on the road, traveling by bus, train, and taxi to various cities surrounding the Gulf Coast.[8] Sometimes gone for a month at a time, his route can be traced to Galveston and through the various revival meetings held through the Trinity Valley Baptist Association churches, of which East Mount Olive was a part. This included stops in Dayton, Texas, and likely many of the Missionary Baptist Churches outlined by the Trinity River south of Lake Livingston where Johnson would not only perform but preach.[9] The couple had even, after moving to the North End of Beaumont, converted their home at 1440 Forrest Street into a church they called The House of Prayer, and Johnson served as its pastor.

Johnson was also frequently a paid guest of a white church in town, the Sabine Tabernacle, when they had their sprawling tent revivals, despite the fact that racial tension in the city was always on the verge of exploding, and did in June 1943.[10] The tabernacle was pastored by Rev. Harry Hodge, and although it was listed as a nondenominational church, Hodge had all the characteristics of a Pentecostal preacher not dissimilar from Sister Aimee Semple McPherson.[11] Hodge, much like McPherson, appealed both to Black and white audiences and held successful tent revival meetings that often took up entire city blocks surrounding his church at the corner of Forrest and Hazel, just a half-mile south from where Angelina and Johnson were living. Some of the accounts of Hodge's services recall members receiving the Holy Ghost through glossolalia, and instruments like the tambourine being part of the worship.[12] Hodge may have also been an advocate for getting Johnson heard on the radio, as he was the host of his own show broadcast from his church in Beaumont and heard across the Texas State Network.[13] Hodge was popular, his show was well-advertised, and it was likely one of many where listeners would have heard Johnson perform.[14] Other stations that likely aired Johnson's voice at this time included WBAP in Fort Worth, which broadcast The Light Crust Doughboys and Bishop R. E. Ranger, a preacher within the Church of God in Christ in Texas; KTEM in Temple; and KPLC in Lake Charles.[15]

Those who would have tuned in for these shows would have heard a diverse mix of what Johnson would have been known for playing in the churches and on the streets. These included many of his recorded songs, including "John the Revelator," "If I Had My Way," and "Nobody's Fault but Mine," as well as a revival of the World War I ballad "When the War Was On," but they also included songs that had become standard for religious singers, some seemingly as old as time itself and others more recent. The loss of one's mother, the importance of keeping faith in the face of life's hardships, and reunification of the familial bonds after death were the most consistent themes in Johnson's repertoire during this period. In partnership with Angelina, who had also lost her mother at a young age, the two frequently performed "Mother's Children" concerning the plight of the child after mother is gone and "Mother's Prayer," a song with lyrics that express a yearning of the singer to be afforded an opportunity to hear their mother's "tender voice" pray again, but knowing this won't happen until they meet in heaven "one sweet day."[16] "Farther Along" was another song they would perform. It deals with the security of God's love in the face of hard trials, and knowing you didn't have to understand everything right away because there was a bigger picture that would become much clearer once the whole race was done.[17] Other songs that Johnson never recorded but would perform regularly on the streets included "99½ Won't Do," "When the Saints Go Marching In," "Blind Man Stood on the Wayside," and "Does Jesus Care When My Heart Is Pained," a hymn penned in 1901 and recorded by "Blind" Willie Harris in New Orleans in 1929.[18]

Please, Don't Pass Me By (Summer, 1945)

> *This may be the last time you hear me sing,*
> *It may be the last time I don't know.*
> *It may be the last time you hear me preach,*
> *It may be the last time I don't know.*

The final phase of the journey is the redemption and reuniting with those who had passed on before, which is symbolized by the Jordan River in spiritual songs like "I Got to Cross the River of Jordan" and by the "swelling tide" the dead must pass over to reach this joyful reunion in "If You See My Savior." The latter is a Thomas A. Dorsey composition Johnson would sing. It places the singer at the bed of a dying neighbor, asking them to carry the message to their loved ones that they'll be coming home someday. It's an emotional triumph of the transformation of pain, a metamorphosis of the internal suffering experienced by a loved one's death to the faith in their eternal presence, a presence that will ultimately be made whole after they are reunited, after the singer crosses over. The path one walks is the test, but the water is the point of passage one must eventually cross for the spiritual renewal to take place, where the bonds that may have been severed in the material world are now reconnected in the sacred one. It's what ultimately pairs the earthly trouble of Johnson's "Mother's Children" with the divine reassurance in "Mother's Prayer." It's a theme that arises once more in "Just a Closer Walk with Thee," another hymn Johnson would sing. It's a song from the stranger on the road reaching out to Jesus with a personal plea for Jesus to walk beside him as he journeys on in this earthly domain. It closes with a prayer that asks, when their time on Earth has ended, to be guided "gently, safely o'er to Thy kingdom's shore."

> *Oh Mary, don't you weep, don't you mourn,*
> *Oh Mary, don't you weep, don't you mourn.*

On the morning of his death, he lay atop their bed that had been covered in the newspapers Angelina had spread in the hope of keeping the water from soaking through into their skin as they slept. She had watched him deteriorate for weeks with pneumonia-like symptoms after the fire destroyed nearly everything, and when the hospital turned him away it was the best she could think to do.[19] Some neighbors assisted in taking up a collection to raise the money needed to pay the costs of burial, which was handled at the funeral home on Gladys Street, four blocks away from where they resided.[20] The official cause of death was listed as malarial fever.[21] The unofficial cause was never recorded. Angelina gave his final profession as "minister" on the death certificate. It was the same one Johnson had used on their marriage license in 1941 and again in 1945 for the city directory when he listed his official name as Rev. W. J. Johnson.

> *Coming home, Coming home,*
> *never more to roam.*
> *Open wide your arms of love,*
> *Lord, I'm coming home.*

The funeral came two days later. Angelina sent a telegram to his father, Dock, telling him what happened and to come to Beaumont, but he didn't make it in time.[22] Shortly after, she moved what she could out of their home, including a charred fragment of his guitar and a few hymn books that hadn't been completely destroyed, and placed them into a trunk.[23] For a few years she even remained in the north part of town not far from their old place, and she would regularly make the trip to the cemetery to clean the modest marker that had been placed at his grave. But as the seasons passed, so did the floods, and with them any evidence of a final resting place.[24]

But, *out of the miry clay . . .* [25]

INTERLUDE 9

Dark Was the Night, Cold Was the Ground

"Dark Was the Night" is a hymn originally composed for Good Friday services and first published by the English clergyman and physician Thomas Haweis in 1792.[1] The words themselves concern the inner anguish Jesus faced as he prayed at the foot of the Mount of Olives before his impending betrayal, arrest, and execution; and where his agony was so deep that "his sweat became like drops of blood, falling down upon the ground."[2] It is a description of Jesus as a flesh and blood man undergoing human suffering both physically and spiritually. In this depth of sorrow, the Black slaves in the United States recognized themselves and converted the hymn in their own image on the plantations, where it was moaned and hummed as a field holler and lined-out in the worship services and funerals.[3] It was a process Zora Neale Hurston described as a "liquefying of words," aimed at arriving at the pure essence of what it felt like for the soul to suffer.[4] The focus here was not on the lyrics or how well they could "sing," but how their expression could match the intensity and depth of not only the emotion conveyed in the biblical scene but something more: a prayer for the strength to turn personal suffering, as Jesus did, into something more beautiful and useful—love.

In the post-slavery era, the symbolism and the dual meaning of the cross became reality through lynchings, imbuing greater significance on the interpretation of the hymn in Black spirituality. Theologian James H. Cone, who made explicit the connection in his book *The Cross and the Lynching Tree*, wrote:

> Christ crucified manifested God's loving and liberating presence *in* the contradictions of black life—that transcendent presence in the lives of black Christians that empowered them to believe that *ultimately* . . . they would not be defeated by the "troubles of the world," no matter how great and painful their suffering.[5]

The hymn during the trials of Jim Crow can be traced to religious work songs where it was sometimes combined with stanzas from "Amazing Grace" or "Am I a Soldier of the Cross?"[6] Mance Lipscomb recalled the hymn as a "moan" he would hear at the start of some Baptist services.[7] Anna Armstrong, who was born in

1887 and was eighty-eight years old when she was interviewed in Panola County in Northeast Texas, said that she would "set there and cry that song" when she was a kid.[8] Langston Hughes included it as a funeral song in his novel *Not Without Laughter*, and Madkin Butler referenced the song in his ballad "Christ Went on Man's Bond."[9] It was sung when Frankie laid Albert down in Mississippi John Hurt's recording of *Frankie* for OKeh in 1928, and "Blind" Joe Taggart converted it to a fiddle song in his recording, *Been Listening All Day*, for Paramount the same year.[10] Mary Price moaned the words as part of a line hymn near Angola, Louisiana, in 1954, just as Rev. Lewis Jackson and Charlotte Rucell did a month earlier in New Orleans.[11]

Johnson's recording of the hymn, as *Dark Was the Night, Cold Was the Ground* in 1927, though, brings us the closest to that "liquefying of words" Hurston talked about and also to how Cone described the wounds from the period when he wrote, "The sufferings of black people during slavery are too deep for words."[12] But there is also something more, for the full story of Christ's Crucifixion would not be complete without what comes out of it, something James Baldwin highlighted when he spoke of using the suffering as an opportunity, as a bridge: "Many people have suffered before you, many people are suffering around you and always will, and all you can do is bring, hopefully, a little light into that suffering."[13] This is the story of redemption, the ultimate promise of the cross; a tale that begins with a deep prayer, but soon is joined by many others in unison through an elongated moan, like the "voice of many waters," in the faith that death is not the end.

It is enough to cause one to tremble.[14]

DARK WAS THE NIGHT

Thomas Haweis 1792.

Dark was the night, and cold the ground
On which the Lord was laid;
His sweat like drops of blood ran down;
In agony He prayed.

"Father, remove this bitter cup,
If such Thy sacred will;
If not, content to drink it up
Thy pleasure I fulfill."

Go to the garden, sinner, see
Those precious drops that flow;
The heavy load He bore for thee;
For thee He lies so low.

Then learn of Him the cross to bear;
Thy Father's will obey;
And when temptations press thee near,
Awake to watch and pray.

These are the original words for the hymn, "Dark Was the Night," but they were likely never seen by those who attended the early Southern Black worship services.

A LOVE SUPREME

I make the guitar say what I say.
If I say 'Our Father' it will say 'Our Father.'
If I give out a hymn it will say it. If I play Amazing Grace it will
　　sing that too.
—FRED MCDOWELL[1]

As the Father has loved me, so have I loved you. Now remain in my love.
— JOHN 15:9[2]

The Anthology of American Folk Music, Song 52

There must always be, in adverse and equal proportion, a counter to destruction and resistance to brutality. Because violence begets violence, creativity and love are its natural opposite.

For Robert Fludd, the seventeenth-century cosmologist, astrologer, and author, the balance of the universe rests, as it was in Genesis, with the harmony of light and darkness.[3] Inspired by Pythagoras's theory of the Music of the Spheres—which states that the proportions of movement in the cosmos creates its own music, and that the perfect harmony is the interval between Earth and the fixed stars—Fludd designed an image of a one-string instrument, which he termed the celestial monochord. It paired two octaves with two cones, one dark and the other light, that all met together in the center at the "sphere of equality." Bringing to mind Emerson's essay "The Over-Soul," it is a visual representation of the all-encompassing universal soul, from Earth up to heaven, all in balance as it is kept in tune by the hand of God. It is an interplanetary vision of the nature of the universe flooded in vibration and uniting the whole soul of existence in sound. And, Fludd wrote, "[i]f struck in the spiritual part, the monochord will give eternal life."[4]

The image of Fludd's monochord would be the symbol that the visual artist and anthropologist Harry Smith would later use to unite the various styles and rhythms of American music. In his compendium released on Folkways in 1952, Smith organized dozens of the songs recorded in the late 1920s and early '30s without regard to race or geography but in accordance with the balance illustrated by Fludd's instrument. Trying to instigate social change, he arranged the three volumes only by one-word headings, classical elements, and their color equivalents.[5]

The *Anthology of American Folk Music*, would be the first compilation on a physical sound record to strive toward a universal language of humanity through music. It was the message of Fludd, as well the Greek philosopher Heraclitus, who believed in the pairing of the individual soul with the soul of the world. But it was also the sentiment voiced in the Great Depression-era novel *The Grapes of Wrath*, when itinerant preacher Casy told Tom Joad that "maybe all men got one big soul ever 'body's a part of."[6]

::

Johnson's "John the Revelator" was included as number fifty-two on the "Social Music" section of the record, represented by the color red, which symbolizes the element of fire and the soul at its least corrupted. Smith noted in his description for Johnson that he may have been from New Orleans, but that "no information is available on . . . one of the most influential of all religious singers." It seemed to be a perfect pairing—this Samson of New Orleans and the ideals Smith hoped to achieve with the *Anthology*: a divine harmony with the sacred and the profane, a conversation of both earthly trouble and spiritual union; the celestial monochord struck at just the right interval.

Samuel B. Charters

The headlights of the Packard sedan came shining over the Texas highway and into the city of Beaumont, finally pulling into the Black district along Forsythe Street in early November 1955.[7] Samuel Charters, a twenty-six-year-old California college student and his wife, Mary, parked and began to walk the street lined with storefronts, searching for a blind gospel singer they had been told used to live in the area and who may still have been around.[8] At first the description of such a person made no impact, as there had been at least a dozen or so singers who fit this vague sketch. It was only after talking with the pharmacist in the local drug store Fowler's that someone seemed to acknowledge that they knew the precise man for whom they were searching. Soon, more of the shopkeepers along the street began to recall this figure they described. He was "a tall, heavy man . . . a dignified man and a magnificent singer," they said.[9] It was the first time Charters was hearing a physical description of the man he had only heard on the records. They were told if they wanted to know more, they needed to go see a woman who was living on the south side of town.

::

The whole journey had begun years before—back in Berkeley—when Charters would spend the nights after jazz rehearsals listening to Robert Johnson's *Stones in My Passway* and a "Blind" Willie Johnson record titled *Dark Was the Night, Cold Was the Ground*.[10] A few years later, when he was alternating between Berkeley and New Orleans, he befriended a fellow jazz enthusiast who was around his age named Richard B. Allen. Allen had moved permanently to New Orleans in the late 1940s and absorbed himself in the scene.[11] He was also an admirer of "Blind" Willie Johnson, and in 1954 told Charters of a story he heard of a blind religious singer getting arrested for trying to start a riot in front of the Custom House on Canal in 1929 while he was singing "If I Had My Way."[12] The location of the Custom House was just a tenth of a mile from Werlein's Music, the location where Johnson presumably recorded the same year. Allen also knew of a blind musician in his early seventies who for decades had dressed in a suit and tie and carried a chair to the corner of Rampart and Canal to play religious songs, including those of "Blind" Willie Johnson, on his guitar. His name was Elder Dave Ross, and Charters had to meet him.

"He came down here and he made a record," Ross told him. "I believe in '29, down here on Canal Street." Charters sat in Ross's kitchen and turned on his Pentron tape recorder to make his first documentary field recording, his microphone resting on a chair while Ross's wife cleaned the dishes.[13] Charters asked him if he had seen Johnson since, but he hadn't. The last time he heard, Johnson was living somewhere in the Dallas area.[14] A few days later, Fred Ramsey, a writer and photographer who was traveling the South making field recordings centered around Black culture, visited Ross and photographed and recorded him singing "He Gave Me a Heart to Love." In the photo, Ross was sitting in his home on Calliope Street wearing dark glasses, a white dress shirt, and suspenders with a guitar laid on his lap.[15]

Over a year would pass before Charters and his wife followed up on Ross's suggestion to go looking for Johnson in Dallas. Beginning with asking around the streets, they were given the suggestion to try the Lighthouse for the Blind. This is where they ran into the director, Abbie Lewis, who had known Johnson and recommended he seek out Adam Booker, a blind preacher who lived some two hundred miles southeast of Dallas in Brenham. When they located Booker, then in his late sixties, he was living in a cabin on the outskirts of the city. Charters once again turned on his recording device as he began to ask about his life and what, if anything, he knew of "Blind" Willie Johnson.

"He was there, you know," Booker told him, meaning in Hearne, where Booker himself could also be found preaching in the mid-1920s. "That being good cotton country, people were all there picking cotton, and they would come on the streets every Saturday and he'd get on the streets and sing and pick the guitar, and they would listen and give him money." Booker went on to tell Charters that, at that time, Johnson could be heard nearly every Saturday in Hearne.[16] Booker also brought up another singer who was well-known in the town, a man by the name of Madkin Butler, and Booker even sang "Everybody Ought to Treat a Stranger Right," one of Butler's ballads. "He would always get on the outside [of the church] and just start to singing," and he was so good, according to Booker, that "if you wasn't a real good preacher he'd close your church up more or less."[17] As for Johnson, Booker suggested they head to Beaumont.

::

Angelina, with her hands crossed in front of her, sat pensively in a chair on the wood floor of her neighbor's home. It was a few weeks before Thanksgiving when the guests arrived, unexpectedly, to ask her questions. It was cold, and she dressed in several layers including an unbuttoned suit jacket that was pulled over her dress as she listened. Her answers ebbed and flowed with emotion over the course of the hour, but her voice always rose with genuine enthusiasm, even frequently breaking into laughter and song, as she recalled her and Johnson's life together.

She met him on the streets, she said. He was singing "If I Had My Way," and she came behind him singing. She spoke of their quick marriage in Houston and of their traveling. They sang on the streets everywhere they went together, including Galveston, Dayton, and Liberty. And Johnson frequently journeyed alone to preach around the revival meetings. "He loved to play on the streets. He certainly did," she remembered, her voice revealing a reverence for a time and a man that existed now only in her memory.[18] When Charters asked if many people liked Johnson playing on the streets, she let out a long "ohhh yes, sir" telling him it was both "the white and colored" including Reverend Hodge's "big fine white church."[19] When asked if anyone played the guitar like him, she simply replied, "No, Sir. They played it but not like him." She sang for him some of the songs they would sing together including "If You See My Savior," "Motherless Children," and "Blind Man Stood by the Wayside." When Charters asked her about "Dark Was the Night," she began to sing and then moan the words in the lined-hymn fashion she knew. And when questioned about recording, she talked about singing on the radio and how some wanted her to sing like Johnson by alternating her pitch which she demonstrated for Charters by singing falsetto on some sections of "When the Saints Go Marching In." The change in tone prompted Charters to inquire about Johnson's vocal pitch variations, which led to Angelina singing a couple of lines of "99½ Won't Do" in her best impression of Johnson.

Figure 8. *Angelina Johnson in 1955. Courtesy of the Samuel and Ann Charters Archives of Blues and Vernacular African American Musical Culture, Archives and Special Collections at the Thomas J. Dodd Research Center, University of Connecticut Libraries.*

She recited a line in a natural tone before moving once again to the falsetto. "He really got me," she laughed.[20] She mentioned a few more songs they would sing together, but there were too many to recall. "I wished I could [remember], but, you see, my remembrance is poor."[21]

When asked about Johnson's death, Angelina told him that he died from pneumonia after they "burned out there in the North End." With the house full of water after the fire was out, she explained that she covered as much of the area as she could with "big clothes with a lot of newspapers" to keep the two of them from getting wet. She continued:

> It didn't bother me but it bothered him, yes. See, he'd turn over you know and I just lay up on the paper, and I thought if you'd put a lot of paper on you know, it was keep us from getting sick. We didn't get wet, but just the dampness you know, and then he's singing and his veins open and everything, and it just made him sick.[22]

Charters asked if Johnson made it to the hospital, to which she answered, "They wouldn't accept him. He'd have been living today if they'd accepted him. 'Cause he's blind. Blind folks has a hard time."

Following the interview and after Charters photographed her, Angelina led Charters to the trunk that she had set outside her home, the one she had hauled from 1440 Forrest containing many of the belongings she was able to recover after the fire. Inside there were over one hundred hymn books that had once belonged to her and Johnson, of which Charters purchased one. She also gave him the charred bridge to Johnson's guitar, and there was one more thing she wished to show him. Likely taken from a coin operated photo booth, she presented to him an image that revealed Johnson as a real man, his "face squarish, but rounded, his hair gone, and his eyes closed."[23]

Alan Lomax

Following the early days of being on the road with his father on trips through the Southern prison system, Lomax had gone on to college and branched out on his own to continue field work separate from his father's expeditions. In 1941, he and the Library of Congress partnered with Fisk University to conduct field recording trips in Coahoma County, Mississippi, a project that produced, over the next year, possibly the largest survey of recorded rural African American artists since before the Great Depression of the 1930s. They spent time recording in both Baptist and Pentecostal churches, plantations, and even at a funeral home. In addition to recording musicians who would become well known like Muddy Waters (McKinley Morganfield), "Son" House (Eddie House), and David "Honeyboy" Edwards, they also made scores of other recordings. Sid Hemphill, a blind multi-instrumentalist, lived outside of the Delta in Senatobia, Mississippi. He was the grandfather of the Mississippi Hill Country sound, a ballad writer, and a keeper of the traditions going back to the slave days, both church songs and reels. Alan Lomax recorded him as part of a fife and drum group screaming out the old work song "John Henry" at one of the traditional Hill Country picnics, his violin blazing through the field with unencumbered intensity:

> *Take this hammer*
> *To the captain,*
> *Tell him he's gone.*
> *Tell him he's gone.*[24]

Turner Junior Johnson, another blind musician, had sent Lomax to Hemphill, whom he referred to as "best musician in the world."[25] Turner Johnson was originally from the northern section of Mississippi, and Lomax first heard him at the corner of an alley in Coahoma County playing harmonica for change that he collected in a tin cup. Lomax noticed his "lusty bass" voice that "sings on forever, growling for food and shelter and a few pennies," and the gaps in his singing where he would let the instrument fill in the words.[26] Turner Johnson sang some of his most contemplative and soulful melodies for Lomax, blowing on his harmonica while beating out time with the pounding of his walking cane.

That same year, 1942, Alan Lomax ran into Charles Haffer Jr., another blind street singer, in Clarksdale. Haffer was standing behind a booth near a Baptist church singing one of his songs about hard times and trouble because of the Second World War, with a sign near his stand introducing him as a "NOTED GOSPEL SONG WRITER AND BIBLE LECTURER."[27] When Lomax asked if he had other songs, Haffer proceeded to open a briefcase filled with ballad sheets. Some were topical, others were warning songs like "The Sinking of the *Titanic*" and "The Natchez Fire," and some were spiritual like "What Is the Soul of Man?" the latter of which had lyrics that paired closely with Johnson's version.[28] Haffer sang for Lomax in a "husky rumble," the "voice of the street evangelist."[29]

When the climate around the second Red Scare began to envelop the United States, Alan Lomax opted to escape to London. Upon returning to New York in 1959, he noticed the burgeoning folk revival scene growing up all around him from the roots of the practitioners he had surrounded himself with for so many years. Determined to go once again searching for what he felt was the "real thing," he decided to embark on a trip through the rural landscape, but this time in a broader way than he had done seventeen years prior.[30] His goal was to reconnect with those out of the purview of the mainstream and record the music of the working people on the margins of American life. It was on this "Southern Journey" expedition that Lomax visited the people in their houses, in the fields, in the prisons, and in their churches.[31] The recordings reveal that the American history reflected in the *Anthology of American Folk Music* was still in flux. There were still traditions important enough to be kept alive outside of all the commercial aspirations, places where slave songs were still being sung in rural churches by groups like the Georgia Sea Island Singers and the remarkable Bessie Jones.[32] Not only that, but there was still genius to be located and recorded that never would be heard if it wasn't for someone who had a yearning to be moved by the truth.

∷

Lomax first recorded Fred McDowell in September 1959. At the time, McDowell was making a living as a farmer in the town of Como in northern Mississippi. Lomax had got word of him from a diddley bow player named Napoleon Strickland who would use a slide to make his one-stringed instrument talk, a style that when transferred to the guitar Lomax described as the guitar "moaning the blues, crying the blues, with a nearly human voice."[33] It was something he had learned from another player nearby, he said, and that was McDowell.

In the early 1940s, after his father's conversation with "Blind" Willie McTell, Alan Lomax may have believed "Blind" Willie Johnson was dead and, therefore, never sought him out in the Texas streets. But he had been collecting Johnson's records for some time, as he found Johnson's singing to be the "most passionate [and] intense . . . he'd ever heard," even wearing down his copy of *I Just Can't Keep from Cryin'*, which, he wrote, was one of his "companions of my lonely nights in the field."[34] Johnson's music to him "wasn't a matter of folklore," but "the way I felt."[35] But here, sitting on McDowell's porch after the sun went down on a late September evening, with only a flashlight to illuminate the equipment he needed to record, he listened to what should be considered to be Johnson's closest spiritual and musical descendant. McDowell played spirituals and blues, but even the blues were inspired with a transcendence that was unique to just him. McDowell was not a preacher like Johnson, but what he possessed was the ability to make his guitar speak lines that would make one feel as though he was leading you right into salvation. Over three recording sessions, McDowell took Lomax on a private journey through his soul, even putting down on tape some songs Johnson had recorded three decades earlier like "Keep Your Lamp Trimmed and Burning," "Jesus Gonna Make Up My Dying Bed," and "Motherless Children." Just like it was with Johnson, McDowell could make one feel as if every note meant something, that he wasn't just a technical practitioner but one of the heart—directing you straight into the poetry and magic that one could forget exists if it's absent for too long. McDowell let you know that it was still there. It was the same thing Lomax must have felt when he sat, weeks earlier, in the Saint James Missionary Baptist Church in Huntsville, Alabama, and listened to the church erupt into "Take Your Stand," the congregation all moaning in triumphant unison, much like Johnson would have experienced for years before turning it into his own rhythmic testament in 1929.

There was something happening here. It was as if he had heard the future on record and then had the opportunity to tour the countryside of the South and witness the places where it started, experiencing firsthand the conscience of America through the sounds of America's neglected poets. Alan Lomax considered himself an ambassador for those he knew may never get their voices heard politically or socially but needed their story told and their song to be sung, and it had all been born in those hellish prison camps where he witnessed the result of what happens to men who stand up to oppression at the hands of the state and institutions. He recalled his memories of hearing the voices in that Central State Farm Prison yard in 1933, in that burning hell, as the men, exploited for their labor, sang out through the brutality in the old call-and-response patterns. He would later write:

I had been listening in the years before to Bach and Beethoven and Stravinsky, but here on a July afternoon . . . these convicts in their shaming stripes out-sang those symphonies. I had been soaked from childhood up in Shakespeare, and here was language as noble and perfect as his.[36]

Mance Lipscomb

Returning once more to the past, we find Mance Lipscomb—the young song-ster who would encounter Johnson on the streets of Navasota on Saturday after-noons and tune his guitar—now in his mid-sixties and working as a tractor driver while overseeing a crew cutting the grass near Texas highways. Tracked down in the fall of 1960 in Navasota by Texas field researcher and writer Robert "Mack" McCormick, Lipscomb recorded dozens of songs for both McCormick and Chris Strachwitz, taking them through the roots of Texas music spawned over the last one hundred years. These included dance songs, train songs, and a couple of numbers he had heard Johnson sing, including "Motherless Children" and "God Moves on the Water." Fourteen of Lipscomb's recordings from the few days they sat with him would be released under the title, *Mance Lipscomb: Texas Sharecrop-per and Songster*. It would be the first album release for the budding roots label Arhoolie Records.

::

A couple of years later in 1962, Lipscomb performed at the annual Hootenanny! Festival put on by the Houston Folklore Society, and it was here that McCormick introduced Lipscomb to Madkin Butler's widow, Ophelia, and his daughter, Mar-tha. McCormick, knowing that the original Texas ballad about the *Titanic*, "God Moves on the Water," was composed by Butler, asked Lipscomb if he'd play it for them as they sat on stage when he performed. "Here they come up on the stage an one got on one side an one got on the othun, I'm in the middle of em," Lip-scomb recalled in his autobiography. "I tuned up the gittah, and stawted ta pla-yin, I knowed ever verse. An knowed ever angle on the gittah. An she knowed ever verse. And she sot there an cried."[37]

Dan Williams

The first news that it was Willie B. Harris, a seventy-five-year-old woman living in Marlin and making a living as a nurse who sang with Johnson on the 1928 and 1930 recording sessions—and not Angelina—came from a series of letters writ-ten in 1977 by a young artist named Dan Williams. In Williams's letters to Nick

Perls, the founder of Yazoo Records and Blue Goose Records, Williams detailed his serious attempt to bring this new discovery to life, but also to advocate for a more intense inquiry than Williams may have felt himself capable at the time. There was also a sense of urgency, as Yazoo was preparing a re-release of Johnson's material on the label the same year.[38]

"I have just returned from an all-too-brief visit with Willie B. Harris in Marlin," Williams wrote to Perls in mid-April 1977. "She was tired and hasn't been feeling real well, so we talked for only a short period of time," he continued before detailing some of the optimistic discoveries Harris was willing to discuss. Johnson "wasn't no preacher, just a songster" and they were both members of the Marlin Church of God in Christ where Johnson would play both guitar and "really tear it up" on piano, Harris told him, mentioning Johnson's association with the Pentecostal Church for the first time.[39]

There was some expected hesitancy on the part of Harris, according to Williams, to discuss a life now fifty years in the past, one that left her to raise many children, including the child she had with Johnson, as a single working mother. He would leave questions for her, hoping they would prompt "more comprehensive remembrance." This sort of full disclosure never occurred, but Williams's genuine pursuit of the truth did open Harris enough to provide a window into those most formative years they spent together. Some of those details included recalling that they first met in 1926 or 1927, Johnson frequently playing on the streets with a "tin cup hung on a wire loop around the neck," and his traveling to church meetings and revivals. She mentioned their trip to Dallas to record. She recalled that they stayed at the Delmonico Hotel, that they had had a run-in with "Blind" Lemon, and of Johnson's "careful" search for guitars in the city. She brought up his friend, the pianist Bob Jackson, who had been killed on the railroad tracks in Marlin, that Johnson's music was "all sacred," and that what he was doing was considered "new," echoing Angelina's assessment of Johnson's ability to Charters when she told him that nobody played like him.[40]

••

On one of his trips, Williams was also able to meet Johnson's daughter, Sam Faye, and even played his 78 copy of *Church, I'm Fully Saved To-Day* for her. Sam, who by this point was nearing fifty years old, had grown up attending Booker T. Washington High School in Marlin and attended college in Seattle and Los Angeles before devoting her life to nursing and the church. In fact, it was the same COGIC church in Marlin her parents attended together where she built the women's ministry through service on the Mothers Board. She would pass away in December of 2005, while her mother, Willie B., died in 1979, just two years after her meeting with Williams.[41]

Figure 9. *Willie B. Harris. Courtesy of Dan Williams.*

In one of his last letters to Perls in 1977, Williams concluded by writing, "I hope this information will be helpful, Dan." Of course, we know that these few months that Williams spent in Marlin and talking to Harris was more than anyone had done since Charters in 1955. But unfortunately, no one followed up with Harris or anyone else around the Central Texas area with regards to Johnson, and Williams's research would be obscured from the wider public view for another decade or so, until later releases of Johnson's music would be forced to reckon with this new world that had come into view. But what had happened to the song collectors in the gulf of years between Charters and Williams, and why did the so-called folk revival nearly miss Texas altogether? These are questions that will have to be dealt with as one determines how "blues" music is defined and where it occurred.[42]

A Love Supreme

What is the role of the artist—of any occupation—if not to free oneself and by doing so, set others free? "And his triumph, when he triumphs, is ours," as we witness the artist "impos[e] order" on "the roar rising from the void," James Baldwin wrote in "Sonny's Blues."[43] But it is not just any "order," mere ritual, instead it *their* order; and once they have discovered this, we too partake in this glorious splendor because we understand, intuitively, that they are saying something which is also in us. But it is the artist who is that original voice, prepared to go where many would never dare, into the "deep," Baldwin wrote of Sonny as he stands, pushed by Creole, onto the bandstand. This is where the artist is willing or, more accurately, *must* go, if they are to distinguish their soul from the many. The artist understands that they cannot be instructed how to feel or think from another soul, or as Emerson put it, to make the "mistake of the infant man, who seeks to be great by following the great."[44] It is a scene rarely captured in person, but in some elements of living and performance, the soul, seemingly spontaneously, but with much solitude kept hidden from view, erupts in a liveliness constituting the true essence of individuation and freedom. Returning to Sonny once more, we can read of such an outburst of spirit in the closing lines Baldwin wrote:

> Sonny's fingers filled the air with life, his life. But that life contained so many others. . . . Then he began to make it his. It was very beautiful because it wasn't hurried and it was no longer a lament. I seemed to hear with what burning he had made it his, with what burning we had yet to make it ours, how we could cease lamenting. Freedom lurked around us and I understood, at last, that he could help us to be free if we would listen, that he would never be free until we did.[45]

The sort of freedom Baldwin speaks about is deeper than any sociological freedom, the kind of latitude offered either by someone else or by recognizing oneself as part of a larger sect of society. Instead, this emancipation is far deeper because it has no use for ideas, theories, philosophy, or any other purely intellectual expression and is focused uniquely on the quest to develop one's acute awareness and identity that remain when the fashions of the day are replaced by new phrases or sentiments that also will be washed away. True expression, to the artist, can never be had first without experience, one that would only be limited by putting that into words. The ones who are truly outcasts and take pride in it are the ones who show us that—because we witness their vulnerability and honesty—we too are capable of such courage in the face of the masses and mediocrity. They are our teachers, but their only instruction is their work, the soul on display.

Acknowledgment

While preachers and street singers, both Baptist and Pentecostal, recorded in the same period as Johnson, no one had the range of Johnson as a combination of all these factors. While he was a street singer, he truly straddled the line between the preacher and the street corner singer. Two of the most prominent street performers known for recording religious material, Joel "Blind" Joe Taggart and Rev. Edward W. Clayborn, both Baptists, made moving records, but they had neither the fire of voice nor feeling of instrument that Johnson brought to his recordings.

It is only after pairing the songster with the Black preacher tradition do we begin to get on solid footing to where Johnson was taking us, something that could not be said of the previously mentioned performers. One merely needs to listen to Rev. F. W. McGee when, in the middle of his sermon on Jonah, the great preacher began to moan out: "The Lord moooooved upon the waaaater."[46] Or the Baptist preacher Reverend Beaumont, who recorded a sermon titled "The Blind Man" that included the roots of Johnson's version of "Let Your Light Shine on Me" six months before Johnson would perform it for his record in New Orleans.[47] But of course there were many more, most of whom Johnson knew the names of and we never shall.

::

To understand the impact Johnson had on the Black artists in the years after his records were released, one would only have to listen to some of the well-known recording artists like Sister Rosetta Tharpe, who came out of the Church of God in Christ, and recorded songs like "What is the Soul of a Man?" and "Nobody's Fault but Mine"; Rev. Gary Davis, who was first recorded as "Blind Gary," and who, like Johnson, would play on the streets and in the Missionary Baptist Church. Davis wasn't fond of open tunings or slide like Johnson, but he would make his guitar "talk" and covered several of the songs Johnson popularized including "If I Had My Way" (which he titled "Samson and Delilah"), "Keep Your Lamp Trimmed and Burning," and "Motherless Children." Son House would record a version of Johnson's "Motherless Children" and "John the Revelator" in 1965, the latter just with punishing a cappella and hand claps.

One of Johnson's greatest disciples was the blind singer Rev. Pearly Brown. Brown was born blind, and like Johnson, his mother died when he was young. "I decided when I got to be a big boy I was gonna sing some of his songs," Brown said of the inspiration he had upon hearing Johnson's records as a young man.[48] On his first album, made in 1961, he recorded five of Johnson's songs including "God Don't Never Change," "Motherless Children," and "By and By (I'm Gonna See the King)."[49] He made a living playing music on the streets of Americus, Georgia, often with a harmonica around his neck and a cup, similar to the way Johnson had, attached to the neck of his guitar. Even though he was blind and often wore a sign that he hung around his chest announcing himself as a blind preacher asking for help, he would still be arrested occasionally for being on the streets.[50] In addition to Johnson's songs on record, Brown also recorded a couple that Johnson would perform but never affix permanently in the studio including "Ninety-Nine and a Half Won't Do" and "Savior, Don't You Pass Me By (Blind Man Stood on the Wayside)." Reverend Davis and Reverend Brown were not alone in their adoption of Johnson's vision as they transported his songs into a new era on city sidewalks and stages. There were many unsung heroes on the street corners who would carry their guitars to where the people were to sing and shout, evangelizing the revelation. Many of them were women.

The Two Gospel Keys (Emma Daniels and "Mother" Sally Jones) recorded songs like "I Don't Feel at Home in This World Anymore," "You've Got to Move," and "Jesus Met the Woman at the Well" while playing tambourines and guitar in the late 1940s. There was Flora Molton out of the Washington, DC, area. She would entertain on the corner of Seventh Street NW and F Street NW and would sing, play guitar, and tap a tambourine with her foot while passersby dropped coins into a plastic pail attached to her guitar.[51] Molton, whose father was a preacher, also ran a ministry out of her home and tuned her guitar to open D tuning, just as Johnson had done. After not being able to find work, Molton "took the street for [hers]."[52] She remarked that, "If it hadn't been for the street, I would have been dead."[53] There was Sister Ola Mae (O. M) Terrell, a "holy ghost preacher" from the same area where the Rev. J. M. Gates preached around Atlanta. She printed ballads, played churches, and performed on the streets playing religious music with a slide. In the 1950s she began a weekly radio show out of Charleston, South Carolina, catching the ear of Columbia Records, which recorded her in 1953.[54]

One could also hear Johnson's influence in the missionary, painter, and singer Sister Gertrude Morgan who was called to preach in 1934 and found the Pentecostal Church after she moved to New Orleans in 1939; and in "Blind" Connie Williams who would play Johnson's songs on the streets of Philadelphia with accordion and guitar.[55] And there was Arvella Gray, the street singer from Texas, who made a name for himself on Maxwell Street in Chicago in the 1960s playing his guitar and singing songs like "Take Your Burden To the Lord," "Motherless Children," and "When the Saints Go Marching In." Bishop Perry Tillis, who was involved with the Pentecostal Church all of his life, played slide guitar, and claimed to have met Johnson in New Orleans, likely in the early 1940s.[56] He would go on to record a foot stomping rendition of "Nobody's Fault but Mine" as well as "Motherless Children" for field recorder Bengt Olsson.

The Reverend Dan Smith was also of the Pentecostal Church—the New Zion Fire Baptized Holiness Church of God in New York—and recorded "Babylon is Falling Down" in 1971 to the same rhythm as Johnson's "If I Had My Way."[57] Around the same time as Smith was recording, there was Rev. Charlie Jackson, who would travel from town to town around Louisiana playing electric guitar and preaching. And then there was Boyd Rivers, who Alan Lomax, John Bishop, and Worth Long first recorded in Mississippi in 1978. Both of these musicians, along with Fred McDowell and the great Rev. Robert Wilkins, could send shivers down your spine as they invoked the spirit of the preacher in ways that hadn't really been heard with such intensity since Johnson's last recordings.[58]

::

The pianist Mercy Dee Walton, from Central Texas, would end up recording the Marlin piano player Bob Jackson's version of "Troublesome Mind" in California in 1961; and Thomas Shaw, Johnson's old friend from Texas, would also finally record.[59] In the early 1970s, Shaw walked into a music store in San Diego to buy guitar strings, and the owner immediately took to him, booking him for the San Diego Folk and Blues Festival, which eventually led to his first record, *Born in Texas*, being recorded in 1971. Shaw recorded both J. T. Smith's "Hungry Wolf" and Johnson's "Motherless Children" for the record. The following year Shaw recorded his album *Blind Lemon's Buddy*, recording a mix of his own songs and those written by Jefferson, Smith, and Johnson. Shaw, by this point, was also a minister and preaching the Pentecostal faith out of his home and would play the guitar for services.[60] His last set of recordings, made in the Netherlands in December 1972, were dedicated to his friends. A portion of the liner notes reads:

> Now this is a song I'm dedication' to some of my friends now, like take Blind Willie Johnson. He was a slide guitar man. Blind Lemon was a bad guitar man, too. He's an old friend o'mine. I'm just dedicatin' this to my friends. . . . Yeah, I remember when Blind Lemon was really goin.' Now he, uh he was good. . . . Yeah now, Blind . . . Blind Willie Johnson, you know, he was a gospel man, he played nothin' but slide guitar mostly. I just like talkin' 'bout them boys, makes me feel good.[61]

But Johnson's sound went further than the angels who performed on street corners or the one-room church houses stretched out along the rural highways and byways; it injected itself right into the core of things when Roebuck "Pops" Staples took it to the mainstream and center stage with the Staple Singers. For Staples, Johnson was "the most moving of all country religious performers" and someone who "exerted a profound and lasting influence" on him, so much so that when someone wondered where he got the guitar sound for the Staples Singers, he played a little bit of "Nobody's Fault but Mine."

"Blind Willie Johnson. That's where I got that from."[62]

Resolution

It was in Baltimore in 1956 when a seventeen-year-old record collector heard Johnson for the first time, and it would change his life. At the time, John Fahey wasn't interested in Black music. "Where I was brought up was very prejudiced towards Negroes," he said. "I was taught to hate and fear them. I didn't like black music very much, I wouldn't even listen to it." But that all changed when, one evening, someone played a copy of Johnson's *Praise God I'm Satisfied* for him. It was as if he had been "smote to the ground by a bolt of lightning."[63] He later said of the experience:

> [Blues connoisseur] Dick Spottswood and I sat in a store where they were selling up old 78s. They weren't catalogued or anything, they were just lying around. We were going through them and I was not picking up any records by Negroes for myself because all I wanted was bluegrass. I found several black records and gave them to Spottswood. Then we went over to this other collector's house and he put on the Blind Willie Johnson. I started to feel nauseated so I made him take it off, but it kept going through my head so I had to hear it again. When he played it the second time I started to cry, it was suddenly very beautiful. It was some kind of hysterical conversion experience where in fact I had liked that kind of music all the time.[64]

A couple years later, Fahey deepened his voice into a growl and began playing in open tunings for his first records. He called himself Blind Thomas, a precursor to Blind Joe Death, and it was the beginning of a whole new genre of playing he would eventually adapt into, what he called American primitive. It was a style of instrumental guitar that wanders out to the edge of the wilderness where there are no demarcations of East or West, and the whole world, including ourselves, is made of an ocean of sound.[65]

Pursuance

It was the year of the Jubilee, one hundred years after the Emancipation Proclamation declared that those who were enslaved would be "forever free," when Rev. Martin Luther King Jr., a Baptist preacher, still in pursuit of that elusive economic and institutional emancipation, delivered his "I Have a Dream" speech. Reverend King was the natural evolution of the spiritual resistance to tyranny that animated Nat Turner but instilled with the love that was at the center of the teachings of Jesus. King was the son of what the author and journalist Louis E. Lomax described as a "'hard' preacher," who "preaches as if Heaven and Hell were coming together." King's opposition was directed not with physical force, though, but with peaceable, nonviolent resistance, which he equated with love.[66] Advocating for a principle of love for love's sake, or *agape*, King wrote:

> If one loves an individual merely on account of his friendliness, he loves him
> for the sake of his benefits to be gained from the friendship, rather than the
> friend's own sake. Consequently, the best way to assure oneself that love is dis-
> interested is to have love for the enemy-neighbor from whom you can expect
> no good in return, but only hostility and persecution.[67]

This love Reverend King advocated for was external, but it also preserved the dignity and devotion of the one who practiced it. In this nonviolent path much of the strength and power, like during the days of slavery, came from the spirituals, songs that were for King, the "soul of the movement" toward freedom.[68] For the songs, like King's vision of resistance, were not passive.

> The way of nonviolent resistance . . . is ultimately the way of the strong man.
> It is not a method of stagnant passivity. . . . For while the nonviolent resister
> is passive in the sense that he is not physically aggressive toward his opponent,
> his mind and his emotions are always active, constantly seeking to persuade
> his opponent that he is wrong. The method is passive physically but strongly
> active spiritually. It is not passive non-resistance to evil, it is active nonviolent
> resistance to evil.[69]

And it was never stagnant, but like all the travelers on the long road of justice everyone had a responsibility to keep advancing, and "not let nobody turn you 'round."[70]

> Keep moving, for it may well be that the greatest song has not yet been sung,
> the greatest book has not been written, the highest mountain has not been
> climbed. This is your challenge! Reach out and grab it and make it a part of
> your life. Reach up beyond cloud-filled skies of oppression and bring out blaz-
> ing stars of inspiration. The basic thing is to keep moving.[71]

King gave his last speech, his "I've Been to the Mountaintop" speech at the Mason Temple (COGIC) in Memphis on April 3, 1968, just a day before he was assassinated. In it he asked, "Who is it that is supposed to articulate the longings and aspirations of the people more than the preacher?" Feeling like his time wasn't long, he reported to his audience that he had seen the coming of the new day, the one he extolled just days earlier at the National Cathedral in Washington, DC, as he recalled the vision of John of Patmos (John the Revelator) out on the island of Patmos. "Thank God for John," he said, "[w]ho centuries ago out on a lonely, obscure island called Patmos caught vision of a new Jerusalem descending out of heaven from God, who heard a voice saying, 'Behold, I make all things new; former things are passed away.'" He closed with his own vision, taken from the book of Job, of "that day [when] the morning stars will sing together and the sons of God will shout for joy."[72]

Psalm

It is this suffering of the soul manifested into love (eventually) that is the fire that burns in the creative artist: to seek and then display, separate from the group or congregation, all of the messiness and beauty of the now transfigured spirit. The African American spirituals understood that this truth, sung as groups, could never be imparted by any formal instruction. The participants in the congregation still had an obligation to express, individually, their own truth, as Zora Neale Hurston explained.

> Glee clubs and concert singers put on their tuxedos, bow prettily to the audience, get the pitch and burst into magnificent song—but not the *Negro* song. The real Negro singer cares nothing about pitch. The first notes just burst out and the rest of the church joins in-fired by the same inner urge. Every man trying to express himself through song. Every man for himself. Hence the harmony and disharmony, the shifting keys and broken time.[73]

This was a lived, personal connection to something higher that sprang from the inner well that danced within each individual and burst out through artistic expression. It was the outward presentation of all the shifting inner keys that ebb and flow within, and there was no school to attend to learn how to sing like someone, for, as Hurston wrote, "Its truth dies under training like flowers under hot water."[74] The only way forward was to listen to the song within, to one's own true identity, which is never fixed but in constant motion, and let it pour forth in one's own voice. This would be a freedom of an uncompromising spiritual union that could never be revoked.

One of the greatest representatives of such a mode of living, in the African American tradition Hurston illustrated, was John Coltrane. Writing on the spirit of the Black jazz musician in 1962, Coltrane said:

> It's [positive and affirmative philosophy] built in us. The phrasing, the sound of the music attest to this fact. We are endowed with it. You can believe all

of us would have perished long ago if this were not so. As to community, the whole face of the globe is our community. You see, it is really easy for us to create. We are born with this feeling that just comes out no matter what conditions exist. . . . Any person who claims to doubt this, or claims to believe that the exponents of our music of freedom are not guided by this same entity, is either prejudiced, musically sterile, just plain stupid or scheming. . . . 'Freedom' has a hell of a lot to do with this musc.[75]

He went further, expounding on what he called "the creative urge":

The creative urge was in the man who found himself so much at odds with the world he lived in, and in spite of all the adversity, frustrations, rejections and so forth—beautiful and living art came forth abundantly . . . if only he could be here today. Truth is indestructible.[76]

And the innovator, he wrote:

is more often than not met with some degree of condemnation. . . . We also see that these innovators always seek to revitalize, extend, and reconstruct the status quo in their given fields, wherever it is needed. Quite often they are the rejects, outcasts, sub-citizens, etc. of the very societies to which they bring so much sustenance. Often they are people who endure great personal tragedy in their lives. Whatever the case, whether accepted or rejected, rich or poor, they are forever guided by the great and eternal constant—the creative urge. Let us cherish it and give all praise to God.[77]

This praise to God would be written again in the liner notes to his album, *A Love Supreme*, recorded two and a half years after that writing, in December 1964. "DEAR LISTENER," he wrote. "ALL PRAISE BE TO GOD TO WHOM ALL PRAISE IS DUE."[78] The album, divided into four parts, was, he wrote, "a humble offering to Him" whose "WAY IS LOVE," and concluded with a prayer titled simply, "Psalm." Composed by Coltrane himself, it is a seven minute transcendent hymn recalling Johnson's record *Dark Was the Night, Cold Was the Ground,* where instead of reciting the words he had written with speech, Coltrane created what he called a "musical narration" in which he moaned out the syllables on the saxophone; just feeling, existence pulsating in vibration, where ordinary language would fall short.[79] It is an understanding shared intuitively with all beings, but especially with those who have had to moan sometimes. Coltrane and King and all those long-ago bards carried with them the same message of hope: that love was the key to true freedom; it is the truest form of resistance, an understanding most familiar to both artists and prisoners, as Baldwin said.[80] The concepts of redemption and freedom are especially pertinent in Black liberation theology, as the theologian James Cone made clear.

> His death is the revelation of the freedom of God, taking upon himself the totality of human oppression; his resurrection is the disclosure that God is not defeated by oppression but transforms it into the possibility of freedom.[81]

It is precisely why Johnson's moan on *Dark Was the Night* is not all sorrow; it is not a defeated moan, but one that in three days shall be redeemed. And what does this freedom sound like after such hard trials? Maybe like Coltrane's "Psalm"; or Johnson's vocal shifts on "Let Your Light Shine on Me"; or Jimi Hendrix painting "The Star-Spangled Banner" as emotion rather than mantra; or Richie Havens marrying "Poor Boy" and "Motherless Children" as if he was in a rhythmic ceremony to the Gods while chanting "Freedom" in glorious repeat; or perhaps it is like Creole and his bandmate Sonny on piano in James Baldwin's story where everything is shaken loose from your soul and allowed to express itself perfectly and at full speed like a prayer.

> He hit something in all of them, he hit something in me, myself, and the music tightened and deepened. . . . Creole began to tell us what the blues were all about. They were not about anything very new. He and his boys up there were keeping it new, at the risk of ruin, destruction, madness, and death, in order to find new ways for us to listen. For, the tale of how we suffer, and how we are delighted, and how we may triumph is never new, it always must be heard. There isn't any other tale to tell, it's the only light we got in all this darkness.[82]

Voyagers

Do you sense the Creator, World?
Seek Him above the canopy of stars![83]

In April of 1960, Alan Lomax, the Texas folklorist and ethnomusicologist, was on St. Simons Island, Georgia, recording the Georgia Sea Island Singers, a group who had preserved in their folk customs a way of life on the island extending back to slavery. Lomax inspired them to perform the song "Moses" when he asked group member John Davis if they knew the song "Go Down, Moses." Davis replied, scornfully:

"Why, everybody know that. Here's one everybody *don't* know." He looked
down. The silence gathered. Then he began to sing in a hoarse whisper. . . . His
text is full of the cryptic language of the freedom movement: Harriet Tubman
and other "conductors" on the Underground Railway were called Moses; the
chariot was a symbol of escape into heaven and at times of the Underground
Railway; horses running, the heavenly river rolling, and the angels moaning
presaged rebellion or war. . . . In no other song they sang was there so much
passionate assenting—groans and aha's from Peter's bass, cooing approval from
the tenor, moaning in the background when the angels were moaning.[84]

Lomax wrote those words in 1977 when he released the album *Georgia Sea
Island Songs*, which included the Singers' "Moses." It was the same year Lomax
would be recruited for a project for NASA led by Carl Sagan, the astronomer
and committee chair for the project, as they were preparing to launch a pair of
spacecraft to explore the larger planets of our solar system. On each craft, they
intended to include a long-playing phonograph record—a gold-plated copper
disc—containing sounds and images selected to portray the diversity of life and
culture on Earth. This wasn't the first time NASA had sent messages into orbit,
but the previous effort had included just information, so Sagan was excited at the
prospect to be able to send a message that transcended our advancement in technology and instead center in on what makes us truly human:

Our previous messages had contained information about what we perceive
and how we think. But there is much more to human beings than perceiving
and thinking. However, our emotional life is more difficult to communicate.
. . . Music, it seemed to me, was at least a credible attempt to convey human
emotions.[85]

Sagan wrote to Lomax that the record would have a "probable lifetime of
a billion years," likely outlasting the continents or any of humanity's artifacts.[86]
It was a similar vision Harry Smith had some twenty-five years earlier when he
arranged all the rough and true sounds of America together on the *Anthology of
American Folk Music* and united them all in the form of Fludd's celestial monochord, but now this would be Earth's music and our message to the cosmos.
Lomax agreed to assist and would end up contributing fifteen of the twenty-seven
musical selections that, along with 115 images, spoken greetings, and twelve minutes of audio labeled "The Sounds of Earth," are now known collectively as the
Voyager Golden Record.

"The Sounds of the Earth" section of the record begins with the auditory ful-fillment of the "Music of the Spheres," the sound of the cosmos as a choir united in perfect harmony from the earth to the fixed stars.[87] This is then followed by the sounds of our particular planet from nature (volcanoes, earthquakes, and thun-der) to our species (laughter, the human heartbeat, and a kiss). The music portion of the record ranged from Western classical selections like Bach's "Brandenburg Concerto No. 2 in F" and the "Queen of the Night aria, no. 14" from Mozart's opera *The Magic Flute*, to the world's folk music, which was mostly chosen by Lomax, including all four selections from the United States. There is percus-sion from Senegal, as well as "Tchakrulo," a Georgian (USSR) song of resistance against a feudal landlord, Chuck Berry's "Johnny B. Goode," Louis Armstrong and His Hot Seven's "Melancholy Blues," a Navajo Yeibichai dance recorded in 1942, and Blind Willie Johnson's "Dark Was the Night, Cold Was the Ground."[88]

Paired with Johnson's song, as the two final selections on the record, was Bee-thoven's "Cavatina," the slow movement, from his "String Quartet No. 13 in B flat, Opus 130." Beethoven composed the piece a year prior to his death through "sorrow and tears," according to his friend, the violinist Karl Holz, and the piece communicates its composer's anxiousness, fears, and fragility through the vio-lin in the same way Johnson's slide trembled alongside its composer's affecting moans.[89] Two voices longing to speak their shifting inner states but finding no words sufficient. They are two men, from two separate worlds, communicating with each other across time, sharing with different instruments their inner hes-itancy and struggle and ultimately the beauty of what it means to be human. Beethoven wrote into the score of this third movement the word *beklemmt*, trans-lating to "oppressed." It was this vibration, this fumbling for language when none is sufficient to truly express what is happening inside that is similar to Johnson's—his quavering slide and moans aiming for clarity and the perfect vocabulary for what was transpiring within. Their aim was not perfection in the typical sense, but that knowingness that our flaws and imperfections and vulnerability *is* what makes us perfect—to be broken and fragile yet resilient. For Beethoven it was the stretching, the reaching out of the violin for the courage and the right words to say, and for Johnson the route was the collective moan of his ancestors and the emotional vibration of what strictly lay between the notes.

For Sagan, these were the two songs—one from an artist who knew what it was like to see and had his sight taken from him, and one from an artist who had hearing and lost it—that were the deepest expression of our human vulnerabili-ties, of our love, of our trials, and our shifting inner states for which, most often, there are no words. That is why Sagan paired them together as the two final selec-tions on the record, writing, "For us they express a longing for contact with other beings in the depths of space, a musical expression of the principal message of the Voyager itself."[90]

::

Timothy Ferris, the producer of the Voyager record, wrote that Johnson's song, "Dark Was the Night," concerned "a situation he faced many times, nightfall with no place to sleep."[91] It was a similar theme invoked by Samuel Charters in *The Country Blues* when he described Johnson's sound as being filled with a "desolate sense of loneliness." Charters also invoked a similar theme on the first release of his research on Johnson in 1957 when he included on the cover of the album a sketch of an African American with eyes closed, his hand grasping his head and his face turned down and away from the viewer in grief. The illustrator also annotated the drawing with these words: "Loneliness is like cold black night—its shadows numb the mind—leaves a man an empty shell." While we can assume that Johnson did experience loneliness—as we all do—this is a weight not derived from Johnson's song, but one that is harnessed to him from the outside. This is a vision of Johnson that sees him as a poor creature, something to be pitied. But if we are to listen to "Dark Was the Night" or any of his recordings, we sense something quite the opposite of this portrayal. Instead, in another example of Beethoven's "Cavatina" and Johnson's "Dark Was the Night" being an ideal pairing, we have to look no further than what Ferris wrote of Beethoven's piece in the same pages he wrote about Johnson and see if the same sentences could not also apply to Johnson's "Dark Was the Night."

> Most listeners would agree that here Beethoven stirs deep emotions . . . but the question is, which emotion? Certainly it is sad. Beethoven wrote it at a heartbreaking time. . . . But sadness alone can't define the Cavatina. Strains of hope run through it as well, and something of the serenity of man who has endured suffering and come to terms with existence perceived without illusion.[92]

For Johnson this "existence perceived without illusion" was born out of his deep faith. It is what St. John of the Cross termed the Dark Night of the Soul, the journey through that Dark Night on its path toward divine union. And "faith, it keeps the lamp alight; in waiting and in expectation keeps the lamp alight," wrote Kierkegaard on the trials and balance of suffering and hope as sustenance for the believer.[93] Continuing, he wrote, "When worldly wisdom is capable of realizing goodness, Faith is not capable of seeing God; but when worldly wisdom cannot see a hand's breadth before it in the dark night of suffering, Faith can see God. For Faith sees best in the dark."[94] With this faith, there can be no true loneliness,

as the burden is light. It is the meaning of the balance of light and dark, of life and death, and the seemingly paradoxical vision of the cross, the extreme suffering of Christ with the loving presence of God. So it is Beethoven and Johnson and two songs—paired as part of possibly our last breath of communication, void of all human sociological separations, of spoken words—sent outward, to the unknown, to only be judged by our souls, through these artists; "the whole cosmos guided, ordered, and interpreted by the spirit of music."[95] It is where the morning stars sing together in harmony, and the monochord is tuned by God, and "[i]f struck in the spiritual part, [it] will give eternal life."[96]

Voyager 2 was launched August 20, 1977; Voyager 1 some two weeks later on September 5, 1977. Each is carrying our letter to the solar system.

On February 14, 1990, just as Voyager 1 was on the edge of the solar system, Sagan requested for the engineers at NASA to have the craft turn around and take a picture of Earth. The result was a vision of our planet almost as a grain of sand, of light, swallowed in the great expanse of space. Upon seeing this image, Sagan termed our planet a "Pale Blue Dot," of which he later wrote, similar to Johnson's ballads, a warning:

> Look again at that dot. That's here. That's home. That's us. . . . Our posturings, our imagined self-importance, the delusion that we have some privileged position in the Universe, are challenged by this point of blue light. Our planet is a lonely speck in the great enveloping cosmic dark. In our obscurity, in all this vastness, there is no hint that help will come from elsewhere to save us from ourselves.[97]

Figure 10. When the Morning Stars Sang Together, by William Blake. Pen and black ink, gray wash, and watercolor, over traces of graphite, 11 x 7 1/16 inches. Courtesy of The Morgan Library & Museum, New York.

EPILOGUE

Jubilee: The Story of the Beggar as Artist

> Some day, in the emergence from this fierce insight,
> let me sing jubilation and praise to assenting Angels.
> Let not a single one of the clearly-struck hammers of my heart
> deny me, through a slack, or a doubtful, or
> a broken string. Let my joyfully streaming face
> make me more radiant: let my secret weeping
> bear flower.
> —RAINER MARIA RILKE, *"Tenth Duino Elegy"*1

> Kyrie, eleison / "Lord, have mercy on us"
> —MATTHEW 20:30, *Greek translation*

Winslow Homer's painting *The Gulf Stream* depicts a man out in the violent waves of the ocean, his fishing boat battered, sharks encircling but his body relaxed; it is a man who is not looking for a way out of reality but to the beauty within, knowing he may never get out alive but remaining spiritually resolute and at ease in the turbulence, untethered but secure in himself and his journey. It is an image that stands in stark contrast to the figure drawn by Ernest York on the Folkways release in 1957. While York's drawing may signify a solitude or inner pain that has turned the physical frame inward toward desolation, the man at sea in Homer's work, while alone, is not lonely; his head is not down but confidently held up and turned not toward the ship in the distance that could signal a possible rescue, but confidently in the opposite direction, already knowing he has been saved. This is the image of the artist.

> *Some are Born to Sweet Delight,*
> *Some are Born to Endless Night.*2

Johnson's legacy should stand on the same high mountain as the world's greatest spiritual artists, with Dostoevsky, Beethoven, Coltrane, and Blake. We know this because of what we hear when we listen to him: a man possessed by a rebel heart and an all-encompassing prophetic vision, someone who, as Baldwin remarked, does "not so much follow [their] vision as find themselves driven by it."[3] We can hear in his voice that he was someone who "must submit [his] will and [his] understanding, not to anything that is, but to the exquisitest suggestion from the unknown that comes upon him."[4] It is a voice carried over from the days of the earliest spirituals of the slave preachers and men and women who labored away in the fields, who strained their voices to release not what was perfect, but what was true. And, in service of what needed to be said, they parted with words altogether and simply moaned and breathed out in exaltation. We can hear Johnson as he reminds us of all of these instruments: of the ancient moan, the antiphonal exchanges, the field hollers, and the line hymn. We lean our ear into him as he audibly exhaled "ahhh" on "Everybody Ought to Treat a Stranger Right," "Keep Your Lamp Trimmed and Burning," and others. But Johnson was not constrained to a period of time, for we hear him also incorporate these same devices into *his* time, through his guitar, which, like Lorca's, is ever weeping, or made to weep, not in sorrow but transcendence, like the songs of all the courageous rebels who walked before him. He straddled the line, through his slide, between East and West, between the unsaid and the unsayable; it is the sound of the soul that few artists have been capable of even daring to approach. And if what Zora Neale Hurston wrote is true, that, "all religious expression among Negroes is regarded as art," because "[t]he individual may hang as many new ornaments upon the traditional form as he likes," then Johnson's ability to assimilate a body of history into his work and perform the work with such original *feeling* must be the most sublime of all art.[5]

⁚⁚

In him we recognize the Black preacher as leader, as agitator, as prophet, who in another life may have been more like Nat Turner, but in his time was more in line with the spirit of Saint Paul after he was converted on the road to Damascus. For like Saint Paul, Johnson, likely through his own conversion, moved toward *becoming*, of individuation, through the transformative experience.[6] In this light, we also observe the revolutionary artist who took the sounds, imagery, and spirit of the Black preacher and was unafraid to link them to what many considered the devil's music. In this way, he compares to Blake who, through many of his own broadsides, sought to unify the material and spiritual worlds. And with Beethoven, he not only shares in the intensity of the emotional resonance of his work, but also in his steadfast resilience when faced with the permanent loss of one of his senses. "I will take fate by the throat; it shall not wholly overcome me," Beethoven wrote in defiance as he began to experience the loss of his hearing.[7] It was the same sort of inner resolve possessed by Dostoevsky when, after nearly being executed, but before being imprisoned in a Siberian labor camp, wrote to his brother: "Brother! I am not despondent and I haven't lost heart. Life is every-where, life is in ourselves, not outside."[8]

We can hear this inner defiance, this love, resounding in perfect equilibrium between the light and the dark, the heavy and the graceful, in Johnson's art. We can also see it when we observe how he reclaimed his name over the years: from Willie Johnson to "Blind" Willie Johnson to "Brother" Johnson and finally to Rev. W. J. Johnson, illustrating the assurance he had in himself, in defense of his humanity, to never be labeled as something other than what he chose for him-self. This in itself is an act of resistance, an act that Reverend King, in his letter penned in the Birmingham Jail, talked about when he mentioned "forever fight-ing a degenerating sense of 'nobodiness.'"[9]

> Hear the voice of the Bard!
> Who Present, Past, and Future sees
> Whose ears have heard,
> The Holy Word,
> That walk'd among the ancient trees.[10]

W. E. B. Du Bois, at the conclusion of *The Souls of Black Folk*, paid tribute to the stranger, to the traveler, the one who "girds himself, and sets his face toward the Morning, and goes his way," as the children stand in the sunshine singing:

> Let us cheer the weary traveler,
> Cheer the weary traveler,
> Let us cheer the weary traveler
> Along the heavenly way.
> I'll take my gospel trumpet,
> And I'll begin to blow,
> And if my Saviour helps me,
> I'll blow wherever I go.[11]

It is the sentiment of the faithful that does not fear death, but instead makes it a point to live, to *shout while I'm here*, to *sing while I'm here*. And what is it that gives sustenance to the wayfarer, the voyager along the way outside of the occasional cheer? It seems to be the same question posed by Johnson in "The Soul of a Man," one that can only be asked and then answered by the one who is inquiring simply because "every man shall bear his own burden" and everyone *must stand his trial in judgment for himself.* [12]

::

Certainly, at the heart of this quest lies the spirit fumbling its way toward the inner light that has the possibility of not only illuminating the sphere of mystery before the seeker, but also of becoming a flood for others to witness, giving proof that there is brilliance even in the darkest of night. Juan Mascaró, in his introduction to an anthology of religious writings, wrote of the itinerant wanderer as they progress toward this:

> Some shine more and some shine less, but they all merge into that vast lamp called by St John of the Cross "the lamp of the being of God." In the limitations of space and time, the soul of man longs for liberty. Here we are in this vast universe, and we do not know what we are, and we do not know what the universe is. Hence the prayer of man for light, his perpetual struggle to learn a little more in the days of his pilgrimage, and his endeavour to hand over the torch of his visions from generation to generation. [13]

And remarking on the separation of the man of the mind and the spirit of the poet, Mascaró wrote:

> The seer and the poet help us in our wanderings towards light, and the thinker gives us theories on the visions the seer has seen. But in these passages we have not theories: we have living words. "He that hath ears to hear, let him hear." . . . In his wanderings towards the Infinite, in the struggle of man for the Highest, there are moments when the spirit of man is filled with the overwhelming joy of an inner vision, the sense of an inner victory. Then he knows that he cannot know with the mind what can only be seen by the spirit, and the words of these lamps of fire become faith, these words in truth become life. [14]

It is this light, springing from nowhere else but inside the traveler, that then becomes transformative; the seeker begins to embody the divine power and become a self, truly free. This may, in truth, be the grand Jubilee, the lived truth, appearing so powerful as to not even be extinguished even in eternity; the spirit breathing fresh life into all who are ready to move; their souls constantly reborn in those who discover their work, proof that death is not the end.

You got to cross that River Jordan,
You got to cross it for yourself.

J. W. Johnson, who paid respect to the "black and unknown bards," and who knew the importance of the leaders of singing and makers of song, understood well the plight of the stranger as they made their way in the weary land Du Bois spoke of. That is why he composed an anthem to guide them on their way toward freedom in this life, which could, itself, be the true fulfillment of the Reverend Willie Johnson's life of song.

Lift every voice and sing,
'Til earth and heaven ring,
Ring with the harmonies of Liberty;
Let our rejoicing rise
High as the skies,
Let it resound loud as the rolling sea.
Sing a song full of the faith that the dark past has taught us,
Sing a song full of the hope that the present has brought us;
Facing the rising sun of our new day begun,
Let us march on 'til victory is won.

It is a hymn for a new generation that mirrors the attitude of the rousing Baptist song of resilience, "Take Your Stand," a version of which was recorded by "Blind" Willie Johnson in 1929, and was, fittingly, the last record of Johnson's music released by Columbia. In it, this maker of songs and leader of singing, was not disheartened as he prepared to take temporary leave of loved ones. Defined by the inner strength and light, Johnson urged those who he may leave behind to not be weary, to live with joy, and in the face of death, take a stand:

Take my hand, take my hand,
If I never see you anymore.
Take my hand, take my hand,
I will meet you on the kingdom's shore.
Sing a song, sing a song
If I never ever see you anymore.
Sing a song, sing a song
I will meet you on the kingdom's shore.
Pray for me, pray for me, pray for me
If I never never see you anymore.

If I may, pray for me, pray for me
I'll meet you on the kingdom's shore.
Tell the truth, tell the truth, tell the truth
If I never never see you anymore.
Tell the truth, tell the truth, tell the truth
I'll meet you on the kingdom's shore.
Take a stand, take a stand, take a stand
If I never ever see you anymore.
Take a stand, take a stand, take a stand
I'll meet you on the kingdom's shore.

W. E. B. Du Bois, writing on the discovery of forgotten Black artists, said that when the recognition comes, "then let the world discover . . . that their art is as new as it is old and as old as new." He compared it to rediscovering the stars that illuminate the heavens, stars that have been lost when "suddenly out of the blackness they looked up and there loomed the heavens; and what was it that they said? They raised a mighty cry: 'It is the stars, it is the ancient stars, it is the young and everlasting stars!'"[15]

When you get down to Jordan
Ask the Ferryman, hired there, to cross.[16]

It is here, under the stars and in the roll of the river, where the pilgrim, like the figure in Homer's painting, still rests in his boat of splinters drifting over the tempestuous sea, God moving him over the face of the waters; this rebel, this artist who is not defined by the battered condition of the boat but by some light that only he can see—somewhere, among the constellations. There is no other guide but the ancestors, whose spirits still sing, now bonded in the present, alive—ever journeying forward; creating and re-creating the tales of the wild wonders, the ageless mysteries of mankind under heaven as we stumble through—our greed, our corruption, our sorrows. Always pushing, knowing some had made it—their way in the dark. Like ripples. Always dancing. Like Blake, like Goya, like Beethoven, like the desert blues of the Tuareg, and the shouts from those storefront saints, and those moaners every Sunday in Amen Corner. The persistent rebels continue to transmute suffering into beauty; their spirits spinning, drifting. Beneath the Southern Cross.

Like Coltrane.
Like Willie Johnson.
Like the hum of the soul.

NOTES

Introduction

1. D. H. Lawrence, "Art and Morality," *Calendar of Modern Letters*, November 1925.

2. Johnson's death certificate was finally looked at during this period, and while it provided a concrete date of death, it seemed to produce more questions than answers. The point is that, up until the late 1970s, only two serious trips were conducted to inquire about Johnson's life.

3. Angelina Johnson, interview by Samuel Charters, 1955, recording, Samuel and Ann Charters Archives of Blues and Vernacular African American Musical Culture, Archives & Special Collections at the Thomas J. Dodd Research Center, University of Connecticut Libraries, Storrs, CT. From this interview with Angelina, Folkways would end up releasing an edited version cut with Charters's narrative in 1957. The issue with this is that the edited version as well as subsequent publications by Charters make no mention of the fact that what one is hearing or reading is not all he had recorded. Although one may expect that audio would be edited, Charters never mentioned it and made no reference to how long the original audio was or even a note referring to the actual content of the missing audio, or how he reconciled the story around contradictory statements.

The issue with this is that more information that could have been researched or debated was in existence, but not in the public domain. Charters also inserted dates that were never spoken by anyone, and he even changed dates that he felt didn't match a cohesive narrative. These included Johnson's death date as 1949 when Angelina said that he passed away in 1941. He also changed the year of her marriage to Johnson to 1927 when she told him they were wed in 1922, and he conveniently cut the audio before she said the year. Angelina also stated that Johnson was from Temple and his father was Dock Johnson, but Charters went with Marlin as his birthplace for one publication—later revised to moving to Marlin as a baby in the Columbia 1993 release—and Temple for another. He also stated that his father was George, choosing Adam Booker's recollection over Angelina's. Early on, he also assumed that Angelina was the one who sang on the records with Johnson, but we would later know that it was Willie B. Harris. And while it is true that Angelina's memory of dates was vastly off, the inaccuracies that were printed generated much speculation that would only be sorted out decades later. It is a tricky thing for someone like me looking at this because it is evident that some truth was sacrificed for a narrative. Truth that was never corrected. In 2010, when Michael Hall was writing a story about Johnson that included my biographical findings, he contacted Charters by email telling him that I had found the name Dock, but when Charters responded he offered no response to the name Dock. Charters would write in the 1993 Columbia release that "Everything that happened [after Johnson]—[Charters's] books, articles, recordings" was because of Johnson. It was Charters's first expedition of true field work, and certainly mistakes can be forgiven, especially for those earlier releases. But I do think, at some point, as more people came to love Johnson's music and write about him, he should have taken a second look at the first discovery.

4. This was amended by Charters when he wrote the liner notes for the 1993 Sony release of Johnson's recordings.

5. I had to come to this conclusion the hard way. Samuel Charters, in his 1957 liner notes to *Blind Willie Johnson: His Story Told, Annotated, and Documented*, wrote that Johnson was born outside of Temple. Then, in his 1959 book, *The Country Blues*, he stated that Johnson was born near Marlin. This created issues, as many future writers on Johnson would write either one or the other depending on which source they were using. Then, the location changed once again after Johnson's death certificate was discovered and placed his location of birth at Independence, Texas. It really took proving that a draft card that belonged to a blind Willie Johnson living in Houston in 1918 was, in fact, the musician "Blind" Willie Johnson. In 2010, when I was researching where Johnson was buried, I began investigating if the Willie Johnson on the draft card was "Blind" Willie Johnson. The key pieces of information came from two Temple city directories linking two known family members (Carl and Robert) to a musician named Johnson in Temple. Both had the same father listed on their draft documents. But I still did not have a mother's name (previously cited as Mary Fields on Johnson's death certificate) until I located death certificates of Johnson's brother (Carl) and his sister (Jettie) proving that Johnson's mother was Mary King. The only way one can arrive at the King name is by piecing this trail together through research, as there is no document that lists her name directly associated with the musician "Blind" Willie Johnson. This information was first printed in December of the same year the research was conducted; see Michael Hall, "The Soul of a Man," *Texas Monthly*, December 2010.

In this case, since we would be using the draft card for Johnson's correct information, the date of birth would also be changed from Angelina's death certificate date of January 22 to a few days later on January 25. For more on that and the family research, see Shane Ford, *Shine a Light: My Year with "Blind" Willie Johnson* (Morrisville, North Carolina: Lulu Press 2011).

But still, as of this writing, this information is still often overlooked, attributed incorrectly, or dismissed. For example, as of this writing in March 2020, and with the benefit of verifiable fact-checking, an article on Johnson was posted on the Document Records website with incorrect basic biographical information including dates, place of birth, and where he was raised. I am only pointing out this specific incident as it was recent. But these sorts of inaccuracies are the norm and not the exception. It is one of the reasons for writing this book.

6. Angelina Johnson, interview.

7. For the Marlin house misinformation, see Michael Corcoran, "He Left a massive Imprint on the Blues, But Little is Known About Blind Willie Johnson," *Austin American-Statesman*, September 28, 2003. Regarding the "false bass," Michael Corcoran, in an interview with Gary Burnett, even refers to Johnson's deep tone as a "gimmick"; see Gary Burnett, "Texas Musical Pioneers: The Legacy of Blind Willie Johnson," *Down at the Crossroads*, May 31, 2019. https://downatthecrossroads.wordpress.com/2019/05/31/texas-musical-pioneers-the-legacy-of-blind-willie-johnson/.

8. Johnson was buried in Blanchette Cemetery in Beaumont in 1945, but for many years

it remained just one of a conglomeration of African American cemeteries in a section of Beaumont, unlisted, unmarked, and unnamed. Anna Obek and I relocated this cemetery in 2009.

9. Dorothy Scarborough, assisted by Ola Lee Gulledge. *On the Trail of Negro Folk-Songs*. (Cambridge, MA: Harvard University Press, 1925), 74–75.

10. Alphonso Smith, "Ballads Surviving in The United States," *The Musical Quarterly*, Volume II, Issue 1 (January 1916): 113.

11. "St. James Infirmary" is derived from the broadside ballad "The Unfortunate Rake" while "The Gallows Pole" has its roots in "The Maid Freed from the Gallows" from Francis James Child's compilation of popular English and Scottish ballads in the late 1800s. This is also a perfect example of a song that became a perfect song for Black Americans in the South—although they more than likely never saw the song written down—as they tried to stay one step ahead of the state and the for-profit prison farms, not to mention the lynch mobs and any accusation that could very well end their life on just such a pole or tree.

12. Of course, there were exceptions, but most of the performers recorded in the late 1920s were lucky to record more than a few sides at one session and most often the pay was royalty free. In a 1962 interview, Frank Walker, the talent scout who recorded Johnson, compared most of the performers' point of view on the opportunity to record to "the next thing to being President of the United States in their mind." See Walker, Frank, 1962, interview, Mike Seeger Collection, University of North Carolina Chapel Hill.

13. *Andrei Tarkovsky: A Poet in the Cinema*, directed by Donatella Baglivo, 1983.

14. Saint John of the Cross, *The Dark Night of the Soul*, ed. Benedict Zimmerman. 4th ed. (London: Thomas Baker, 1916), 199.

15. Saint John of the Cross, *The Dark Night*, 108.

16. William Blake, *The Complete Poetry and Prose of William Blake*, eds. Harold Bloom and David V. Erdman (New York: Doubleday, 1988). In 2010, when finalizing the cenotaph for Johnson, I used Blake's grave marker as a model for the inscription. Like Johnson, Blake's exact burial location was unknown. Since 2010, the actual location of Blake's burial site has been located and a new memorial installed.

17. LeRoi Jones, *Blues People* (New York: William Morrow and Company, 1963), 55.

18. Leo Tolstoy, *"The Kingdom of God is Within You": Christianity Not as a Mystic Religion But as a New Theory of Life.* (United Kingdom: William Heinemann, 1894) 40.

19. The *Crisis*, Vol. 32, October 1926, 290–297. Du Bois, speaking at the NAACP conference about Black artists in 1926, said "It is not simply the great tenor of Roland Hayes that opened the ears of America. We have had many voices of all kinds as fine as his and America was and is as deaf as she was for years to him."

Prologue: Dark Was the Night

1. Blake, *The Complete Poetry and Prose*, 17.

2. Barbara Ann Holmes, *Joy Unspeakable: Contemplative Practices of the Black Church* (Minneapolis, MN: Fortress Press, 2017), 73.

3. Harold Courlander, *Negro Folk Music U.S.A.* (New York: Columbia University Press, 1966), 25.

4. Lead Belly, *Lead Belly: The Smithsonian Folkways Collection*. Produced and liner notes by Jeff Place. Smithsonian Folkways Recordings, SFW40201, 2015.

5. Blind Willie McTell, *Blind Willie McTell—Complete 1940 Library of Congress Recordings*. Recorded November 5, 1940, in Atlanta, Georgia.

6. John Wesley Work, *Folk Song of the American Negro* (Nashville, TN: F. A. McKenzie, 1915).

7. Jones, *Blues People*, 26–27.

8. John G. Van Deusen, *The Black Man in White America* (Washington, DC: Associated Publishers, 1938), 230.

9. DuBois, W. E. Burghardt. *The Souls of Black Folk* (Chicago: A. C. McClurg & Co., 1903).

10. Frederick Douglass, *Narrative of the Life of Frederick Douglass, an American Slave* (Boston, MA: Published at the Anti-slavery Office., 1846), 14.

11. Jones, *Blues People*, 26.

12. Courlander, *Negro Folk Music*, 23.

13. James Wentoworth Leigh, *Other Days* (New York: Macmillan, 1921), 156.

14. *Negro Work Songs and Calls*, The Library of Congress Archive of Folk Culture, Rounder Records, CD 1517, 1993.

15. Courlander, *Negro Folk Music*, 140.

16. Frederick Law Olmsted, *A Journey in the Seaboard Slave States with Remarks on Their Economy* (New York: Dix and Edwards, 1856), 394.

17. Courlander, *Negro Folk Music*, 140.

18. Alan Lomax, *The Rainbow Sign* (New York: Duell, Sloan and Pearce, 1959), 21–22.

19. Courlander, *Negro Folk Music*, 141–143. A few more remarkable renditions of "Black Woman" were recorded by folklorists David Evans and George Mitchell, respectively, when they recorded Othar Turner in Mississippi in the late 1960s. Turner, mostly revered for his fife and drum performances, recorded the song both a cappella and with guitar. When Harold Courlander recorded Rich Amerson for Folkways, Amerson sang a version of "Black Woman" that no doubt was the basis for Hall's. The most moving of the recorded versions of the field holler though may be those of Annie Grace Horn Dodson, who sang an example of "Field Calls" when she recorded "Father's Field Call" a rendition of a call her father would use when calling her mother to the fields to work, along with a children's call and a greeting call. See *Negro Folk Music of Alabama, Vol. 1: Secular Music*. Recorded by Harold Courlander, Folkways Records, FW04417, 1951.

20. The result of the ban on the use of the drum was a radical cultural theft for the African in America and the beginning of new forms of communication that would replace the stolen rhythm. The drums in Africa are the center of making music, ritual, and dance. The talking drum itself, constructed by tightening the skin around it to increase tension, was able to mimic the change in pitch of speech, thus giving it its name. But slavery did not put an end to percussion; new ways were constructed to provide rhythm including by "patting juba" or "hambone"—using the body as the drum by stomping, hand clapping, and thigh slapping. But the "talking" instruments would also later return, most notably in the guitar in the early 1900s.

21. Davis J. McCord, *The Statutes at Large of South Carolina*, vol. seven (Columbia, SC: A. S. Johnston, 1840), 410.

22. Robert B. Winans "Black Instrumental Music Traditions in the Ex-Slave Narratives." *Black Music Research Journal* 10, no. 1 (1990): 43–53. Accessed June 11, 2020.

23. Solomon Northup, *Twelve Years a Slave* (Bedford, MA: Applewood Books, 2008) 24, 217. One such documented instance is that of Solomon Northup, who was kidnapped and sold into slavery in 1841 and was rescued from a cotton plantation near the Red River in Louisiana. In his account of his captivity, he described his fiddle playing as "notorious" and confessed that "if it had not been for my beloved violin, I scarcely can conceive how I could have endured the long years of bondage."

24. Northrup, *Twelve Years*, 217.

25. Reed Parker, "The Instrument with a Fascinating Past—The Banjo" *History Is Now Magazine*, August 23, 2015, http://www.historyisnowmagazine.com/blog/2015/8/23/the-instrument-with-a-fascinating-past-the-banjo.

26. John P. Kennedy, *Swallow Barn* (New York: G. P. Putnam & Co., 1872), 101–103.

27. Jason Lee Oakes, "The Banjo at the Crossroads: Smithsonian Year of Music Object of the Day, August 27," *Smithsonian Music*, September 9, 2019, https://music.si.edu/story/banjo-crossroads-smithsonian-year-music-object-day-august-27.

28. Garnett Andrews, *Reminiscences of an Old Georgia Lawyer*, ed. S. Kittrell Rushing (Knoxville: University of Tennessee Press, 2009), 8–9.

29. *Federal Writers' Project: Slave Narrative Project, Vol. 1, Alabama, Aarons-Young*. 1937. Manuscript/Mixed Material. https://www.loc.gov/item/mesn010/.

30. Du Bois, *The Souls of Black Folk*, 190.

31. Nicholas May, "Holy Rebellion: Religious Assembly Laws in Antebellum South Carolina and Virginia." *The American Journal of Legal History* 49, no. 3 (2007): 237.

32. Nat Turner and Thomas R. Gray, *The Confessions of Nat Turner: the Leader of the Late Insurrection in Southampton, VA* (Baltimore, MD: Lucas and Deaver, 1831), 8–9.

33. Turner and Gray, *The Confessions*, 8–9.

34. Turner and Gray, *The Confessions*, 11.

35. Turner and Gray, *The Confessions*, 11.

36. Thomas Wentworth Higginson, "Nat Turner's Insurrection," *The Atlantic*, August 21, 2018, https://www.theatlantic.com/magazine/archive/1861/08/nat-turners-insurrection/308736/.

37. Higginson, "Nat Turner's Insurrection." These are the words of Charity Bowery quoted by Higginson in the 1861 *Atlantic* article.

38. William Frances Allen, Charles Pickard Ware, and Lucy McKim, eds. *Slave Songs of the United States* (New York: A. Simpson & Co, 1867), 89. This is one of the most cited songs as remembered in many slave narratives, which is telling for all the reasons one could imagine. But it is also a song that would be changed and rearranged as the years went by, as the theme of running was a constant in Black folklore and song. For just a few examples see versions performed by Mance Lipscomb ("Run, Sinner, Run"), Nina Simone ("Sinnerman"), and "Blind" Willie Johnson ("I'm Gonna Run to the City of Refuge").

39. Jones, *Blues People*, 46. The physical movement of the body was most often in the participation in the "ring shout," a form of worship that involved the hambone style of rhythm generated by the dancers clapping and stomping as they moved in a circular pattern either in a church or outdoors. This form of worship is a celebration of bodies, which can be contrasted with the moan in a more contemplative section of the service.

40. Peter Randolph, *From Slave Cabin to the Pulpit* (Boston: J. H. Earle, 1893), 202–203.

41. *Federal Writers' Project: Slave Narrative Project, Vol. 16, Texas, Part 2, Easter-King*. 1936. Manuscript/Mixed Material. https://www.loc.gov/item/mesn162/.

42. Clifton H. Johnson, ed., *God Struck Me Dead: Religious Conversion and Autobiographies of Ex-Slaves* (Nashville, TN: Fisk University Social Science Institute, 1945), 45.

43. Allen, Ware, and Garrison, *Slave Songs of the United States*, v, vi.

44. Allen, Ware, and Garrison, *Slave Songs of the United States*, v.

45. William T. Dargan, *Lining Out the Word: Dr. Watts Hymn Singing in the Music of Black Americans* (Berkeley: University of California Press, 2006), 4.

46. Dargan, *Lining Out the Word*, 26.

47. William St. Clair Gordon, *Recollections of the Old Quarter* (Lynchburg, VA: Moose Brothers, 1902), 109–110.

48. Gordon, *Recollections of the Old Quarter*, 110

49. Gordon, *Recollections of the Old Quarter*, 111.

50. Du Bois, *The Souls of Black Folk*, 251.

51. Jones, *Blues People*, 41.

52. James H. Cone, *The Spirituals and the Blues: an Interpretation*. (Maryknoll, NY: Orbis Books, 1992), 29.

53. There are numerous spirituals that serve to subvert coercion on the plantation, function as resistance, and veil meanings. Some include "Wade in the Water," "O Rocks Don't Fall on Me," and "My Father, How Long."

54. Lawrence W. Levine, *Black Culture and Black Consciousness: Afro-American Folk Thought from Slavery to Freedom* (Oxford: Oxford University Press, 2007), 51.

55. Levine, *Black Culture*, 50.

56. Carol V. R. George, *Segregated Sabbaths: Richard Allen and the Emergence of Independent Black Churches 1760–1840* (New York: Oxford University Press, 1973).

57. As in the case of "Ol' Tom," a slave on a plantation in Fayette County, Texas, who was both a preacher and musician. See George P. Rawick, *The American Slave: A Composite Autobiography: Supplement, Series 2*, (Westport, CT: Greenwood Press, 1979), 2111. Accessed March 29, 2021, on the Baylor University Texas Collections website, https://digitalcollections-baylor.quartexcollections.com/Documents/Detail/the-american-slave-a-composite-autobiography-supplement-series-2/840265?item=840275.

58. Rawick, *The American Slave*, 45–46.

59. James Weldon Johnson and J. Rosamond Johnson, *The Books of American Negro Spirituals* (New York: Viking Press, 1969), 29.

60. Du Bois, *The Souls of Black Folk*, 261.

61. Cone, *The Spirituals and the Blues*, 56.

62. Work, *Folk Song of the American Negro*, 19.

63. Rich Amerson, "When You Feel Like Moaning," on *Negro Folk Music of Alabama, Vol. 1: Secular Music*, Recorded by Harold Courlander, Folkways Records, FW04417, 1951.

64. Cone, *The Spirituals and the Blues*, 48–49.

65. Viktor E. Frankl, *Man's Search for Meaning* (New York, NY: Pocket Book, 1963), 59.

66. Andrei Tarkovsky, *Sculpting in Time: Reflections on the Cinema*, trans. Kitty Hunter-Blair (New York, NY: Knopf, 1987), 41.

67. Cone, *The Spirituals and the Blues*, 61.

68. Ralph Waldo Emerson, "Experience," in *Essays and Poems by Ralph Waldo Emerson*, (New York: Barnes and Noble Classics, 2004): 251–52.

69. Cone, *The Spirituals and the Blues*, 49.

70. Cone, *The Spirituals and the Blues*, 47.

71. This song has several variants including "He Never Said a Mumbalin' Word," "Crucifixion," and "Easter."

72. Lawrence W. Levine, *Black Culture and Black Consciousness: Afro-American Folk Thought from Slavery to Freedom* (Oxford: Oxford University Press, 2007), 33–34.

73. Emily Hallowell, *Calhoun Plantation Songs, Second Edition*. (Boston: C. W. Thompson Co., 1907).

Tell 'Em I'm Gone

1. Mark Twain, Lin Salamo, and Harriet Elinor Smith. *Mark Twain's Letters 1872–1873*. (Berkeley: University of California Press, 1997), 315.

2. There are also criticisms of the way many of the songs were performed by the singers of Fisk under George L. White, the university's treasurer and vocal instructor, who also traveled with The Singers. John Wesley Work II, who would later direct The Singers, described some of the early training as a "smoothing down of their voice." For Work, though, it was not a disparagement. He recognized that it was White who kept his faith against protest from some parents of the group's members who felt that the world was "not worthy" of the songs, and that the world would be as moved as he was from what he heard. He actually credited White's training for maintaining the songs "reverential" and "serious" nature in the face of popularizing them for entertainment purposes. See: Work, *Folk Song of the American Negro*, 104.

3. General Orders, No. 3. US House, 54th Cong., 1st sess. H. Doc. 369, pt. 2 (1896). "General Order Number 3." US Documents Collection. Y 1.1/2: SERIAL 3437.

4. *The Galveston Daily News* , July 7, 1865, p. 1; Claude Elliott, "The Freedmen's Bureau in Texas," *The Southwestern Historical Quarterly* 56, no. 1 (1952): 1–24.

5. William E. Strong to Major General O. O. Howard, January 1, 1866, in US Congress, Senate, *Message from the President of the United States, Communicating, in Compliance with a Resolution of the Senate of the 27th of February Last, a Communication from the Secretary of War, Together with the Reports of the Assistant Commissioners of the Freedmen's Bureau Made since December 1, 1865*, Senate Executive Documents, 39th Cong., 1st sess., no. 27, serial 1238, 81–86.

6. Disobedience was defined as: "Failing to obey reasonable orders, neglect of duty, leaving home without permission, impudence, swearing or indecent language to, or in the presence of the employer, his family or agent, or quarrelling and fighting with one another. . . . For any disobedience, a fine of one dollar shall be imposed on, and paid by the offender." In addition, the laws regulated the behavior of the freedmen: "It is the duty of this class of laborers to be especially civil and polite to their employer, his family and guests, and they shall receive gentle and kind treatment."

7. Hans Peter Mareus Neilsen Gammel. *The Laws of Texas, 1822–1897 Volume 5* (Austin: The Gammel Book Company, 1898), https://texashistory.unt.edu/ark:/67531/metapth6727/, accessed August 26, 2020, University of North Texas Libraries, The Portal to Texas History.

8. *Journal of the Reconstruction Convention, Which Met at Austin, Texas, Dec. 7, A. D. 1868* volume 2. (Austin: Tracy, Seimering, and Co. Printers, State Journal Office, 1870), 111.

9. Barbara Leah Clayton, "The Lone Star Conspiracy: Racial Violence and the Ku Klux Klan Terror in Post-Civil War Texas, 1865–1877⊠ (master's thesis, Oklahoma State University, 1979), iv.

10. *Journal of the Reconstruction Convention (1868–1869),* 111.

11. Springfield, now a ghost town, was the Limestone County seat beginning in 1847 but, like Eutaw, was bypassed by the H&TC, and after the courthouse burned, the county seat was shifted a few miles south to Groesbeck.

12. James Smallwood, Barry A. Crouch, and Larry Peacock. *Murder and Mayhem: The War of Reconstruction in Texas.* (College Station: Texas A&M University Press, 2003), 121.

13. US Census of Bosque County, 1870. It's very possible that Dock and Ellen, while in Valley Mills, became a part of an all-Black community being formed in Rock Springs just a few miles from Valley Mills proper. The freedom community was founded by former slave and preacher James B. Sadler who, by 1878, bought land in the area to build a school and later the Cumberland Presbyterian Church. Two of Dock's daughters were buried here years later: Amanda, who died in 1929 and was born in the early 1870s, and Sarah, who died in 1941.

14. William C Pool, *The History of Bosque County, Texas* (San Marcos, TX: San Marcos Record Press, 1954), 51.

15. John A. Lomax, *Adventures of a Ballad Hunter* (Austin: University of Texas Press, 2017), 11.

16. In the 2017 printing of Lomax's autobiography, the forward mentioned that Lomax may have borrowed from *The Adventures of Huckleberry Finn* in his descriptions of his friend Blythe. This may be true, especially in his descriptions of a young John (half Nat's age) being the one who taught Blythe to read, etc. As much as I searched, I could find no reference to Nat Blythe in census documents, but I did finally find who Colonel Blythe was, and it seems unlikely that Nat would be a made-up figure altogether, which leads me to believe that, although there may be some myth mixed with truth, Nat himself was a real person.

17. James Miller Guinn, *Historical and Biographical Record of Southern California* (Chicago, IL: Chapman Publishing Co., 1902), 1136–37.

18. Lomax, *Adventures of a Ballad Hunter,* 9.

19. Lomax, *Adventures of a Ballad Hunter,* 9.

20. Lomax, *Adventures of a Ballad Hunter*, 10.

21. Lynching in Texas Staff, "Lynching of Ed Sayles," *Lynching in Texas* website, accessed August 13, 2024, https://lynchingintexas.org/items/show/222.

22. *St. Paul Globe*, July 12, 1886.

Interlude 1: Keep Your Lamp Trimmed and Burning

1. Mary Dickson Arrowood and Thomas Hoffman Hamilton, "Nine Negro Spirituals, 1850–61, from Lower South Carolina," *The Journal of American Folklore* 41, no. 162 (1928): 579–84. https://doi.org/10.2307/535022.

2. Thomas Wentworth Higginson, "Army Life in a Black Regiment," 1869, Project Gutenberg, March 23, 2009. Accessed December 18, 2019. https://www.gutenberg.org/files/6764/6764-h/6764-h.htm#link2HCH0009.

3. Gustavus D. Pike, *The Singing Campaign for Ten Thousand Pounds: Or the Jubilee Singers in Great Britain* (New York, NY: American Missionary Association, 1875), 272.

Blind Man Sat in the Way and Cried: The Preacher and the Song Leader

1. Paul Oliver, Mack McCormick, Alan B. Govenar, and Kip Lornell, *The Blues Come to Texas: Paul Oliver and Mack McCormick's Unfinished Book* (College Station: Texas A&M University Press, 2019), 314.

2. Johnson, *God Struck Me Dead*, 45.

3. Johnson, *God Struck Me Dead*, 45.

4. Karen O'Dell Bullock, "Journey to Galveston and Houston: Oldest black Baptist churches in Texas," *Baptist Standard*, July 27, 2016. Accessed September 17, 2020. https://www.baptiststandard.com/news/texas/journey-to-galveston-and-houston-oldest-black-baptist-churches-in-texas.

5. DuBois, *The Souls of Black Folk*, 191.

6. *Fort Worth Gazette*, August 15, 1890. Nicknames were also popular among the old-time Black preachers.

7. *San Antonio Express*, 1908. There are countless newspaper articles of Griffin's sermons as he was a much in-demand and celebrated preacher and attracted massive crowds up until his legal troubles.

8. *Fort Worth Gazette*, August 15, 1890.

9. Change is larger, but his time at Central State Farm resulted in nicknaming Huddie Ledbetter as "Leadbelly." See Charles K. Wolfe and Kip Lornell, *The Life and Legend of Leadbelly* (New York: HarperCollins Publishers, 1992), 32.

10. James Weldon Johnson and J. Rosamond Johnson, *The Books of American Negro Spirituals* (New York: Viking Press, 1969), Book One, 21–22.

11. Johnson and Johnson, *The Books of American Negro Spirituals*, 22.

12. Johnson and Johnson, *The Books of American Negro Spirituals*, 22.

13. Johnson and Johnson, *The Books of American Negro Spirituals*, 23.

14. It's very possible, although she did not mention the pastor of the church in her writ-

ings, that the preacher was Arthur Armstead (A. A.) Gundy, who would record for Columbia Records in 1929, and the church that Bales walked into was New Elam Baptist where Gundy preached in the late 1920s. See Mary Virginia Bales, "Some Negro Folk-Songs of Texas," in *Follow De Drinkin' Gou'd*, edited by J. Frank Dobie. Austin: Texas Folklore Society (1928): 85–112, 88.

15. Bales, "Some Negro Folk-Songs of Texas," 89.

16. Bales, "Some Negro Folk-Songs of Texas," 89.

17. There are numerous papers, including quite a few from the *Dallas Express* (many listed in these notes) that chronicle Butler's extensive travels and name. "Jubilee" was a term derived from the Fisk Jubilee Singers and was used to describe a cappella religious music prior to the word "gospel" being introduced; it would later evolve into the quartet style. Most often the term jubilee was used in the public sphere while the term "sanctified" was preferred in private. There were many newspapers that described Butler as a jubilee singer. For one example, see the *Weekly Advocate* (Victoria, Texas), September 9, 1911.

18. *Houston Post*, July 8, 1915.

19. *Houston Daily Post*, July 9, 1917.

20. *Houston Post*, July 8, 1915.

21. William T. Dargan, *Lining Out the Word: Dr. Watts Hymn Singing in the Music of Black Americans* (Berkeley: University of California Press, 2006), 23. The hymns most often lined-out are few, but some of the more prominent ones include "Amazing Grace," "I Love the Lord, He Heard My Cries," "Father, I Stretch My Hands to Thee," and "A Charge to Keep I Have."

22. Many Black preachers were recorded in the late 1920s because of their popularity among the African American buying public. Some of the best examples of what the congregations would have experienced were Rev. J. C. Burnett, Rev. J. M. Gates, and Rev. A. W. Nix, among many others. While these recordings can provide a sense of what it may have felt like to be a witness to the sermon, keep in mind that time limitations on recordings resulted in truncated versions of a typical sermon, thus nothing, of course, would take the place of actually experiencing a service in person.

23. *Dallas Express*, August 23, 1924.

24. *Dallas Express*, January 15, 1921.

25. *Palestine Daily Herald*, September 10, 1910.

26. Emancipation Park in Houston was the site for many yearly celebrations of Juneteenth. The land was purchased, in part, by Rev. Jack Yates of the Antioch Baptist Church in 1872 for just this purpose.

27. *Houston Daily Post*, June 19, 1911.

28. McCormick and Oliver, *The Blues Come to Texas*, 314.

29. *Weekly Advocate*, September 9, 1911

30. *Dallas Express*, May 1, 1920, and *The Dallas Express*, January 7, 1922.

31. *Kansas City Sun*, June 2, 1917.

32. McCormick and Oliver, *The Blues Come to Texas*, 314–15. Mack McCormick states in *The Blues Come to Texas* that "some residents of Hearne recall him occasionally playing guitar or piano, . . . [but] he seldom used an accompaniment."

33. One of their houses, maybe their only one at the time, caught fire in 1916. The local paper, *The Hearne Democrat*, bemoaned the fact the house was, most likely, a total loss and that Black citizens could not purchase home insurance at the time. See *The Hearne Democrat*, September 1, 1916.

34. McCormick and Oliver, *The Blues Come to Texas*, 315.

35. Scarborough, *On the Trail of Negro Folk-Songs*, 75.

36. Madkin Butler biography card, James Avery Lomax Family Papers, 3D178, Folder 6 1842, 1853–1986, Dolph Briscoe Center for American History, University of Texas at Austin.

37. McCormick and Oliver, *The Blues Come to Texas*, 315.

38. McCormick and Oliver, *The Blues Come to Texas*, 315. Also see in this text under the song titles for more information on the origins of the Titanic ballad.

39. For the additional ballad sheets, see James Avery Lomax Family Papers, 3D178, Folder 6.

40. C. Michael Hawn, "History of Hymns: 'Pass Me Not, O Gentle Savior,'" June 14, 2013. https://www.umcdiscipleship.org/resources/history-of-hymns-pass-me-not-o-gentle-savior. For the original hymn, see W. Howard Doane, *Songs of Devotion for Christian Associations: A Collection of Psalms, Hymns, and Spiritual Songs with Music: for Church Service, Prayer and Conference Meetings, Religious Conventions, and Family Worship* (New York: Biglow & Main, 1870), 39.

41. McCormick and Oliver, *The Blues Come to Texas*, 315. See also Isaac White, who sold his broadsides on the streets in and around Hempstead in 1910. His broadsides can be found in the James Avery Lomax Family Papers, 3D178, Folder 6.

42. Johnson and Johnson, *The Books of American Negro Spirituals*, Book One, 108–09.

43. McCormick and Oliver, *The Blues Come to Texas*, 314.

Interlude 2: If I Had My Way, I'd Tear the Building Down

1. Emily Hallowell, *Calhoun Plantation Songs, Second Edition* (Boston: C. W. Thompson Co., 1907).

2. Hallowell, *Calhoun Plantation Songs*, 72

3. Howard Washington Odum, *Religious folk-songs of the Southern negroes*. 1909, Smithsonian Libraries website, 10.5479/sil.357411.39088007768757

4. "My Soul is a Witness," Fisk University Jubilee Singers, Discography of American Historical Recordings, Victor matrix B-9925, accessed October 22, 2021.

5. Dorothy Scarborough, *From a Southern Porch* (New York: The Knickerbocker Press, 1919).

6. Scarborough, *From a Southern Porch*, 298–99.

7. Scarborough, *From a Southern Porch*, 298–99.

8. *If I Had My Way*, Rev. T. T. Rose and Gospel Singers, Paramount, 1927; *Samson and The Woman*, Rev. J. M. Gates, Victor, 1927; August Wilson, *Ma Rainey's Black Bottom: A Play in Two Acts* (New York: Plume, 1985), 71.

9. *Pressure and Baldwins Nigger: Two Films by Horace Ové.* (BFI Video Publishing, 1969 and 1975), DVD.

Poor Boy Long Ways from Home

1. This is a fictionalized account of William Christopher (W. C.) Handy's story of hearing the sound of slide guitar for the first time in a Tutwiler train station in 1903. See W. C. Handy, Arna Bontemps, and Abbe Niles. *Father of the Blues: An Autobiography* (New York: Macmillan Company, 1944).

2. Joplin died at only age forty-eight after being admitted into a mental institution as a result of dementia brought on by syphilis. He was of the same age as both John Lomax and Dock Johnson, and like Willie Johnson his grave was left unmarked for decades following his death.

3. Samuel Barclay Charters, *Jazz—New Orleans: An Index to the Negro Musicians of New Orleans* (Bellville, NJ: Walter C. Allen, 1958), 2–3.

4. These were the three terms that Howard Odum used to describe the type of performer in the Black community in the early twentieth century. The songster was anyone who "regularly sings or makes songs." The musicianer "applies often to the expert with the banjo or fiddle," and the music physicianer traveled from place to place and was a combination of the two. This follows closely—but on the secular end—with James Weldon Johnson's "maker of songs" and "leaders of singing." See Howard W Odum, "Folk-Song and Folk-Poetry as Found in the Secular Songs of the Southern Negroes." *The Journal of American Folklore* 24, no. 93 (1911): 255–294.

5. Guido van Rijn, "From the Vaults . . . Thomas Shaw Interview." *Blues & Rhythm* no. 193 (Oct 2004): 4–8.

6. Mance Lipscomb and Glen Alyn. *I Say Me for a Parable: The Oral Autobiography of Mance Lipscomb, Texas Bluesman.* (New York: W. W. Norton & Company, Inc., 1993), 246.

7. Odum, "Folk-Song and Folk-Poetry," 258.

8. This last line was one added by her son, Mance, when he went further in personalizing the Crucifixion lyrics in his recording of the song under the title, "I Just Hang Down My Head and I Cry." Here he transformed the line "hung his head and died" concerning the death of Christ in the "Mumblin' Word" spiritual to the personal "I just hung my head and cried." See Mance Lipscomb, "I Just Hang Down my Head and Cry," *Mance Lipscomb Volume 6*, track 2, recorded May 1973, Arhoolie Records 1069, 1974; and Lipscomb and Alyn, *I Say Me for a Parable*, 62.

9. Both "Spanish" and "Sevastopol" (Vastopol) were open tunings that found prominence with the introduction of two popular instrumental parlor guitar pieces published by Henry Worrall, an Ohio music teacher, around the mid-1850s. The first was "Spanish Fandango," which had a tuning that was also adopted by banjo players and would later be recorded by Elizabeth Cotten, Mississippi John Hurt, and Mance Lipscomb under the title "Spanish Flang Dang." The second was "Sabastopol. A Descriptive Fantaisie for the Guitar," a military march that became one of the most popular pieces for solo guitar in the nineteenth century. Its sheet music was frequently included with many of the mass-produced guitars of the 1890s. See Henry Worrall Collection, Kansas Historical Society, item number 208635, accessed October 16, 2020. https://www.kansasmemory.org/item/208635. For "Hawaiian" tuning, the extent of the influence of Hawaiian guitarists on the early blues, as it relates to the slide style of playing

brought to the mainland by Joseph Kekuku and his steel bar style of playing, likely can never be known for certain. But the style was most certainly included in the mix of sounds going around at the time and everything was up for grabs if you could figure out a way to make it your own. Much of the early writing on the slide playing references "Hawaiian style" as if to say there was no other antecedent, but the bending of pitches and talking instruments was certainly nothing new. In Africa they already had the talking drum, which could be made to "speak" or hum by creating tension by tightening the skin around it. The bending of pitches was also not unique to societies that relied on oral rather than written communication. The performers knew that—like human emotions that are not always so articulately expressed in words or only in major or minor scales—it was also what happens between the pitches that matters.

10. One of the more popular songs that almost always was played with a knife in this style.

11. Odum, "Folk-Song and Folk-Poetry," 261.

12. *Minglewood Blues* was first recorded by Cannon's Jug Stompers, a band that included the banjo player Gus Cannon, who adopted the slide style to his banjo, in 1928 for Victor Records.

13. Odum did not mention a song title but included the lyrics in his article. See Odum, "Folk-Song and Folk-Poetry," 363.

14. Odum, "Folk-Song and Folk-Poetry," 270.

15. Norm Cohen, *Long Steel Rail: The Railroad in American Folksong*, ed. David Cohen. (Urbana: University of Illinois Press, 2000), 427.

16. Ralph Waldo Emerson, "Experience," in *Essays and Poems by Ralph Waldo Emerson* (New York: Barnes and Noble Classics, 2004), 251–52.

Interlude 3: Lord, I Just Can't Keep from Crying

1. Rev. H. R. Tomlin, *Lord, I Just Can't Help from Crying*, Columbia Records, 1927. See also Laura Henton's 1929 version of the song for a stark comparison of what Johnson recorded in 1928: Laura Henton, *Lord, I Just Can't Keep from Crying Sometime*, Brunswick Records, 1929.

Willie Johnson: The Birth of the Bard, Part I

1. These lines are taken from J. W. Johnson's text of sermons. James Weldon Johnson, *God's Trombones: Seven Negro Sermons in Verse* (New York: Viking Press, 1927), 40.

2. This sermon is drawn from J. C. Burnett's recording, *The Great Day of This Wrath Has Come*. Rev. J. C. Burnett, *The Great Day of This Wrath Has Come*, Columbia 14225-D, New York, May 17, 1927.

3. Steve Olafson, "Unimaginable Devastation: Deadly Storm Came with Little Warning," *Houston Chronicle*, August 28, 2000.

4. *Houston Daily Post*, "Graphic Stories Told By Refugees From Galveston," September 10, 1900.

5. Paul Lester. *The Great Galveston Disaster, Containing a Full and Thrilling Account of*

the Most Appalling Calamity of Modern Times. 1900, University of North Texas Libraries, The Portal to Texas History, https://texashistory.unt.edu/ark:/67531/metapth26719/m1/1/?q=negro, accessed October 27, 2020.

6. For birth details see footnote 3 in the Introduction to his book as well as Ford, *Shine a Light*, 29. All other family information is put together from various 1870 and 1880 census records as well as marriage certificates.

7. US Census of Bell County, 1900.

8. Zora Neale Hurston, *Dust Tracks on a Road: An Autobiography* (New York: Harper Perennial, 1995), 269–70.

9. Hurston, *Dust Tracks on a Road*, 269–70.

10. Hurston, *Dust Tracks on a Road*, 269–70.

11. It is uncertain the exact year or cause of Mary King's death. No records have yet surfaced. All we have to go on is the timeline provided by Angelina Johnson in her interview with Samuel Charters. In it she said that Johnson was blinded at seven years old, and this was following his mother's death. According to other records, we know his mother was alive in 1900, so her death could be put at any point from 1900 to around 1904. An earlier date seems like it would be the most accurate considering no more children were born to Dock and Mary after Jettie, who was born in 1900.

12. Concerning Johnson's blinding, Johnson would most likely have been blinded around 1904 or 1905. There is a broader timeline that could stretch anywhere from 1904 to 1910, which would account for all the possibilities and confusion surrounding this incident. The exact reason for Johnson's blinding will never be known but, in brief, here is what we know: Angelina stated that he was seven years old when this happened, which would put the year around 1904. Johnson himself, in his 1918 draft card, stated that he had been blind for either thirteen years, putting the date around 1905, or at age thirteen, putting the date in 1910. Also, the exact reason of Johnson's blinding will never be known, but through interviews with people who knew him, three different causes have been cited. The first and most often cited cause originated from Angelina Johnson in her interview with Samuel Charters in 1955. In the interview she stated that Johnson's father told her that Johnson was blinded following his mother's death when his father "married" another woman named Betty, who was seeing other men. Angelina did not state in the audio that there was a beating that ensued, but Charters did in his writings, so it is possible that this was something communicated privately. See Angelina Johnson, interview. Whatever the case, in this scenario, something occurred to make his stepmother become outraged and, in revenge, she threw lye into Willie's eyes, blinding him. The other two reasons that have been stated are from Willie B. Harris, Johnson's wife in the late 1920s, who said Johnson went blind from looking at an eclipse through a piece of glass. See Dan Williams to Nick Perls, February 22, 1977. The Williams letters are photocopies supplied to me by Randy Harper, a fan of Johnson's, who reached out to me when I was researching the grave and getting the cenotaph support. Since then, I have resupplied them to Williams himself who, for a time, did not have access to what he had written while out of the United States.

The final possible reason for his blindness originated from his friend Thomas Shaw, who said that Johnson had led him to believe that picking up discarded spectacles led to his impairment, matching more closely with what Harris said. For the Thomas Shaw information, see "Blind" Willie Johnson, *Praise God I'm Satisfied*, Yazoo Records 1058. Notes by Steve Calt, 1977. First, the eclipse scenario is definitely possible. There were several partial solar eclipses visible in the Temple region while Johnson was young. Two significant ones occurred in 1900 and 1908, and a common way that many were advised to view them was through smoked glass. But, it is not *how* Johnson was blinded, but what the blinding signified in Johnson's life, that is the most important question to ask. Johnson, like Madkin Butler and most preachers or evangelists, most likely interpreted his blinding as a sign from God, and the eclipse would have fit this narrative, just as Nat Turner saw the eclipse as a sign. This does not dismiss the stepmother and lye story, but of course, we must also recognize that the evil stepmother theme is common in both myth and literature. Some examples can be found in the plays of Euripides, writings of Seneca, the Roman declamations, and, of course, later fairy tales such as *Snow White*. A final explanation never mentioned for Johnson's blindness may be found in the less sensational story that it was caused from congenital syphilis, a common ailment among poor African Americans who lacked access to safe living conditions and proper health care.

13. The Santa Fe passenger station was completed in 1911.

14. The "Temple Colored School" was first organized in 1885 and was located on the east side of town. The school was officially sanctioned and was mentioned in newspapers as the only segregated Black school in the city. But a close look at the Sanborn Fire Insurance Maps shows that the location of the Mount Zion Church on the west side also served as a public school in the community as early as 1915. The story of Black churches stepping up in the absence of options for formal education for Black citizens is an untold history of early Black education in the southern United States. Starting with early Sabbath schools, the church made it a priority to build a path to freedom through education and literacy, and this was done in many Black community churches, Mount Zion being only one of them.

15. While the first-class passengers were able to fully enjoy all the luxuries, the third-class passengers, including immigrants, were kept segregated in lower decks.

16. *Abilene Semi Weekly Farm Reporter*, July 26, 1910.

17. *The Crisis* vol. 11, no. 3, January 1916, p. 145.

18. Washington was accused of the rape and murder of Lucy Fryer, who along with her husband George, was the proprietor of the land that Washington's family worked on as tenant farmers.

19. "The Waco Horror," *The Crisis*, vol. 12, no. 3, July 1916.

20. Patricia Bernstein, *The First Waco Horror: The Lynching of Jesse Washington and the Rise of the NAACP* (College Station: Texas A&M University Press, 2006), 108.

21. Statistics provided by the Archives at Tuskegee Institute. https://archive.tuskegee.edu/repository/wp-content/uploads/2020/11/Lynchings-Stats-Year-Dates-Causes.pdf

22. McCormick and Oliver, *The Blues Come to Texas*, 81.

23. McCormick and Oliver, *The Blues Come to Texas*, 81.

24. The notes on Johnson teaching himself to play originate from Dan Williams to Nick Perls, February 22, 1977. Regarding Johnson's first playing guitar, it is probable that after his blinding, his father feared that he would not be able to make a living, and this worry led him

to construct the guitar for his son. It certainly would be a justified concern as there were few options and no government assistance available for those who suffered from impairments precluding them from the manual labor or domestic occupations fated to many African Americans at the time. The result was that the blind were thrust onto the streets and forced to rely on passersby for charity.

25. Johnson and Johnson, *The Books of American Negro Spirituals*, Book One, 22–23.

26. Lipscomb and Alyn, *I Say Me for a Parable*, 218.

27. Friedrich Wilhelm Nietzsche, *The Complete Works of Friedrich Nietzsche: the First Complete and Authorised English Translation*, ed. Oscar Levy, trans. Adrian Collins, 2nd ed., vol. 5 (New York: The Macmillan Company, 1974), 106.

28. Jer. 1:8; Mark 16:15.

Interlude 4: Let Your Light Shine on Me

1. Matthew 5:16. Lucie Eddie Campbell and Allen Griggs, "Please Let Your Light Shine on Me," notated music (Memphis, TN: Campbell-Griggs Publishing Co., 1919), https://www.loc.gov/item/2013571026/.

2. Campbell and Griggs, "Please Let Your Light Shine on Me."

3. *The King of Kings: a choice collection of gospel songs, standard hymns, choruses, children's songs, solos, duets, and quartets together with responsive readings for use in evangelistic meetings* (Indianapolis: Hackleman Music Co., 1915), 14.

4. *Songs & Spirituals* (Chicago: Overton-Hygienic Co., 1921).

5. Wiseman Sextette, *Shine on Me*, Rainbow Records, 1923.

6. Rev. E. D. Campbell, *Escape for Your Life*, Victor Records, 1927.

7. Rev. Beaumont, *The Blind Man*, Paramount Records,1929; John 9:1–12.

8. See Leadbelly, "Let It Shine on Me," Smithsonian Folkways Recordings, SFW40044, 1996. This version, recorded sometime between 1941 and 1947,was likely based on Johnson's version because he performed the song in a similar fashion to Johnson's but led the listener through the different styles he was playing in—from the Baptist line hymn, to Methodist, to the "Holy Ghost" people. Leadbelly inserted two hymns ("Amazing Grace" and the Isaac Watts hymn, "Am I A Soldier on The Cross," as verses), but while Leadbelly explained the song, Johnson just performed it, and we have to catch up.

Willie Johnson: The Birth of the Bard, Part II

1. Brandon Allen, "Fourth Ward, Houston, Texas (1839-)," BlackPast, July 16, 2019, https://www.blackpast.org/african-american-history/fourth-ward-houston-texas-1839/#:~:text=By%201920%2C%20Fourth%20Ward%20was,baseball%20venue%2C%20West%20End%20Park.

2. *Brenham Daily Banner*, "Address is Made by Moderator of the Lincoln Association," July 6, 1923. Antioch, by 1917, was being pastored by Rev. Frederick Lee (F. L.) Lights, president of the Baptist Foreign Mission Convention, following the death of Rev. Yates in 1897.

3. While fellow musicians may have crossed paths with each other in church, the two worlds remained vastly separated when it came to performing. Many of the musicians who played piano and guitar inevitably found one another in the underground circuit, but Johnson's insistence on performing only religious spirituals and ballads would have kept him outside the secular network. This separation, along with the fact that so little research was put into Texas, would also explain why the blues performers who were later interviewed were familiar with other secular performers, but their awareness of Johnson was minimal at best.

4. Tomico Meeks, "Freedmen's Town, Texas: A Lesson in the Failure of Historic Preservation," *Houston History*, 8 (2), (April 2011): 42–44.

5. Mack McCormick's notes. See John Jeremiah Sullivan, "The Ballad of Geeshie and Elvie," *New York Times*, April 12, 2014, https://www.nytimes.com/interactive/2014/04/13/magazine/blues.html. Also see Mack McCormick, "Lightnin' Hopkins: Blues," *The Jazz Review*, no. 1, January 1960.

6. McCormick and Oliver, *The Blues Come to Texas*, 125.

7. McCormick, "Lightnin' Hopkins: Blues."

8. Lipscomb and Alyn. *I Say Me for a Parable*, 217–18; McCormick and Oliver, *The Blues Come to Texas*, 316.

9. Lipscomb and Alyn, *I Say Me for a Parable*, 217–18

10. McCormick and Oliver, *The Blues Come to Texas*, 316.

11. McCormick and Oliver, *The Blues Come to Texas*, 316.

12. *Treasury of Field Recordings Vol. 1*, compiled and with liner notes by Mack McCormick, 77 Records, 77-LA-12-2, 1960.

13. Guido van Rijn, "From the Vaults . . . Thomas Shaw Interview," *Blues & Rhythm* no. 193 (October 2004): 4–8.

14. Tom Mazzolini, "L. C. 'Good Rockin' Robinson," *Living Blues* no. 22 (July/August 1975). The memory of Johnson playing music for the Robinsons originated with L. C., who in the same 1975 interview made the claim that Johnson was his "brother-in-law." Tom Mazzolini, the author of the article, even referenced A. C. (L. C.'s brother) who confirmed this fact while mentioning that the relationship stemmed not from a sister but from a sister's daughter. The name "Alberta Jones" is mentioned, but it is not clear if this was the sister or the daughter. In this case it is most likely the sister, as the brothers did have an older sister named Alberta who was born around 1898. She is mentioned in both the 1900 and the 1910 Washington County censuses. With this information, we must surmise that Johnson would certainly have been with Alberta and not one of her daughters, considering Alberta would have been only a year younger than Johnson himself. Unfortunately, I could not locate any records of a marriage between the two or a record of a child, which certainly is no evidence that none exists. In fact, it is most likely true that Johnson was involved in a relationship with one of the Robinson women. Johnson himself, in the 1930 census, listed his first marriage at age twenty, which would correspond to around 1917, a time when Johnson would have frequently been in the area. It is also unclear how long such a relationship continued, but if this was the 1917 marriage Johnson listed, we would have to assume that it lasted for at least a few years, at least long enough for L. C. Robinson (born in 1915) to remember it and take anything of substance from Johnson's guitar skills.

Although Robinson did not mention a year with regards to when Johnson would stay over, based on the two brothers' ages, one would assume it would be somewhere between 1919 to the early 1920s, which means that it could have been after Johnson was with the COGIC and his slide skills excelled.

15. McCormick and Oliver, *The Blues Come to Texas*, 316.

16. *Temple Daily Telegram*, "Negro Lynched in Galveston by Mob Obtaining Entrance to Jail by Ruse; Race Riots Threatened," June 26, 1917.

17. Rev. Elijah C. (E. C.) Branch, a Missionary Baptist minister also out of Galveston, established the International Relief Company in 1917 to do just this. Steven A Reich, "Soldiers of Democracy: Black Texans and the Fight for Citizenship, 1917–1921," *The Journal of American History* 82, no. 4 (1996): 1478–504.

18. *Houston Daily Post*, "The 'Exodus' in Texas," June 28, 1917.

19. *Houston Daily Post*, June 28, 1917.

20. *Houston Daily Post*, June 28, 1917.

21. *Houston Daily Post*, "Negro Praises Post Editorials," July 9, 1917.

22. Record Groups 153 and 393, Modern Military Records Branch, Textual Archives Services Division, National Archives Services Division, National Archives and Records Administration, College Park, Maryland. This digital reproduction is found on reel 6 images 173–175.

23. *The Crisis*, November 1917. It would be the NAACP again, led by James Weldon Johnson, that would eventually secure over fifty pardons as well as the freedom for twenty of the soldiers after meeting with President Calvin Coolidge in 1924.

24. Robert V. Haynes, "The Houston Mutiny and Riot of 1917," *The Southwestern Historical Quarterly* 76, no. 4 (1973): 418–39. Accessed November 30, 2020. http://www.jstor.org/stable/30238208.

25. "The 1917 Houston Riots/Camp Logan Mutiny," Prairie View A&M University, May 21, 2020. https://www.pvamu.edu/tiphc/research-projects/the-1917-houston-riotscamp-logan-mutiny/.

26. "United States World War I Draft Registration Cards, 1917–1918," database with images, August 14, 2019); Texas, Houston City no. 4; B-Sowell, Thomas W. image 3099 of 5863; citing NARA microfilm publication M1509 (Washington, D.C.: National Archives and Records Administration).

27. Theodore Kornweibel, *"Investigate Everything": Federal Efforts to Ensure Black Loyalty During World War I* (Bloomington: Indiana University Press, 2002), 152–57.

28. "Food Conservation During WWI," The Library Company of Philadelphia, 2016, https://togetherwewin.librarycompany.org/food-conservation-during-wwi-post/.

29. *Houston Chronicle*, September 24, 1918; *Houston Chronicle*, October 9, 1918.

30. Centers for Disease Control and Prevention, National Center for Immunization and Respiratory Diseases (NCIRD).

31. Hurston, *Dust Tracks on a Road*, 103.

32. *Los Angeles Times*, "New Sect of Fanatics is Breaking Loose," April 18, 1906.

33. *The Apostolic Faith*, "Pentecost Has Come," September 1906

34. *The Apostolic Faith*, September 1906.

35. *The Apostolic Faith*, September 1906.

36. Acts 2:3

37. Cecil M. Robeck, *The Azusa Street Mission and Revival: The Birth of the Global Pentecostal Movement* (Nashville, TN: Emanate Books, 2006), 35.

38. *The Apostolic Faith*, September 1906

39. *COGIC Official Manual* (Memphis, TN: Board of Publication of the Church of God in Christ, 1973), 26.

40. *COGIC Official Manual*, 27. See Acts 2:4: "All were filled with the Holy Spirit. They began to express themselves in foreign tongues and make bold proclamations as the Spirit prompted them."

41. *COGIC Official Manual*, 27.

42. Anthea D. Butler, *Women in the Church of God in Christ: Making a Sanctified World* (Chapel Hill: The University of North Carolina Press, 2012).

43. See Psalm 150:3–5, which reads, "Praise Him with the sound of the trumpet; praise Him with the psaltery and Harp. Praise Him with the timbrel and dance. Praise Him with stringed instruments and organs."

44. For examples of Mason's powerful sermons, listen to his "Yes, Lord" prayer.

45. *COGIC Official Manual*, 138; Sherry Sherrod DuPree, *African-American Holiness Pentecostal Movement: An Annotated Bibliography* (New York: Routledge, 2013), xlv.

46. James Baldwin, "Sonny's Blues," *The Jazz Fiction Anthology*, eds Sascha Feinstein and David Rife (Bloomington: Indiana University Press, 2009), 38–39.

47. Robert R. Owens, *Never Forget: The Dark Years of COGIC History* (Fairfax, VA: Xulon Press, 2002), 84.

48. Karen Kossie-Chernyshev, "Constructing Good Success: The Church of God in Christ and Social Uplift in East Texas, 1910–1935," *East Texas Historical Journal* 44 (2006): issue 1, article 11, 51.

49. Kornweibel, *"Investigate Everything,"* 152–157.

50. Elaine J. Lawless, *God's Peculiar People* (Lexington, KY: The University Press of Kentucky, 1988).

51. Hurston, *Dust Tracks on a Road*, 104.

52. See Acts 2:20 when Peter addresses the Apostles by quoting Joel: "The sun will be turned to darkness and the moon to blood before the coming of the great and glorious day of the Lord" and compare it to the line in "When the Saints Go Marching In": "when the moon turns red with blood."

53. This was a common refrain within the COGIC and likely sung many times, but for an early example, within the context of a sermon on recording, see Rev. Shy (E. S.) Moore, *Christ, The Teacher*, Victor Records, 21737, September 22, 1928.

54. Dan Williams to Nick Perls, April 1977; Lipscomb and Alyn, *I Say Me for a Parable*, 218.

55. Kossie-Chernyshev, "Constructing Good Success," 50–51.

56. *Yearbook of the Church of God in Christ*, compiled by Lillian Brooks Coffey (Memphis, TN: Church of God in Christ, 1926).

57. *Yearbook of the Church of God in Christ*; *Dallas Express*, "The Apostolic Church in Texas—It's Rapid Growth and Membership," October 9, 1920.

58. Kossie-Chernyshev, "Constructing Good Success," 52.

59. Kossie-Chernyshev, "Constructing Good Success," 52. Dranes was mentioned several times in the Black weekly newspaper, the *Dallas Express*, with regards to the church in Sherman and in conjunction with Page. See *Dallas Express*, February 15, 1919.

60. *Houston Informer*, July 28, 1923.

61. *Cleveland Gazette*, March 11, 1922.

62. While there may have been musicians who played slide guitar in Texas, the only evidence we have to rely on is what has been recorded. So, although it is possible that there were numerous musicians in the state who were influential on slide guitar by the early 1920s who never made it to a recording studio, one would think that more Texas musicians who would have learned from them would have made some recordings. But this is not the case. Although Lemon Jefferson was known to play a couple of songs using the knife, it was not a style that either the state or he was known for. A couple more slide guitar players, Oscar "Buddy" Woods and Ramblin' Thomas, played in Texas, but they did not record religious music. Their slide styles lent themselves more to the Hawaiian sound than what was happening in Memphis or northern Mississippi with musicians such as Robert Wilkins, Furry Lewis, and others. Johnson, in fact, was the one known Texas guitar player who followed the COGIC and recorded. So, while it may have been from direct experience with Memphis or the northern Mississippi region, or just from being in contact with traveling musicians from the church visiting Texas, there can be little doubt on the association between the influence of the COGIC church on Johnson's proficiency with slide guitar.

63. The COGIC also would be the church that would later allow electric guitars into churches and change music once again.

64. James Avery Lomax Family Papers, 3D178, Folder 6.

65. Butler was still active, at least until the mid-1920s, but his travel became shorter and less frequent. Some examples of these trips included his assisting Rev. Drisdale in Taylor, Texas, in 1922; reciting a prayer following the opening choir at the Colored National Woodmen Convention at his home church in Hearne in August of 1922; entertaining in Bryan, Texas, in March 1924; conducting a rally at Pleasant Grove Baptist Church in Thornton in Limestone County in June 1924; and leading a "song service" for Ebenezer Baptist Church in Mexia in early December 1925.

66. McCormick and Oliver, *The Blues Come to Texas*, 318.

67. Charters, *Blind Willie Johnson: His Story Told, Annotated, and Documented*.

68. See the *Houston Informer*, March 29, 1924, for details on The Colored Relief Department in Houston, which in 1924 began to qualify some blind citizens from the street by offering a pension and offered housing in "Old Folks Homes."

Interlude 5: Bye and Bye, I'm Goin' to See the King

1. Odum, *Religious folk-songs of the Southern negroes*.97

2. Odum, *Religious folk-songs of the Southern negroes*, 97.

3. Odum, *Religious folk-songs of the Southern negroes*, 52. For other variants, see also J. W.

Johnson's inclusion of "Zekiel Saw De Wheel" as part of his collection of spirituals: Johnson and Johnson, *The Books of American Negro Spirituals*, 22, and Ezekiel 1:15.

4. Newman Ivey White, *American Negro Folk-Songs* (Cambridge: Harvard University Press, 1928), 117.

5. A. E. Perkins, "Negro Spirituals from the Far South," *Journal of American Folklore* 35 (July 1, 1922): 241–43.

6. Roland Hayes, *My Favorite Spirituals: 30 Songs for Voice and Piano* (Mineola, NY: Dover Publications, 2001), 26.

The Marriage of Heaven and Hell: The Recordings of "Blind" Willie Johnson

1. "Columbia Recording Laboratory Opened in Chicago," *The Talking Machine World*, (August 15, 1915); 67. See also Frieberg, who died the same month and year as Johnson in 1945.

2. For information on Frank Walker and recording see Walker, Frank, 1962, interview, Mike Seeger Collection, University of North Carolina Chapel Hill.

3. *Afro-American Blues & Game Songs, From the Archive of Folk Song*, ed. Alan Lomax, Library of Congress AFS L4, 1942.

4. Mark Twain, Letter to *Daily Alta California* Newspaper, San Francisco, August 1, 1869.

5. Twain, Letter.

6. Deirdre O'Connell, *The Ballad of Blind Tom* (New York, NY: Overlook Press, 2009), 54. Wiggins's popularity grew, and he was soon one of most celebrated pianists of his era. Consequently, his performance schedule expanded further into North America and Europe where he was consistently performing to packed concert halls with a repertoire that, in addition to his own compositions, included works by Beethoven, Bach, and Liszt. Wiggins was also the first African American to give a musical performance at the White House in 1860. See, "'Blind Tom' Music Sheet," The Columbus Museum, Accessed October 13, 2020, https://columbusmuseum. catalogaccess.com.

7. There is still somewhat of a contradiction here, and that is that although they may have outwardly expressed through advertising that they would strictly go on merit, Boone was still marketed as "Blind John" and later "Blind Boone" and not just John Boone. See Ann Sears, "John William 'Blind' Boone, Pianist-Composer: 'Merit, Not Sympathy Wins.'" *Black Music Research Journal* 9, no. 2 (1989): 225–47. Accessed October 13, 2020.

8. Melissa Fuell-Cuther, *Blind Boone, His Early Life and His Achievements* (Robbins, TN: Evangel Pub. Society, 1918), 27.

9. Mary Collins Barile and Christine Montgomery, eds., *Merit, Not Sympathy, Wins: The Life and Times of Blind Boone* (Kirksville, MO: Truman State University Press, 2012), 90.

10. Barile and Montgomery, *Merit, Not Sympathy*, 6.

11. Ed Komara, "'Crazy Blues'—Mamie Smith (1920)." Library of Congress website, 2005. https://www.loc.gov/static/programs/national-recording-preservation-board/documents/CrazyBlues.pdf

12. According to reports, Bessie Smith sold two million records in the first six months and

six million over the next four years. Also, while *Cemetery Blues* was recorded under Columbia's "race records" 13000D series, the label quickly migrated their "race records" to the 14000D series, and Bessie Smith, once again, was the first to record for the series. For information on sales, see Gwen Thompkins, "Forebears: Bessie Smith, The Empress of The Blues," *NPR*, January 5, 2018. https://www.npr.org/2018/01/05/575422226/forebears-bessie-smith-the-empress-of-the-blues#:~:text=Within%20a%20reported%2010%20months,%2C%20later%2C%20in%20jazz%20clubs.

13. While Dranes takes the title for her record, *My Soul is a Witness for the Lord*, from earlier versions of the song that had been both written about and recorded previously, lyrically the song was very much changed as she removed the theme of Samson while still keeping lines that referred to the walls falling down, which could reference Samson or the walls of Jericho. She also recorded her version of the spiritual *John Said He Saw a Number*, a song transcribed from earlier folklorists that referenced the book of Revelation and included the repeated response line of "way in the middle of the air" sung by the singers of the small congregation (including Sara Martin) that either the label or Dranes had assembled for the recording. It was a line similar to one that would also be found when singers sang of Ezekiel witnessing the wheel as well as other versions of spirituals as lyrics became shared and used in other religious songs such as "I Wouldn't Mind Dying If Dying Was All."

14. This upbeat, sanctified piano take on the Crucifixion can also be heard in Jessie Mae Hill's 1927 OKeh recording of *The Crucifixion of Christ* as well as in the Pentecostal preacher Rev. D. C. Rice's *Were You There When They Crucified My Lord?* recorded for Brunswick in 1930.

15. See Arizona Dranes, "He's Got Better Things for You," Dec. 27, 1926; E 654882; Consolidated Music Publishing House, Chicago.

16. Alan B. Govenar, *Texas Blues: The Rise of a Contemporary Sound* (College Station: Texas A&M University Press, 2008), 86.

17. The account of Johnson hearing Rev. J. C. Burnett is fictional, but it is certainly possible. Burnett was from Mobile, Alabama, but he frequently traveled on the tent circuit in Louisiana, Mississippi, and Texas after joining the ministry in 1911. It was the early jazz singers like Mamie Smith who gave him the inspiration to record for the first time in 1926. His lining-out hymn and sermon *The Downfall of Nebuchadnezzar* became a massive seller for Columbia. Burnett said of recording, "If the devil could make such success with this popular invention there was no reason why the Lord could not do the same." For quote see: "Jazz Singer Gave Preacher His Tip," *Afro-American* May 19, 1928.

18. See the similar lyric "got to go by yourself" in Arizona Dranes's *Bye and Bye We're Going to See the King*, in which McGee was also present as choir director.

19. Ozro Thurston (O. T.) Jones became the assistant state overseer of Oklahoma under Bishop Page in the 1920s. His style was also characterized by a gravelly, musical tone. Although he was not recording in the 1920s, he would end up succeeding Bishop C. H. Mason following Mason's death, and Jones's powerful style can be heard in his eulogy for Mason in Memphis in 1961.

20. For more on "I Know His Blood Can Make Me Whole," see Mark 5:29 and its description of the woman who was an outcast and cut off from society due to illness until she

touched the hem of Jesus's garment and was freed from suffering. Compare this song to "Blind Man Sit in the Way," and one may come to understand what a song like this would have meant to Johnson. Also see versions of "The Hem of His Garment" published by George Frederick Root as well as Rev. E. D. Campbell's recording in November 1927 of *The Hem of His Garment*, which began with his version of "When the Saints Go Marching In."

21. Rawick, *The American Slave*, 121.

22. This research on Clayborn is my own derived from piecing together facts of his life, including his being born in Richmond, Alabama, anytime from 1880–1885, and living with his mother for many years in Pittsburgh while preaching at St. Luke's Baptist Church. He was living in Chicago by 1930, likely due to his recording as he recorded a number of his sides in Chicago. Death records reported that he died in Pittsburgh in January 1978.

23. J. Frank Dobie, ed., *Tone the Bell Easy* (Dallas: Southern Methodist University Press 1932), 56. Accessed July 12, 2020, through the University of North Texas Libraries, The Portal to Texas History, https://texashistory.unt.edu/ark:/67531/metadc38876.

24. The antecedents of *Jesus Make Up My Dying Bed* included "When I's Dead an' Gone," a song collected by Howard W. Odum and Guy B. Johnson for their book, *Negro Workaday Songs*, in 1926. In this version the parable of Jesus meeting the woman at the well is combined with Jesus as a dyin' bed maker. It has many lyrics in common with Johnson's version including the idea of being "lost," the scene of Jesus at the Crucifixion, and crossing Jordan. This version also pairs more lyrically with Charley Patton's *Jesus Is a Dying-Bed Maker* recorded for Paramount Records in 1929. See Howard W. Odum and Guy B. Johnson, *Negro Workaday Songs* (Chapel Hill: The University of North Carolina Press, 1926), 197–198. Also see Dobie, *Tone the Bell Easy*, which took its title from the song that was collected in Texas and printed in an essay by Martha Emmons for the Texas Folklore Society and pairs very closely to Johnson's version.

25. Meritt was a local Kansas City "race" label started by the musician and entrepreneur Winston Holmes.

26. John 3:1–4. See also Rev. Gatewood's *The New Birth*, which was released on Paramount Records. For Rev. Gatewood in Kansas City.

27. Listen also in this recording for the voice of the great sanctified singer Bessie Johnson, who would record several sides for both Victor and OKeh in the coming years. Here, they are just labeled as the "Holy Rollers."

28. A version of this song was mentioned in the Lou Austin slave narrative as well, but as "Sometimes I Feel Like a Motherless Child," which was the spiritual from which Johnson's version originated, although they are two distinct songs. See Federal Writers' Project, *Slave Narrative Project*, vol. 16, Texas, Part 1, Adams-Duhon. 1936. Manuscript/Mixed Material. https://www.loc.gov/item/mesn161/. Laura Clark, a blind woman and former slave from Livingston, Alabama, also recalled hearing the song sung in a version closer to Johnson's with the lyrics, "A motherless chile sees a hard time." See Work Projects Administration, *Slave Narratives: A Folk History of Slavery in the United States From Interviews with Former Slaves*, vol. I, Alabama Narratives, Project Gutenberg, May 3, 2011, https://www.gutenberg.org/files/36020/36020-h/36020-h.html. The song was also distinct in the recordings of Johnson for its

blues structure, with repeated lines in an AAB pattern, which was atypical for Johnson's delivery. But on that point it is necessary to call attention once again to Lemon's *All I Want Is That Pure Religion* to hear a striking resemblance to Johnson's version both in structure and sound, although Johnson's tempo is sped-up, and he used a slide.

29. For more on *Dark Was the Night, Cold Was the Ground*, see the song section.

30. For more on *If I Had My Way, I'd Tear the Building Down*, see the song section.

31. Walker interview, 1962. Walker would pick "the three or four [songs] that were the best . . . [and] you were through with that man as an artist."

32. Johnson's complete title is "O Black and Unknown Bards." Johnson and Johnson, *The Books of American Negro Spirituals*, Book One, 11.

33. Johnson and Johnson, *The Books of American Negro Spirituals*, Book One, 12.

34. Johnson and Johnson, *The Books of American Negro Spirituals*, Book One, 11.

35. Jones, *Blues People*, 26.

36. A note here also about ballad sheets, which did not include musical notation, meaning that if one was not able to hear a performer, they'd have to put their own music in place. For someone blind, like Johnson, who probably learned from hearing a song first (versus having it read to him), one can see how memorizing all the precise lyrics was never a point that was important, nor had it been for the entire history of folk culture when it came to song. In addition, for a more modern example of this, see Jim Hendrix's 1968 recording of "All Along the Watchtower." Hendrix had only heard the tapes of Bob Dylan's song in 1967 but had never seen the lyrics. So, in the Jimi Hendrix Experience version, lines may be sometimes mumbled or rearranged without a second thought, always in pursuit of the main goal of creating something completely original strictly based on the emotional interpretation.

37. *Louisiana Weekly*, January 14, 1928.

38. It was Columbia's best seller in the "race" category the first two months of 1928. See "Blind" Willie Johnson, *Sweeter as the Years Go By*, with liner notes by David Evans, Yazoo Records, Columbia Race Records 1078, 1990.

39. Abbe Niles, "Ballads, Songs, and Snatches," *Sights and Sounds* (June 1928): 423; Abbe Niles, "Ballads, Songs, and Snatches," *Sights and Sounds* (November 1928): 328.

40. Harris in her interview with Dan Williams mentioned Johnson was excellent at the piano and, in her words, could "really tear it up." Dan Williams to Nick Perls, April 18, 1977.

41. *Sanborn Fire Insurance Map from Marlin, Falls County, Texas*. Sanborn Map Company, March 1916. Map. https://www.loc.gov/item/sanborn08642_007/.

42. Dan Williams to Nick Perls, February 22, 1977.

43. The lyrics and title for the song were taken from the spiritual "Trouble in Mind," but according to Mercy Dee Walton, a musician who grew up in the area and heard him play, Jackson's version was a "different kind of deal." Thomas Shaw also was in Waco often, and it was here that he met Lemon Jefferson and bought his first guitar, an eight-dollar Stella from bluesman Aulies Patterson. See Tom Shaw, *Tom Shaw: Blind Lemon's Buddy*, Blue Goose Records BG-2008, 1972, with liner notes by Stephen Calt. For Walton interview, see "Marcy Dee Walton Interview," The Chris Strachwitz Collection, Arhoolie Foundation website, https://arhoolie.org/mercy-dee-walton-interview/. Johnson's association with Jackson came from Dan

Williams interview with Willie B. Harris: Dan Williams to Nick Perls, February 22, 1977.

44. The "½" on the address signifies the fact that the hotel occupied the entire upstairs of a warehouse-like building, and, according to the 1928 Dallas City Directory, the lower floor was unoccupied at the time.

45. Dan Williams to Nick Perls, February 22, 1977.

46. Scarborough, *On the Trail of Negro Folk-Songs*, 208–09.

47. Johnson and Harris's *I'm Gonna Run to the City of Refuge* is a combination of the common slave patrol song "Run, Nigger, Run," one of the most mentioned songs in the slave narratives sung as a warning concerning the patrol hired by plantations in order to ensure those enslaved were not holding meetings to plan escape or insurrections, and in the case that one did escape they would be in charge of locating them, and the need to "run" to God by being baptized before the end of days. The religious motif of "run" also originated in the antebellum period as "Run, Sinner, Run," which implored the sinner to listen to God lest the "fire'll over-take you." In 1923, there was an a cappella version of the song with the same title recorded by the Wiseman Sextet (with writing credits to Homer Rodeheaver), and while their chorus is the same as Johnson's, this version lyrically more resembled "My Soul is a Witness," with its lyrics of Samson, than what Harris and Johnson were doing. Instead, Johnson's recording pointed to the COGIC, and in particular, the Pentecost. The biblical reference is Acts 2:14 in which Peter spoke to the eleven men and lead them in his speech to baptism.

48. Evangelist R. H. Harris was recorded for Gennett, and her recording of *Jesus is Coming Soon* resembled more the message of the spiritual "Keep Your Lamp Trimmed and Burning" and its message of being "ready when he comes again" opposed to a specific incident, like a plague, that was taking lives.

49. Johnson mentioned the book of Zechariah at the end of the song, a book of the Bible that shares similar prophecies to that of Ezekiel in that both centered on apocalyptic warnings of destruction and visions for a peace to follow. See also the hymn "Jesus is Coming Soon," attributed to Thoro Harris and Howard B. Smith in 1914. This hymn also is a warning that "war and commotion" is in every land pointing to the end times and the return of Jesus.

50. When Rev. Grimke spoke of the "evil" ways he was specifically referring to whites who believed that they were made from "better clay" than the Black man. Francis James Grimké and Charles Simpson Butcher, *Some Reflections, Growing Out of the Recent Epidemic of Influenza That Afflicted Our City: a Discourse Delivered In the Fifteenth Street Presbyterian Church, Washington, DC, Sunday, November 3, 1918*. [Washington, D.C.]: [publisher not identified], 1918.

51. For more on *Lord I Just Can't Keep from Crying* and *Keep Your Lamp Trimmed and Burning*, see the song section.

52. As for the speculation that if the unissued sides were, in fact, Johnson's, that they would be secular is probably a leap too far. Harris herself said about Johnson's music, that "all was sacred," and it would also overlook the possibility that it was not Johnson at all. Another distinct possibility is, because these were two recordings at the close of the session, that they were another blind singer Johnson and Harris had brought to Dallas with them, and who was given a chance to record at the end of the session. It is interesting to note that the songs have no titles, and only that they were "to be named," which seems strange when one looks at other

unreleased songs from labels, including Columbia, which were (almost always) titled. So, it is certainly likely that it was a favor to Johnson, but upon hearing the output he had no intention of releasing them, much less getting the titles. For an example of who it could be see Mack McCormick's mention of the blind street singer "Blind Barber," who frequently visited Madkin Butler and Ophelia in Hearne, and was not named Willie Johnson. See McCormick and Oliver, *The Blues Come to Texas*, 315; *Discography of American Historical Recordings*, s.v. "Columbia matrix W147572. Unknown titles / Blind Texas Marlin," accessed April 12, 2021, https://adp. library.ucsb.edu/index.php/matrix/detail/2000037136/W147572-Unknown_titles; and Dan Williams interview with Willie B. Harris in Dan Williams to Nick Perls, February 22, 1977.

53. Rev. Gundy would end up leaving Hearne to start the Greater St. Stephen Missionary Baptist Church on South Liberty Street in New Orleans in 1937.

54. It is unknown where Columbia set up its studio in New Orleans. The Werlein's music store as the location came from the singer Dave Ross, who was around at the time and gave this information to Samuel Charters. It is a very likely location because Columbia had recorded jazz musician Sam Morgan in the store in 1927. In addition, the store was huge, having several stories and floors. While specializing in selling musical instruments as well as sheet music, it also held performances in the spaces. As a note—I did an extensive search on other artists who recorded at this time for Columbia and OKeh and came up empty with an exact location. In addition, Johnson's reason for recording in New Orleans, as opposed to Dallas, may be because he was in or around Beaumont, according to Elder Dave Ross, who told Charters this in 1954. It is unlikely though that he was living in Beaumont though due to his relationship with Willie B. Harris, which began as late as 1928 and stretched to 1931.

55. Brown also recorded a version of a Titanic ballad titled *Sinking of The Titanic* in the same session as *James Alley-Blues*.

56. John 9:3

57. For more on *Let Your Light Shine on Me*, see the song section.

58. This is a song that may have been recited in both the Baptist and Pentecostal tradition. In the *COGIC Yearbook* of 1926, a section within the section titled "Doctrinal Subjects" references God's healing of those who were faithful (sick, blind) and reminds the readers that "God has not changed." *Yearbook of the Church of God in Christ*, 1926, 37. In addition, the song can still be located under the title "I Know God is God" with additional and separate lyrics to Johnson at the Holiness Preaching Online site at http://holiness-preaching.org/.

59. "Sweeter as the Years Go By" was published numerous times in various hymnals over the years and was sung at revival and camp meetings. A point to note is that Mrs. Morris herself would also become blind at age fifty-two, two years following her publication of the song. See recording by the song publisher and evangelist Homer Rodeheaver in 1926.

60. For more on *Bye and Bye I'm Going to See The King*, see the song section.

61. Although we will likely never know the name of the woman who sang with Johnson in 1929, it would make the most sense (based on her shouting style of singing common to the street versus the church) that she was someone Johnson met on the streets on that first day of recording. This seems the most plausible, because while she was familiar enough with the songs to sing them, she could never quite keep up with what Johnson was doing with them. She

seemed most comfortable in a response pattern say in *When the War Was On*, but completely out of her element and lost on *Take Your Burden to the Lord* or *Praise God I'm Satisfied* as she tangled her voice with Johnson's in a way that betrayed any sense of intimacy between them. Another possibility—although slightly less likely—is that she is either one of the Sisters (Jordan or Norman) who frequently traveled and recorded with Rev. J. M. Gates and recorded with the great Sister Clara Hudmon, "The Georgia Peach," in Atlanta as well. Gates would be in town to record for OKeh five days after Johnson's session, and if he was around earlier it seems impossible that both Johnson and Gates (two of Columbia/OKeh's biggest sellers) would not meet up. This hypothesis is hardly definitive though.

62. Johnson and Johnson, *The Books of American Negro Spirituals*, Book One, 22–23.

63. For other versions of "Bond," see the Fisk Jubilee Singers *You Better Get Somebody on Your Bond* (1924) and Charley Patton's 1929 recording *You're Gonna Need Somebody When You Die*." Patton recorded the song similar to a preacher's sermon by taking a talking break in the middle of the song unaccompanied by instrumentation. Also, John Henry Faulk recorded a version at Rose Hill Baptist Church near Navasota, Texas, in Grimes County in 1941 for the Library of Congress.

64. William and Versey Smith, a couple of religious street singers, recorded a variant of the ballad with many similarities to Johnson's for Paramount in 1927 titled *Everybody Help the Boys Come Home*, and although there were plenty of lyrical similarities between the two songs, the separation in both the quality of the recording and the performances were stark. They only had one session where they recorded three other sides, including a Titanic ballad, *When That Great Ship Went Down* and *Sinner You'll Need King Jesus*, a version of "You'll Need Somebody on Your Bond."

65. The hymn "Praise God I'm Satisfied" looks to have been first published in 1922 by the preacher and missionary worker Herbert Buffum. See also Johnson's line, "For he bowed his head and died," which does not appear in the original hymn, but one that Johnson (or the version that he heard in the Black church) decided to insert to rhyme with "satisfied" and taken from the spiritual "He Never Said a Mumbalin Word."

66. Prior to Johnson, it had already been recorded by the Baptist singers Joel Washington "Blind Joe" Taggart in 1926, Washington Phillips in 1927, and "Blind" Roosevelt Graves with his brother (Uaroy Graves) a few months prior to Johnson's version.

67. See Rev. Shy E. S. Shy Moore's *Christ, the Teacher* recorded for Victor in Memphis in 1928; Rev. J. C. Burnett's *Stand Your Ground* for Columbia in 1927; Charley Patton's *I'm Goin' Home* and *Prayer of Death Part I* recorded for Paramount in 1929. See also *Take a Stand* recorded by the Pentecostal, COGIC singers Elders McIntorsh and Edwards along with Bessie Johnson and Melinda Taylor for OKeh in Chicago 1928. There was also at least one instance of the song being sung under the title "Mother's There" recounted by Tony Lott for the *Slave Narratives*. See Alan B. Govenar, *African American Frontiers: Slave Narratives and Oral Histories* (Santa Barbara, CA: ABC-CLIO Interactive, 2000), 285.

68. Mark 16:16–18. See also the themes of the Pentecostal Church: speaking in new tongues and laying-on of hands for healing.

69. "Canaan's shore" designated the place of freedom either in this life or beyond, and

it was no coincidence that the "Battle Hymn of the Republic" was a derivative of the songs "Canaan's Happy Shore" and "John Brown's Body," and was composed by the abolitionist Julia Ward Howe as a marching song.

70. For more on *God Moves on The Water*, see the song section.

71. Willie B. Harris to Dan Williams in Dan Williams to Nick Perls, February 22, 1977. The biblical reference for the woman, an outcast due to her mixed race, comes from John 4:1–40. It is interesting to note here the parable of the Good Samaritan as detailed in Luke 10:25–37 in which Jesus related to a lawyer the story of a man who had been robbed and left for dead on the road but who was passed by on several occasions by people unwilling to lend him a hand. In each, Jesus and the Samaritans are compared to each other—each were outcasts and each were willing to assist those who are also rejected. It is a similar theme in Johnson's recording of *Everybody Ought to Treat a Stranger Right*, and of course, in the latter example, its similarity to Jesus on the road as he passed Blind Bartimaeus.

72. Some of these healings, including "the lame made to leap for joy," and the "Blind made to declare, 'I see,'" are recorded at least as early as 1925 at the annual Holy Convocation held in Memphis; *Yearbook of the Church of God in Christ*, 1926.

73. It has been written and promoted that Johnson and Harris lived together at 817 Hunter Street in Marlin, but it was simply not the case. No evidence has been presented to prove this, and the facts are that the 1930 census, which is the only census that does have them living together, does not have house numbers for this address. Furthermore, and most importantly, the house at Hunter Street was not even constructed until 1951, according to deed records. The date of departure comes from that same census, which was conducted only six days before the recording session on April 20.

74. *If It Had Not Been for Jesus* explicitly referenced the Pentecostal Church in its lines about going to the "meeting / Just to hear them sing and shout" and was published by the Metropolitan Church Association in the Holiness hymn book *The Joy Bells of Canaan or Burning Bush Songs No. 2* in 1905 with nearly identical lyrics to Johnson's recording. *Go With Me to That Land* is a derivative of the hymn "On Jordan's Stormy Banks I Stand," which was published in numerous songbooks and credited to Samuel Stennett in 1787 with the "land" meaning the "promised land," or Canaan. See also "I Want to Go There" published in *The Joy Bells of Canaan or Burning Bush Songs No. 2* listed above. On a more contemporary note, the activist, composer, and singer Bernice Johnson Reagon-also recorded the song for her album *River of Life: Harmony One*. This song was definitely sung in the COGIC churches. Arizona Dranes also recorded a version, *Don't You Want to Go*, for OKeh in 1928 as a stomping call-and-response song that in tone was the antithesis of Harris and Johnson's recording.

75. See the "former rain" and "latter rain" in Joel 2:23. See also a reference in *The Whole Truth* newspaper published by the Church of God in Christ in Memphis, and their reference to "The latter rain is falling and our souls are rejoicing" in Port Arthur, Texas. *The Whole Truth*, March 1934. Also see Aimee Semple McPherson's "Latter Rain" from her *Pentecostal Foursquare* hymnal.

76. See similarities in the hymn "By and By" with the lyrics "our bondage it shall end" and "and our sorrows have an end." Also, the hymn "We Have but The One More River to Cross," around since at least 1859, begins with the line "My suff'ring time will soon be o'er," while

others substitute "trials" for suffering. See also Matthew 11:29. See also Rev J. C. Burnett's *The Christian's Trouble Is Soon Ended*, recorded for Columbia in May 1927.

77. Adam Booker was a blind preacher who lived in Hearne in the mid-1920s when Butler lived there and Johnson visited. In an interview with Charters, he recalled Butler singing this song outside churches. See Charters, *Blind Willie Johnson: His Story Told, Annotated, and Documented*. See also the "long ways from home" pulled from *Poor Boy* and Rev. Edward Clayborn's *Everybody Ought to Treat Their Mother Right*, recorded for Vocalion in 1927.

78. For *Church I'm Fully Saved Today*, the most relevant hymn is "I Am Fully Saved Today" composed by an early leader of the white Holiness movement, William J. Henry (and Clarence E. Hunter) published in 1900. "The Blood of Jesus," composed by F. M. Atkinson, which was published as early as 1910, also contained elements of Johnson's rendition with its references to the blood as the answer to what saves and includes the line, "Precious blood that makes me whole."

79. This form is similar in the way Son House performed "Grinning in Your Face" in 1965 when House used hand claps instead of the guitar to add a percussive element but otherwise sang a cappella.

80. See Luke 2:41–50 and for more on *The Soul of a Man*, see the song section.

81. For more on *John the Revelator*, see the song section

82. *Barefoot Bill's Hard Luck Blues*, Mamlish Records S-3812. Notes by Don Kent, Pat Conte, Gayle Dean Wardlow, Bengt Olsson, 1984.

83. The two-week length of stay in Atlanta comes from Willie B. Harris in her interview with Dan Williams; Dan Williams to Nick Perls, February 22, 1977. It is likely that Harris and Johnson met up with "Blind" Willie McTell (William Samuel McTier) while in Atlanta, although Harris didn't recall it years later in her recollections with Dan Williams. But it would make sense, as McTell recorded for Columbia just three days prior to Johnson, and it would have been surprising if they did not find each other on the streets (if not in the studio) during this time period. Ora Sam Faye Johnson was born June 23, 1931. There are two certificates of birth for her. One listed Johnson's occupation as musician (and another even said "Blindman" next to musician) and Willie Johnson's birthplace as Temple.

84. See the lawsuit concerning Bessie Smith's lack of royalty payments—Gee v. CBS—against Columbia Records at Justia US Law website, https://law.justia.com/cases/federal/district-courts/FSupp/471/600/1804873/.

85. For Dock Boggs's issues with payments, see Dock Boggs, *His Folkways Years, 1963–1968*, Smithsonian Folkways SFW40108, notes by Barry O'Connell, 1998. Regarding fiddlers Sady Courville and Dennis McGee not getting any payment from Vocalion for at least their first recordings, see Ann Allen Savoy, ed., *Cajun Music: A Reflection of a People*, vol. 1 (Eunice, LA: Bluebird Press, 1984), 40.

Interlude 6: God Moves on the Water

1. Perkins, "Negro Spirituals from the Far South," 223. A. E. Perkins was a Black folk song and story collector as well as the principal of Daneel Public School in New Orleans.

2. Lead Belly combined both Jack Johnson and the Titanic when he sang his version of

the Titanic ballad for a Black audience. See Lead Belly, *Lead Belly: The Smithsonian Folkways Collection*.

3. *Chicago Defender*, April 20, 1912.

4. *Chicago Defender*, April 20, 1912.

5. *Chicago Defender*, April 20, 1912.

6. *The Pittsburgh Courier*, May 4, 1912.

7. Mack McCormick, *The Unexpurgated Folk Songs of Men*, recorded in 1959 in Texas, no label, vinyl LP, 1960.

8. Lightning Washington, *God Moves on the Water*, audio recorded by John A. Lomax and Alan Lomax at Darrington State Prison, Sandy Point, Texas, 1933. American Folklife Center, https://www.loc.gov/item/ihas.200197230/.

The Sun Will Never Go Down

1. Lomax Family Papers, 3D178, Folder 6.

2. Lomax, *Adventures of a Ballad Hunter*, 96.

3. Lomax, *Adventures of a Ballad Hunter*, 89.

4. Lyrics from the singer are pulled from two separate sources. While the first half of the song is taken from John Lomax's account from his autobiography, the second half is drawn from Alan Lomax's account from a *Radio Times* piece. See Alan Lomax, "From a Great Dark River," *Radio Times* (November 23, 1951): 6; and Lomax, *Adventures of a Ballad Hunter*, 98.

5. John Darrington purchased Darrington Plantation in 1835 and continued to operate with leased convict labor after slavery until the leasing system was abolished and the plantation sold to the Texas Prison Commission.

6. Washington, *God Moves on the Water*.

7. There is no indication that John Lomax was familiar with the firebrand preacher who had been such a pivotal figure in Texas decades before, as Lomax makes no mention of the name J. L. Griffin or any of *that* Griffin's past success or controversies. It is my belief that this "Sin-Killer" Griffin is not the same as the earlier Griffin although they share the same nickname.

8. Lomax, *Adventures of a Ballad Hunter*, 191.

9. The song leader in the Darrington service is not identified; the recording is only labeled as "Sin-Killer," but this is inaccurate as Griffin only appeared at the end of the service with his sermon.

10. Lomax, *Adventures of a Ballad Hunter*, 192.

11. Sin-Killer Griffin, "Moaning," recorded by John and Alan Lomax at Darrington State Prison, Sandy Point, Texas, 1934. Alan Lomax would again record a version of this hymn but in the style of Johnson's slide guitar when he recorded Sampson Pittman's "Brother Low-down and Sister Doo-dad" in Detroit in 1938. See: Sampson Pittman, "Brother Low-down and Sister Doo-dad," recorded by Alan Lomax in Detroit, MI, November 1, 1938. https://www.loc.gov/item/afc1939007_afs02483a/.

12. Lomax, *Adventures of a Ballad Hunter*, 193.

13. Lomax, *Adventures of a Ballad Hunter*, 193.

14. Lomax, *Adventures of a Ballad Hunter*, 193.

15. Sin-Killer Griffin, "Church Service, Easter," recorded by John A. Lomax at Darrington Prison Farm in Sandy Point, Texas, 1934.

16. Isaac Watts, *The Psalms and Hymns of Isaac Watts* (Grand Rapids, MI: Christian Classics Ethereal Library, 1806), 23. Hymn 116.

17. Lomax, *Adventures of a Ballad Hunter*, 198.

18. John A. Lomax, *Our Singing Country: A Second Volume of American Ballads and Folk Songs* (New York: The Macmillan Company, 1949), 9.

19. Lomax, "From a Great Dark River."

20. Alan Lomax, *The Land Where the Blues Began* (New York: The New Press, 1993), 283.

Interlude 7: John the Revelator

1. *Yearbook of the Church of God in Christ*, 1926.

2. Exodus 3:1–8

Brother Willie Johnson

1. Franklin D. Roosevelt, "Oglethorpe University Address: The New Deal," Atlanta, Georgia, May 22, 1932. Pepperdine School of Public Policy website, https://publicpolicy.pepperdine.edu/academics/research/faculty-research/new-deal/roosevelt-speeches/fr052232.htm

2. *San Antonio Register*, May 27, 1932. Union Baptist was located at the corner of Pine and Center streets at exactly where Johnson resided at 815 N. Center. The Union Baptist Church at the time was pastored by Rev. J. L. Taylor, the moderator of the Guadalupe Association.

3. Little Hat Jones, *Cherry Street Blues*, OKeh, 1930.

4. The church was first organized as the Olive Street Colored Methodist Episcopal Church around 1918 where they initially worshiped in a tent in the 400 block of Cherry Street before moving to their brick location at 133 Gibbs, at Olive and Gibbs. The church is still standing today, although the building has been repurposed as part of the Little Carver Civic Center. The Fields name also brings up interesting questions with regards to Johnson family scholarship. Johnson's death certificate listed Johnson's mother as Mary Fields from Moody, Texas. And while we now know that Mary King was Johnson's mother and not Mary Fields, I would argue against easily dismissing some sort of connection due to Johnson's closeness with the family and the CME church in San Antonio. According to the church's history, a Ms. Lottie Fields was one of the first prominent members in 1918, and by the early 1930s John and Maggie Fields, along with John's daughters Bessie and Josephine were living there. Maggie was born Maggie Sadler, according to her death certificate, in Valley Mills, Texas, before becoming Washington and then widowed by 1920, when she was rooming in the same place as John Fields, a former section laborer on the Santa Fe Railroad, and his two daughters in Crawford, Texas (a city equidistant from Valley Mills and Moody) in 1920. John was born in Seguin, just east of San Antonio, and

the next records of them showed them living together in 1932 in San Antonio. I am positive that there is a connection and have done my best to go down many routes to see what it may be, but the road is rough after so many years. I leave this note to any future researcher who seeks to understand the Fields and Johnson connection. An interesting side note though is that, according to census and World War II draft data, John Fields was working at Fort Sam Houston by the early 1940s, the same location of the execution of the men who were found guilty in the Houston riot of 1917. For the record on Johnson's marriage, see *San Antonio Register*, December 2, 1932. See his marriage to Mary Brown at the Fields's home on Potomac Street on Sunday, November 27, 1932. The ceremony was overseen by the head pastor of the Olive Street Church, Rev. Abner (A. M.) Lee.

5. For Johnson's singing partner, see McCormick and Oliver, *The Blues Come to Texas*, 317. In *The Blues Come to Texas*, McCormick mentioned a woman by the name of Sara Lee Montgomery as a singing partner of Johnson's who was "a Schulenberg-born girl who was about thirty-five when she met . . . [Johnson] there in the year 1933–34." Willie B. Harris also recalled hearing that Johnson had found a new singing partner when she spoke to Dan Williams in 1977. See Dan Williams to Nick Perls, April 18, 1977. According to my own research, Montgomery was born in 1906 and would have been around twenty-seven in 1933. She was married to a public-school teacher named Grover C. Montgomery, and they had a son born in Schulenberg in 1928 and another child born in Waelder, a city located just east of Schulenberg, in 1930. But by October 1931, when another child was born, they resided in Liberty, Texas, and were still living there in 1933, according to birth records. The 1933 document also stated that Sara Lee was born in Schulenberg. McCormick's note that, by 1933, she was no longer living in Schulenberg but returned there to sing on weekends would be confirmed by these documents. For the source on Johnson's performance in Shiner, see *Shiner Gazette*, October 26, 1933. "Blind" Willie McTell mentioned that he played with Johnson on *Blind Willie McTell— Complete 1940 Library of Congress Recordings*, recorded in Atlanta on November 5, 1940.

6. Michael Gray, *Hand Me My Travelin Shoes: In Search of Blind Willie McTell* (Chicago, IL: Chicago Review Press, 2009), 214.

7. For Johnson's run-in with The Lighthouse, see Charters, *Blind Willie Johnson: His Story Told, Annotated, and Documented*. The church basement in San Antonio where Johnson attended, Olive Street C. M. E., also became the location for a Lighthouse for the Blind workshop where mops were constructed for the war effort during World War II. See "Eastside Churches," Historic and Design Review Commission, April 15, 2027, p. 12. https://sanantonioreport.org/wp-content/uploads/2017/05/Eastside-Churches-1.pdf).

8. 1935 City of Temple directory. The house where they were listed was at 308 S. Fifth Street in the same neighborhood where they spent much of their time growing up—off of Avenue D.

9. Mazzolini, "L. C. 'Good Rockin' Robinson."

10. Lou Curtiss, "Tom Shaw Talks," *Living Blues* no. 9 (Summer 1972): 24–27.

11. See Bob Jackson's death certificate dated September 8, 1936, "Texas Deaths, 1890–1976," FamilySearch website, entry for Bob Jackson and J. A. Jackson, September 8, 1936.

12. For sources on Carl Johnson, see his son's birth certificate, "Texas Birth Index,

1903–1997," FamilySearch, James Lester Johnson, January 4, 1935; from "Texas Birth Index, 1903–1997," database and images, on Ancestry.com, http://www.ancestry.com, citing Texas Department of State Health Services as well as Carl's death certificate dated February 27, 1937, "Texas, Death Certificates, 1890–1976," digital image "Carl Johnson" (1896–1937), *Ancestry. com*. As a note of interest, Carl's birthplace is listed as Pendleton, Texas. As for Carl's son, James, he died at only twenty-five after being stabbed to death in the early morning hours of August 21, 1960, in Waco.

13. Lynn Abbott, *I Got Two Wings: Incidents and Anecdotes of the Two-Winged Preacher and Electric Guitar Evangelist Elder Utah Smith* (Montgomery, AL: CaseQuarter, 2008), 4.

14. Abbott, *I Got Two Wings*, 11. For one of Smith's stays in Dallas, see *The Whole Truth*, Vol. 9, no. 1, 1933.

15. Bruce Nemerov, "I'm a Holy Ghost Preacher," *Blues & Rhythm* 141 (August 1999): 5.

Interlude 8: The Soul of a Man

1. Roland Hayes, *My Favorite Spirituals: 30 Songs for Voice and Piano* (Mineola, NY: Dover Publications, 2001), 103; Luke 2:41–50.

2. Hayes, *My Favorite Spirituals*.

3. Luke 2:48–50.

4. Luke 24:5. For two striking versions of this song, each with different lyrics, see the 1941 recording of "What Kind of Soul Hath Man" sung by Anne Graham and accompanied on guitar by Leadbelly for the WNYC American Music Festival series, https://ezproxy.library.und. edu/login?url=https://www.wnyc.org/story/king-twelve-string-guitar-wnyc-regular-through -1940s/; and the ballad sheet, "What Is the Soul of Man?" composed by Charles Haffer. For Haffer's ballad, see Alan Lomax, *Alan Lomax Collection, Manuscripts, Mississippi, Tennessee and Arkansas,-1942.* to 1942, 1941. https://www.loc.gov/item/afc2004004.ms090438/

Coming Home: Reverend Willie Johnson

1. Blind Willie McTell, *Complete 1940 Library of Congress Recordings*, Recorded in Atlanta, GA., November 5, Document Records, 1940.

2. Blind Willie McTell, *Complete 1940 Library of Congress Recordings*.

3. Michael Gray, *Hand Me My Travelin' Shoes: In Search of Blind Willie McTell* (Chicago: Chicago Review Press, 2009), 272.

4. Amanda Jettie Johnson was working as a cook in Temple when she passed away in February 1940. She was buried in Temple.

5. Angelina Johnson, interview. Though her name has been written several ways, if we are to mention her in future writings it should be as Angelina. It is how she signed Johnson's death certificate and the name on their marriage license.

6. Johnson and Angelina Broussard were married in Houston on September 15, 1941. Johnson used the title "Rev." on the official document.

7. Charters, *Blind Willie Johnson: His Story Told, Annotated, and Documented*.

8. See the *Victoria Advocate*, "State Takes Over Support," May 21, 1942, for reporting on the aid provided to the blind, money which was withheld if one chose to remain on the streets. Also see Angelina Johnson, interview, for Angelina's details on how and where they would travel at this time.

9. Angelina Johnson, interview.

10. The tensions of white and Black shipyard workers competing for the same jobs (as well as food shortages) came to a head in mid-June 1943 when a white woman accused a Black man of rape. The incident was the final spark that caused the white workers to walk off the job and join a mob of thousands in front of city hall. Once the alleged attacker was not found to be in police custody, violence ensued resulting in Black homes and businesses looted or being burned to the ground. Several were injured, and many were killed. Martial law was declared, and the Texas National Guard was sent in to keep the peace. See: Tabitha Wang, "Beaumont Race Riot, 1943," BlackPast website, July 3, 2008, https://www.blackpast.org/african-american-history/beaumont-race-riot-1943. Johnson's affiliation with the Hodge church comes from Angelina's recollection with Sam Charters in 1955. See: Angelina Johnson, interview.

11. Aimee Semple McPherson was the founder of the Foursquare Church in Los Angeles in the early 1920s. See also Harry Hodge's involvement with the Latter Rain Pentecostal movement post-World War II in Jon Rising, "The Latter Rain Movement of '48, How It Started— the Basic Facts," May 22, 2013. https://lrm1948.blogspot.com/2013/05/how-it-started-basic-facts.html.

12. David Rhew, *Crumbs From the Cookie Jar* (Bloomington, IN: West Bow Press, 2015). Jeannie Williams, church member, interview with the author, early 2020.

13. *Waxahachie Daily Light*, February 5, 1943.

14. Angelina Johnson, interview. She mentioned several times when they would record, and the locations were spread out from Beaumont to Fort Worth. These were likely radio broadcasts, and definitely were not for Johnson's recordings with Columbia. Again, this was a source of confusion when Charters initially wrote that Angelina was the woman who sang on the recordings from 1927 to 1930.

15. The radio sources of KTEM and KPLC come from Texas music researcher Mack Mc-Cormick. See: Michael Corcoran, "He Left a massive Imprint on the Blues, But Little is Known About Blind Willie Johnson," *Austin American-Statesman*, September 28, 2003.

16. See a version of this song, "Mother's Prayer," written in 1922, recorded by the street singer A. C. Forehand for Victor in 1927.

17. The information about all these additional, non-recorded songs that Johnson was known for singing come from Angelina in her uncut interview with Sam Charters in 1955. See: Angelina Johnson, interview. For the song "99½ Won't Do," compare Dan Pickett's (James Founty) 1949 recording for the Gotham label of this song to what Johnson may have been doing, but with Johnson performing a call-and-response with his voice—one low, one high, as this was the way Angelina sang it in her interview with Charters.

18. "Blind" Willie Harris is possibly a pseudonym for Richard "Rabbit" Brown, the New Orleans street singer.

19. Charters, *Blind Willie Johnson: His Story Told, Annotated, and Documented.* Angelina

Johnson said the hospital turned him away because he was blind, but it also could have been because of race. It's a story that would have not been unique in the South at the time, especially in Texas. For one example, see the story of Clarence Halliday, a musician and Billie Holiday's father, who was turned away from a hospital in Dallas only to be finally admitted to the St. Paul Sanitarium for a couple of days right before he passed. This incident is one of the reasons Holliday said that she sang the anti-lynching anthem, "Strange Fruit." See also Johnson's death certificate for length of illness, which was recorded as three weeks. A note on the fire: Although fire records were checked and none were found that seemed to place a fire at this residence, there must have been one for two main reasons. First, that would account for the amount of water that would have been in their home and why Angelina was putting newspapers around the home to stay dry. But more importantly, in the complete Angelina Johnson interview, she made several unprompted references to a fire. Besides, a fire in a Black neighborhood not being recorded or possibly not even attended to by a white fire department was likely nothing unique. A last note: There was a category-four hurricane that struck at Matagorda on the Texas coast on August 27, 1945, and caused extensive damage along the Gulf Coast and into San Antonio. Beaumont seems to have been saved from the worst of it, but the timing would make sense if, in any way, the storm was the impetus for the fire.

20. Angelina Johnson, interview; Willie Johnson 1945 death certificate.

21. Angelina had told Charters that the cause of death was pneumonia, which shares many of the same symptoms as malarial fever including chills and excess fluid in the lungs. Johnson died on September 18, 1945, but he had been suffering for weeks, according to Angelina, putting his initial contraction of the illness likely in late August or early September, the prime months for the disease. See: Paulo Carrasco and Wayne X Shandera, "The past and present of malaria in Houston," *Tex Med*, 108(7), July 1, 2012.

22. Dock Johnson died in Temple in 1949, according to his death certificate. "Texas, Death Certificates, 1890–1976," digital image. "Dock Johnson" (1873–1949), Ancestry.com. "Texas Deaths, 1890–1976."

23. Angelina was living near the cross streets of Forrest and Evalon, just south of Gladys in 1947.

24. Angelina Johnson, interview. Johnson's death certificate listed Blanchette Cemetery as Johnson's burial place. It was a cemetery owned by the proprietor of Flemings Fraternal Undertaking at the time. Later, any records pertaining to Johnson's exact burial location were lost as was any public record of Blanchette. For a more in-depth narrative of this discovery, see Ford, *Shine a Light*.

25. Psalm 40:1–3.

Interlude 9: Dark Was the Night, Cold Was the Ground

1. Many have written the name of the hymn as "Gethsemane," but there is no listing for a song with this title in the 1792 publication, instead it is "Dark Was the Night." See Rev. Thomas Haweis, *Carmina Christo; or Hymns to the Saviour: Designed for the Use and Comfort of Those Who Worship the Lamb That Was Slain* (Bath: S. Hazard, 1792), 9. https://archive.org/details/

bim_eighteenth-century_carmina-christo-or-hym_haweis-thomas_1792/mode/2up.

2. Luke 22:39–46

3. The examples of the hymn on plantations come from several slave narratives; see the Federal Writers' Project: *Slave Narrative Project, Vol. 10, Missouri, Abbot-Younger*, 1936. Manuscript/Mixed Material, https://www.loc.gov/item/mesn100/; and the collection Library of Congress collection, *Slave Narratives: A Folk History of Slavery in the United States From Interviews with Former Slaves: Volume I, Alabama Narratives*, Work Projects Administration, 1936–1938. See also the slave narrative of Jim Davis, who recalled playing both "Dark Was the Night" and "Amazing Grace," two line hymns, on his banjo during the Civil War days. "I could pick a church song just as good as I could a reel," he recalled. And after playing a little of "Amazing Grace," he added, "I used to talk that on my banjo just as I talked it there." *Federal Writers' Project: Slave Narrative Project, Vol. 2, Arkansas, Part 2, Cannon-Evans.* 1936. Manuscript/Mixed Material. https://www.loc.gov/item/mesn022/

4. Zora Neale Hurston, *The Sanctified Church* (Berkeley, CA: Turtle Island Foundation, 1981), 82–83.

5. James H. Cone, *The Cross and the Lynching Tree* (Maryknoll, NY: Orbis Books, 2013), 2.

6. Newman Ivey White, *American Negro Folk-Songs* (Cambridge: Harvard University Press, 1928), 105.

7. McCormick and Oliver, *The Blues Come to Texas*, 317

8. *Black Gold*, Volume 1, Number 1, Spring 1975.

9. Langston Hughes, *Not Without Laughter* (United Kingdom: Dover Publications, 2012), 166. Madkin Butler Broadside Ballad card, James Avery Lomax Family Papers, 3D178, Folder 6.

10. Mississippi John Hurt, *Frankie*, OKeh Records, 1928; Blind Joe Taggart, *Been Listening All Day*, Paramount Records, 1928

11. Various artists, *Music from the South, Vol. 7: Elder Songsters*, 2, Smithsonian Folkways, FW02656, 1956.

12. Cone, *The Cross and the Lynching Tree*, 2.

13. James Baldwin and Nikki Giovanni, *James Baldwin, Nikki Giovanni: A Dialogue* (Philadelphia, PA: Lippincott, 1973), 74.

14. Revelation 14:2

A Love Supreme

1. Mississippi Fred McDowell, *I Do Not Play No Rock 'N' Roll*, Capitol Records ST-409. 1969.

2. John 15:9

3. Dante Diotallevi, "A Modern Interpretation of Robert Fludd's Symbolic Illustrations," (master's thesis, Queen's University, Kingston, Ontario, Canada, September 2015). https://www.academia.edu/109884708/A_modern_interpretation_of_Robert_Fludds_symbolic_illustrations

4. Manly Palmer Hall, *An Encyclopedic Outline of Masonic, Hermetic, Qabbalistic, and Rosicrucian Symbolical Philosophy* (San Francisco, CA: H. S. Crocker Company, 1928), 617.

5. John Cohen, "A Rare Interview with Harry Smith," *Sing Out!* 19, no. 1 (April/May 1969): 2–11, 41 and vol. 19, no. 2 (June/July 1969).

6. John Steinbeck, *The Grapes of Wrath* (New York: Penguin Books, 1992), 32–33.

7. Samuel Charters, *A Language of Song: Journeys in the Musical World of the African Diaspora* (Durham: Duke University Press, 2009), 72.

8. Charters, *A Language of Song*, 78.

9. Charters, *Blind Willie Johnson: His Story Told, Annotated, and Documented*.

10. Blind Willie Johnson, *The Complete Blind Willie Johnson*, Roots N' Blues—Columbia Legacy, C2K 52835, Sony Music. Notes by Samuel Charters, 1993.

11. Allen would become a pivotal authority on the history of jazz in New Orleans and went on to write about the music as well as help curate the William Ransom Hogan Jazz Archive at Tulane University.

12. Charters, *Blind Willie Johnson: His Story Told, Annotated, and Documented*. The story of Johnson's arrest came from Allen, but Allen would have been only two in 1929, and he never specified where he "heard" the story. The most logical assumption would be that he heard it from Ross, but it is still far from certain. It is also not certain that it was, in fact, Johnson who was arrested in 1929. An arrest wouldn't have been out of the question, as vagrancy of any sort by a Black man around a government building may have prompted an arrest and even more so if the song was perceived as a veiled threat, which "If I Had My Way" surely would have. As Lawrence Levine wrote in *Black Culture and Black Consciousness*, "veiled meanings by no means . . . eluded the whites," and slaves, even at the outbreak of the Civil War, were jailed for singing religious songs of freedom that were interpreted as being on the topic of emancipation from slavery. See Lawrence W. Levine, *Black Culture and Black Consciousness: Afro-American Folk Thought from Slavery to Freedom*. (Oxford: Oxford University Press, 2007), 51.

13. Charters, *A Language of Song*, 73.

14. Charters, *A Language of Song*, 73.

15. *Music from the South, Vol. 9: Song and Worship*, Smithsonian Folkways FW02658, 1956. In Charters's notes for the *His Story Told, Annotated* release, he mentioned that Ross was "a man of deep religious conviction" and that he would go on "long fasts" that had weakened his health. Ross, like Johnson, was, for at least a decade, a member of the Church of God in Christ and fasting was one of their core tenants. Other information about Ross came from his World Wars I and II draft documents, which stated that he was about fourteen years older than Johnson and had been blind since he was twenty.

16. Charters, *A Language of Song*, 75.

17. Charters, *Blind Willie Johnson: His Story Told*. In the audio for the 1957 Folkways release, Charters made the leap on his own that Butler was the one who had the biggest impact on Johnson's vocal stylings, but it was never mentioned in the released audio of Booker. The truth is we will never know what Butler sounded like, and he very well may have been (and probably was) influential to Johnson vocally, but the great Black preachers, in general, must have made the most impact on what Johnson was doing. That specific "style" came down through the ages and didn't start with Butler or Johnson. They were carriers of the tradition, but definitely superior vessels.

18. Angelina Johnson, interview.

19. Angelina Johnson, interview.

20. Angelina Johnson, interview.

21. Angelina Johnson, interview.

22. Angelina Johnson, interview.

23. *The Complete Blind Willie Johnson*, 1993.

24. Lomax, *The Land Where the Blues Began*, 318.

25. Lomax, *The Land Where the Blues Began*, 37.

26. Lomax, *The Land Where the Blues Began*, 32–34.

27. Lomax, *The Land Where the Blues Began*, 48. Haffer's ballad was titled "These Days Got Every Body Troubled."

28. Lomax, *The Land Where the Blues Began*, 49; Alan Lomax Collection, Manuscripts, Mississippi, Tennessee and Arkansas to 1942, 1941. Manuscript/Mixed Material. https://www. loc.gov/item/afc2004004.ms090438/.

29. Alan Lomax Collection.

30. Alan Lomax, *Selected Writings: 1934–1997*, ed. Ronald D. Cohen (New York: Routledge, 2005), 333.

31. On the first half of the trip, Lomax was joined by the folk singer Shirley Collins and on the second, his daughter, Anna Lomax.

32. Bessie Jones would end up recording "I'm A Rollin,' I'm A Rollin' (Everybody's A Rolling Stone)" in Lomax's New York apartment in 1961. The song included lines from "Motherless Children."

33. Lomax, *The Land Where the Blues Began*, 351.

34. Lomax, *The Land Where the Blues Began*, 13; John F. Szwed, *Alan Lomax: the Man Who Recorded the World* (London: William Heinemann, 2010), 21.

35. Szwed, *Alan Lomax*, 21.

36. Szwed, *Alan Lomax*, 285.

37. Lipscomb and Alyn, *I Say Me for a Parable*, 221.

38. This release included liner notes by Steve Calt, who rightly questioned Charters's assumption that Johnson's "singing style" derived solely from Madkin Butler pointing out that the inferred source of this idea (Adam Booker) doesn't meet Johnson until 1925. Another issue, obviously, is when one listens to the actual interview, one can hear that Booker never actually said this, and the information was only inferred by Charters.

39. This information relating to Johnson and the COGIC was never really followed up on, at the time, unfortunately. Even by the time of the Columbia/Sony compilation in 1990, Charters (who wrote the liner notes) or someone else still may have been able to flesh out some history here, but it was a subject largely left as a data detail and not something to explore.

40. Angelina Johnson, interview.

41. The details of Sam Fay Kelly (Johnson) come from her obituary written by Ken Gates after a memorial celebration was held for her life on December 22, 2005, at the COGIC church she attended in Marlin.

42. Dan Williams to Nick Perls, February through April 1977.

43. Baldwin, "Sonny's Blues," 45.

44. Ralph Waldo Emerson, "An Address," in *Essays and Poems by Ralph Waldo Emerson* (New York: Barnes and Noble Classics, 2004), 70.

45. Baldwin, "Sonny's Blues," 47.

46. Rev. F. W. McGee, *Jonah in The Belly of The Whale*, Victor Matrix BVE-38650, Chicago, Illinois, June 7, 1927.

47. Rev. Beaumont, *The Blind Man*, Cameo Records, 1929.

48. Rev. Beaumont, *The Blind Man*.

49. Blind Pearly Brown, *Georgia Street Singer*, Folk-Lyric FL 108, 1961. This album was recorded by Harry Oster and Sam Charters's friend Richard Allen in Macon, Georgia. The title, in a subsequent release, was changed from "Blind" Pealy Brown to Rev. Pearly Brown.

50. *It's A Mean Old World*, Folkstreams, film by John English, William VanDerKloot, Robert L. Williams, Education Through Visual Works, Inc, 1977. Also see his recordings with his wife, Christine, including when they both attended the Newport Folk Festival in 1966.

51. Bart Barnes, "Popular D.C. street singer Flora E. Molton dies" *Washington Post*, June 22, 1990.

52. Bernice Reagon, "Lady street singer," *Southern Exposure*, March 1, 1974.

53. Reagon, "Lady street singer."

54. Bruce Nemerov, "I'm a Holy Ghost Preacher," *Blues & Rhythm* 141 August 1999, 5–6.

55. For Sister Gertrude Morgan, see Lynda Roscoe Hartigan, *Made with Passion: The Hemphill Folk Art Collection in the National Museum of American Art* (Washington, DC: National Museum of American Art with the Smithsonian Institution Press, 1990); Blind Connie Williams, *Philadelphia Street Singer*, Testament Records, TCD 5024, with notes by Pete Welding, 1995.

56. Various artists, *Old Country Blues*, Flyright Records, FLY 537, with notes by Bengt Olsson, 1979.

57. Dan Smith, *God Is Not Dead*, Biograph BLP-12036, 1971.

58. See both McDowell and Wilkins in the northern Mississippi and the Memphis area, in the land of the slide guitar and of course, the Church of God in Christ. These men may have been the last of the truly great musicians who embodied that blend of the religious and secular at the scale they did. And while McDowell didn't mind playing "blues," it was something Wilkins had given up for decades after his initial recordings in the late 1920s and early '30s. By the time Wilkins recorded in 1964, he had become a minister with the COGIC, and it was all sacred music. As an example of what he was doing by this point, one can listen to his "That's No Way to Get Along," recorded in 1929 about longing for a train to take him away (a song that also incorporates the lyrics to "Blind Man Stood on the Road") and compare it to his "The Prodigal Son" recorded in 1964 which moved lyrically away from the personal and into the spiritual while maintaining a similar emotional feeling. Piedmont PLP 13162, 1964.

59. Mercy Dee, *Mercy Dee*, Arhoolie Records F1007, 1961. See also Walton's comments on hearing Bob Jackson's version of the song. He said in an interview that although it was a well-known song, "the way he sang it it was a different kind of deal. It was a real blues the way he sing it." Strachwitz, "Mercy Dee Walton Interview."

60. Connie Bruck, "National City's Protege of Blind Lemon Jefferson, Friend of Howlin' Wolf." *San Diego Reader*, July 5, 1973. https://www.sandiegoreader.com/news/1973/jul/05/cover-a-right-to-sing-the-blues/#.

61. Thomas Shaw, *Do Lord Remember Me*, Blues Beacon 1932 123, 1973.

62. Greg Kot, *I'll Take You There: Mavis Staples, the Staple Singers, and the Music That Shaped the Civil Rights Era* (New York: Scribner, 2014), 13. Jas Obrecht. *Early Blues: The First Stars of Blues Guitar* (Minneapolis: University of Minnesota Press, 2015), 127.

63. John Fahey, *Dance of Death and Other Plantation Favorites*, Takoma C 1004, 1965.

64. Edwin Pouncey, "Blood on the Frets," *The Wire* no. 174, August 1998.

65. See also the amazing Jack Rose, who recorded "Dark was the Night, Cold was the Ground" for his *Red Horse, White Mule* album in 2002 and again in 2006 under the title "Dark was the Night." See also Max Ochs's "Ain't Nobody High Raga," on the Tompkins Square website, https://tompkinssquare.bandcamp.com/track/aint-nobody-high-raga. It's a take on Johnson's "Can't Nobody Hide from God."

66. Louis E. Lomax, *The Negro Revolt* (New York: Harper & Row, 1962), 86. Martin Luther King Jr., *A Testament of Hope*, ed. James Melvin Washington (New York: HarperOne, 1986), 19.

67. King, *A Testament of Hope*.

68. Martin Luther King Jr., *Why We Can't Wait* (New York: Penguin Books, 1963).

69. King, *A Testament of Hope*, 18.

70. Lyrics from a well known song during slavery and the civil rights movement, "Don't You Let Nobody Turn You Round." Paul Harvey, *Freedom's Coming: Religious Rulture and the Shaping of the South from the Civil War through the Civil Rights Era* (UNC Press Books, 2012), 174.

71. Martin Luther King Jr., "'Keep Moving from This Mountain" (Address at Spelman College, April 10, 1960). The Martin Luther King Jr., Research and Education Institute website., https://kinginstitute.stanford.edu/king-papers/documents/keep-moving-mountain-address-spelman-college-10-april-1960.

72. Martin Luther King Jr., "Remaining Awake Through a Great Revolution," speech on March 31, 1968, at the Washington National Cathedral.

73. Zora Neale Hurston, *The Sanctified Church* (Berkeley, CA: Turtle Island Foundation, 1981), 80–81.

74. Hurston, *The Sanctified Church*, 80.

75. Cuthbert Ormond Simpkins, *Coltrane: A Biography* (Baltimore, MD: Black Classic Press, 1975), 159–160.

76. Simpkins, *Coltrane*, 160.

77. Simpkins, *Coltrane*, 160–161.

78. John Coltrane, *A Love Supreme*, Impulse! A-77, ABC Paramount Records,1965.

79. John Coltrane, *A Love Supreme*.

80. James Baldwin, "Of the Sorrow Songs: The Cross of Redemption," in *The Cross of Redemption*, ed. Randall Kenan (New York: Pantheon Books, 2010), 247.

81. James H. Cone, *A Black Theology of Liberation* (Maryknoll, NY: Orbis Books, 2005), 118.

82. Baldwin, "Sonny's Blues," 46. See Richie Havens's performance of "Freedom" at Woodstock in 1969 when he tangled up the two songs "Poor Boy" and "Motherless Children."

83. Friedrich Schiller's "Ode to Joy" was quoted in Ludwig van Beethoven's "Ninth Symphony."

84. Various artists, *Georgia Sea Island Songs*, New World Records 80278, with notes by Alan Lomax, 1977.

85. Carl Sagan, *Murmurs of Earth* (New York: Random House, 1978), 13. Also see other NASA messages sent into space including Pioneers 10 and 11 and the Arecibo message in 1974.

86. Carl Sagan to Alan Lomax, June 6, 1977, in Alan Lomax Collection, Library of Congress. June 6, 1977. https://www.loc.gov/item/cosmos000113/.

87. The Music of the Spheres, in this sense, is based on astronomer Johannes Kepler—one of Robert Fludd's contemporaries—and his vision of cosmic harmony, or the *Harmonice Mundi*: of Mars, Saturn, Jupiter, Mercury, Venus, and the Earth.

88. Regarding the Georgian song, "Tchakrulo," it is a song that recalls the armed revolt against a tyrant echoing much of the sentiment in African American songs from the time of slavery in the United States. See Sagan, *Murmurs of Earth*, 21. The particular selection of the Louis Armstrong performance must have been difficult as there were likely many that Lomax and the committee could have chosen as, for Lomax, Armstrong's trumpet was "the only American sound that could match" the depth of what he heard in the Texas prison camps. See: Lomax, *The Land Where the Blues Began*, 285. Armstrong also had something in common with Johnson in that he growled on his trumpet like Johnson roared with his voice; and Armstrong was also inspired by the Sanctified Church. In 1967, he wrote a letter to a marine in Vietnam, telling him that it "all came from the Old 'Sanctified Churches. I can remember—'way back in the 'old days in 'New Orleans, La—' My home town. And I was a little Boy around 'ten years old. My Mother used to take me to 'Church with her, and the Reverend ('Preacher that is') used to 'lead off one' of those 'good ol good 'Hymns. And before you realized it—the 'whole 'Congregation would be "Wailing—'Singing like 'mad and 'sound so 'beautiful. 'I 'being a little boy that would 'Dig' 'Everything and 'everybody, I'd have myself a 'Ball in 'Church, especially when those 'Sisters 'would get 'So 'Carried away while 'Rev' (the preacher) would be 'right in the 'Middle of his 'Sermon. 'Man those 'Church 'Sisters would 'begin 'Shouting 'So—until their 'petticoats would 'fall off. Of course 'one of the 'Deacons would 'rush over and 'grab her—'hold her in his 'Arms and 'fan her until 'she'd 'Come 'to." See Louis Armstrong, *Louis Armstrong, in His Own Words* (New York: Oxford University Press, 1999), 170. And the Navajo night chant was one that would be chanted to cure sickness and restore harmony and balance in the winter.

89. Elliot Forbes, ed., *Thayer's Life of Beethoven* (Princeton, NJ: Princeton University Press, 1964, rev. Ed. 1967), vol. 2, 975.

90. Sagan, *Murmurs*, 20.

91. Sagan, *Murmurs*, 178.

92. Sagan, *Murmurs*, 203.

93. Søren Kierkegaard, *The Gospel of Suffering*, trans. A. S. Aldworth and W. S. Ferrie. (Cambridge, UK: James Clarke & Co., 1955), 35.

94. Kierkegaard, *The Gospel of Suffering*, 36.

95. Hermann Hesse, *The Glass Bead Game*, trans. Richard Winston and Clara Winston (New York: Henry Holt and Co., 1990), 55.

96. Manly Palmer Hall, *An Encyclopedic Outline of Masonic, Hermetic, Qabbalistic, and Rosicrucian Symbolical Philosophy* (San Francisco, CA: H. S. Crocker Company, 1928), 617.

97. Carl Sagan, *Pale Blue Dot: A Vision of the Human Future in Space.* (New York: Ballantine Books, an imprint of The Random House Publishing Group, a division of Random House, 1994), 6–7.

Epilogue: Jubilee, the Story of the Beggar as Artist

1. Rainer Maria Rilke, *The Selected Poetry of Rainer Maria Rilke*, trans. Stephen Mitchell (New York: Vintage Books, 1982), 205.

2. Blake, *The Complete Poetry and Prose*, 492.

3. James Baldwin, "No Name in the Street," in *Price of the Ticket: Collected Nonfiction, 1948–1985* (New York: St. Martin's Press, 1985), 540.

4. David Herbert Lawrence, "The Reality of Peace," in *Phoenix: The Posthumous Papers* (New York: Viking, 1972), 670.

5. Hurston, *The Sanctified Church*, 83.

6. Acts 9:3–9.

7. Alexander Wheelock Thayer, *The Life of Ludwig Van Beethoven*, trans. Henry Edward Krehbiel (New York: The Beethoven Association, 1921).

8. Fyodor Dostoyevsky, *Fyodor Dostoevsky: Complete Letters*, edited and translated by David Allan Lowe and Ronald Meyer (Ann Arbor, Michigan: Ardis Publishing, 1988), 178.

9. Martin Luther King Jr. "Letter from a Birmingham jail," The King Center, 1963.

10. Blake, *The Complete Poetry and Prose*, 18.

11. DuBois, *The Souls of Black Folk*, 264. The hymn, *"Let Us Cheer the Weary Traveler,"* derives from Frederick Jerome Work and John Wesley Work, *Folk Songs of the American Negro No. 1.* (Nashville, TN: Work Bros. & Hart Co., 1907).

12. Galatians 6:5.

13. Juan Mascaró, *Lamps of Fire: From the Scriptures and Wisdom of the World* (London: Methuen & Co Ltd, 1961), 9.

14. Mascaró, *Lamps of Fire*, 10.

15. W. E. B. Du Bois, "Criteria of Negro Art," *The Crisis*, October 1926.

16. "Blind" Willie Johnson, *Jesus Make Up My Dying Bed*, Columbia Records, 1927.

BIBLIOGRAPHY

Abbott, Lynn. *I Got Two Wings: Incidents and Anecdotes of the Two-Winged Preacher and Electric Guitar Evangelist Elder Utah Smith*. Montgomery, AL: CaseQuarter, 2008.

Allen, Ann Savoy. *Cajun Music: A Reflection of a People*. Eunice, LA: Bluebird Press, 1984.

Allen, William Frances, Charles Pickard Ware, and Lucy McKim, eds. *Slave Songs of the United States*. New York: A. Simpson & Co, 1867.

Andrews, Garnett. *Reminiscences of an Old Georgia Lawyer*. Edited by S. Kittrell Rushing. Knoxville: University of Tennessee Press, 2009.

Armstrong, Louis. *Louis Armstrong, in His Own Words*. New York: Oxford University Press, 1999.

Bales, Mary Virginia, "Some Negro Folk-Songs of Texas." In *Follow De Drinkin' Gou'd*, edited by J. Frank Dobie. Austin: Texas Folklore Society, 1928.

Baldwin, James. *The Cross of Redemption, Uncollected Writings*. Edited by Randall Kenan. New York: Vintage International, 2010.

———."Sonny's Blues." In *The Jazz Fiction Anthology*, edited by Sascha Feinstein and David Rife. Bloomington: Indiana University Press, 2009.

Barile, Mary Collins, and Christine Montgomery, eds. *Merit, Not Sympathy, Wins: The Life and Times of Blind Boone*. Kirksville, MO: Truman State University Press, 2012.

Blake, William. *The Complete Poetry and Prose of William Blake*. Edited by David V. Erdman. New York: Doubleday, 1988.

Butler, Anthea D. *Women in the Church of God in Christ: Making a Sanctified World*. Chapel Hill: The University of North Carolina Press, 2012.

Charters, Samuel Barclay. *Jazz—New Orleans: An Index to the Negro Musicians of New Orleans*. Bellville, NJ: Walter C. Allen, 1958.

———. *A Language of Song: Journeys in the Musical World of the African Diaspora*. Durham: Duke University Press, 2009.

Clayton, Barbara Leah. "The Lone Star Conspiracy: Racial Violence and the Ku Klux Klan Terror in Post-Civil War Texas, 1865–1877." Master's thesis, Oklahoma State University, 1979.

Cohen, Norm. *Long Steel Rail: The Railroad in American Folksong*. Edited by David Cohen. Urbana: University of Illinois Press, 2000.

Cone, James H. *A Black Theology of Liberation*. Maryknoll, NY: Orbis Books, 2005.

———. *The Spirituals and the Blues: an Interpretation*. Maryknoll, NY: Orbis Books, 1992.

Courlander, Harold. *Negro Folk Music U.S.A*. New York: Columbia University Press, 1966.

Dargan, William T. *Lining Out the Word: Dr. Watts Hymn Singing in the Music of Black Americans*. Berkeley: University of California Press, 2006.

Doane, W. Howard. *Songs of Devotion for Christian Associations: A Collection of Psalms, Hymns, and Spiritual Songs with Music: for Church Service, Prayer and Conference Meetings, Religious Conventions, and Family Worship*. New York: Biglow & Main, 1870.

Douglass, Frederick. *Narrative of the Life of Frederick Douglass, an American Slave*. Boston, MA: Published at the Anti-slavery Office, 1846.

Du Bois, W. E. Burghardt. *The Souls of Black Folk*. Chicago, Ill: A. C. McClurg & Co., 1903.

DuPree, Sherry Sherrod. *African-American Holiness Pentecostal Movement: An Annotated Bibliography*. New York: Routledge, 2013.

Emerson, Ralph Waldo. *Essays and Poems by Ralph Waldo Emerson*. New York: Barnes and Noble Classics, 2004.

Frankl, Viktor E. *Man's Search for Meaning*. New York: Pocket Book, 1963.

Ford, Shane. *Shine a Light: My Year with "Blind" Willie Johnson*. Morrisville, North Carolina: Lulu Press, 2011.

Fuell-Cuther, Melissa. *Blind Boone: His Early Life and His Achievements*. Robbins, TN: Evangel Pub. Society, 1918.

George, Carol V. R. *Segregated Sabbaths: Richard Allen and the Emergence of Independent Black Churches 1760–1840*. New York: Oxford University Press, 1973.

Gordon, William St. Clair. *Recollections of the Old Quarter*. Lynchburg, VA: Moose Brothers, 1902.

Govenar, Alan B. *African American Frontiers: Slave Narratives and Oral Histories*. Santa Barbara, CA: ABC-CLIO Interactive, 2000.

———. *Texas Blues: The Rise of a Contemporary Sound*. College Station: Texas A&M University Press, 2008.

Gray, Michael. *Hand Me My Travelin' Shoes: In Search of Blind Willie McTell*. Chicago: Chicago Review Press, 2009.

Hall, Manly Palmer. *An Encyclopedic Outline of Masonic, Hermetic, Qabbalistic, and Rosicrucian Symbolical Philosophy*. San Francisco, CA: H. S. Crocker Company, 1928.

Hallowell, Emily. *Calhoun Plantation Songs, Second Edition*. Boston: C. W. Thompson Co., 1907.

Handy, W. C., Arna Bontemps, and Abbe Niles. *Father of the Blues: An Autobiography*. New York: Macmillan Company, 1944.

Hesse, Hermann. *The Glass Bead Game*. Translated by Richard Winston and Clara Winston. New York: Henry Holt and Co., 1990.

Holmes, Barbara Ann. *Joy Unspeakable: Contemplative Practices of the Black Church*. Minneapolis, MN: Fortress Press, 2017.

Hurston, Zora Neale. *Dust Tracks on a Road, A Memoir*. Urbana and Chicago: University of Illinois Press, 1984.

———. *The Sanctified Church*. Berkeley, CA: Turtle Island Foundation, 1981.

Johnson, Clifton H., ed. *God Struck Me Dead: Religious Conversion and Autobiographies of Ex-slaves*. Nashville, TN: Fisk University Social Science Institute, 1945.

Johnson, James Weldon, ed. *The Books of American Negro Spirituals*. Musical arrangements by J. Rosamond Johnson. New York: Viking Press, 1969.

———. *God's Trombones: Seven Negro Sermons in Verse*. New York: Viking Press, 1927.

Jones, LeRoi. *Blues People*. New York: William Morrow and Company, 1963.

Kennedy, John P. *Swallow Barn*. New York: G.P. Putnam & Co., 1872.

Kierkegaard, Søren. *The Gospel of Suffering*. Translated by A.S. Aldworth and W.S. Ferrie. Cambridge, UK: James Clarke & Co., 1955.

King, Martin Luther. *A Testament of Hope*. Edited by James Melvin Washington. New York: HarperOne, 1986.

———. *Why We Can't Wait*. New York: Penguin Books, 1963.

Kornweibel, Theodore. *Investigate Everything: Federal Efforts to Ensure Black Loyalty During World War I*. Bloomington: Indiana University Press, 2002.

Kot, Greg. *I'll Take You There: Mavis Staples, the Staple Singers, and the Music That Shaped the Civil Rights Era*. New York: Scribner, 2014.

Lawless, Elaine J. *God's Peculiar People*. Lexington: The University Press of Kentucky, 1988.

Leigh, James Wentoworth. *Other Days*. New York: Macmillan, 1921.

Lomax, Alan. *The Land Where the Blues Began*. New York: The New Press, 1993.

———. *The Rainbow Sign*. New York: Duell, Sloan and Pearce, 1959.

———. *Selected Writings: 1934–1997*. Edited by Ronald D. Cohen. New York: Routledge, 2005.

Lomax, John A. *Adventures of a Ballad Hunter*. Austin: University of Texas Press, 2017.

———. Alan Lomax, and Ruth Crawford Seeger. *Our Singing Country: A Second Volume of American Ballads and Folk Songs*. New York: The Macmillan Company, 1949.

Lomax, Louis E. *The Negro Revolt*. New York: Harper & Row, 1962.

Levine, Lawrence W. *Black Culture and Black Consciousness: Afro-American Folk Thought from Slavery to Freedom*. Oxford: Oxford University Press, 2007.

Lipscomb, Mance, and Glen Alyn. *I Say Me for a Parable: The Oral Autobiography of Mance Lipscomb, Texas Bluesman*. New York: W. W. Norton & Company, Inc., 1993.

McCord, Davis J. *The Statutes at Large of South Carolina, Volume Seven*. Columbia, SC: A. S. Johnston, 1840.

Nietzsche, Friedrich Wilhelm. *The Complete Works of Friedrich Nietzsche: The First Complete and Authorised English Translation*. Edited by Oscar Levy. Translated by Adrian Collins. 2nd ed., vol. 5. New York: The Macmillan Company, 1974.

Northup, Solomon. *Twelve Years a Slave*. Bedford, MA: Applewood Books, 2008.

Obrecht, Jas. *Early Blues: The First Stars of Blues Guitar*. Minneapolis: University of Minnesota Press, 2015.

O'Connell, Deirdre. *The Ballad of Blind Tom*. New York: Overlook Press, 2009.

Odum, Howard W., and Guy B. Johnson. *Negro Workaday Songs*. Chapel Hill: The University of North Carolina Press, 1926.

Oliver, Paul, Mack McCormick, Alan B. Govenar, and Kip Lornell. *The Blues Come to Texas: Paul Oliver and Mack McCormick's Unfinished Book*. College Station: Texas A&M University Press, 2019.

Olmsted, Frederick Law. *A Journey in the Seaboard Slave States With Remarks on Their Economy*. New York: Dix and Edwards, 1856.

Owens, Robert R. *Never Forget: The Dark Years of COGIC History*. Fairfax, VA: Xulon Press, 2002.

Pool, William C. *The History of Bosque County, Texas*. San Marcos, TX: San Marcos Record Press, 1954.

Randolph, Peter. *From Slave Cabin to the Pulpit*. Boston: J. H. Earle, 1893.

Rhew, David. *Crumbs From the Cookie Jar*. Bloomington, IN: West Bow Press, 2015.

Robeck, Cecil M. *The Azusa Street Mission and Revival: The Birth of the Global Pentecostal Movement*. Nashville, TN: Emanate Books, 2006.

Sagan, Carl. *Murmurs of Earth*. New York: Random House, 1978.

———. *Pale Blue Dot: A Vision of the Human Future in Space*. New York: Ballantine Books, 1994.

Scarborough, Dorothy, assisted by Ola Lee Gulledge. *On the Trail of Negro Folk-Songs*. Cambridge, MA: Harvard University Press, 1925.

Simpkins, Cuthbert Ormond. *Coltrane: A Biography*. Baltimore, MD: Black Classic Press, 1975.

Smallwood, James, Barry A. Crouch, and Larry Peacock. *Murder and Mayhem: The War of Reconstruction in Texas*. College Station: Texas A&M University Press, 2003.

Steinbeck, John. *The Grapes of Wrath*. New York: Penguin Books, 1992.

Szwed, John F. *Alan Lomax: the Man Who Recorded the World*. London: William Heinemann, 2010.

Tarkovsky, Andrei. *Sculpting in Time: Reflections on the Cinema*. Translated by Kitty Hunter-Blair. New York: Knopf, 1987.

Thayer, Alexander Wheelock. *Thayer's Life of Beethoven, Volume Two*. Edited by Elliot Forbes. Princeton, 1967.

Turner, Nat, and Thomas R. Gray. *The Confessions of Nat Turner, the Leader of the Late Insurrection in Southampton, VA*. Baltimore, MD: Lucas and Deaver, 1831.

Twain, Mark, Lin Salamo, and Harriet Elinor Smith. *Mark Twain's Letters 1872–1873*. Berkeley: University of California Press, 1997.

Van Deusen, John G. *The Black Man in White America*. Washington, DC: Associated Publishers, 1938.

Work, John Wesley. *Folk Song of the American Negro*. Nashville, TN: Press of Fisk University, 1915.

INDEX